MASS
COMMUNICATION
THEORY

MASS COMMUNICATION THEORY
AN INTRODUCTION

DENIS McQUAIL

 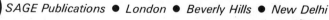 *SAGE Publications* ● *London* ● *Beverly Hills* ● *New Delhi*

For information address:

SAGE Publications Ltd 28 Banner Street London EC1Y 8QE

SAGE Publications Inc 275 South Beverly Drive Beverly Hills California 90212

SAGE Publications India C-236 Defence Colony New Delhi 110 24

British Library Cataloguing in Publication Data

McQuail, Denis
Mass communication theory
1. Mass media
I. Title
302.2'34   P90

Library of Congress Catalog Card Number 82-04288

ISBN 0-8039-9770-1
ISBN 0-8039-9771-X PbK

Printed in Great Britain by J. W. Arrowsmith Ltd, Bristol

To my fellow members of the European
Election Project team, whose periodic
good company was much appreciated
during the time of preparation of this
book: Jay Blumler; Giovanni
Becchelloni; Frans Bergsma; Kees
Brants; Roland Cayrol; Anthony Fox;
Mary Kelly; Walter Kok; Gianpietro
Mazzolini; Marie-Claude Noël-Aranda;
Vibike Petersen; Philip van Praag; Steen
Sauerberg; Klaus Schönbach; Winfried
Schulz; Joanna Spicer; Gabriel
Thoveron

CONTENTS

FIGURES

PREFACE

This book was conceived initially as a successor to my earlier *Towards a Sociology of Mass Communications* (Collier Macmillan, 1969) and is intended to serve in a similar way as a general introduction to a branch of study which appears under a number of titles, including 'mass communication', 'mass media studies', perhaps 'communication science'. The earlier book was based, implicitly at least, on a view of mass media study as a field of research to which many disciplines contributed but which had no disciplinary 'status' and, consequently, no theory of its own. An attempt was made to supply coherence by drawing on sociological theory and by summarizing the directions and main themes of research within a sociological framework, with particular reference to mass society theory and structural-functionalism. The original aim of the revision was to expand and update the earlier book by incorporating more recent research results. It was soon apparent, however, that it could not be done in this way, partly because the earlier framework proved inadequate and partly because media research had become too large in quantity and too diverse to be adequately summarized in a book of this scope.

The alternative strategy which has been adopted is to develop a better framework and to summarize work according to its theoretical yield rather than its empirical substance. This is something more than a response to practical difficulties, since it involves the assumption that media study has come to depend on, and in some degree contribute to, a body of theory which makes it more than a collection of loosely related research problems. In effect, it is assumed that we are dealing with something more than a research field. There is certainly no one theory of mass communication and much of what passes for theory is little more than a set of alternative perspectives or generalizations, whose applicability or validity depends on variations of social and historical circumstances and on the immediate conditions of time and place. It is difficult, in consequence, to offer a coherent thread beyond what is suggested by the familiar sequence 'society-sender-message-receiver-effect' which can be recognized in the table of contents. Even so, there is something more than this, set out in Chapter 2 and involving, in brief, a view of mass communication as the production, distribution and formation of 'public knowledge' under conditions of inequality in society which play a key part in the shaping of media processes.

13

It is in the nature of a book of this kind that the largest debt is one which cannot be fully acknowledged, since it is owed to the many researchers and writers whose work has been referred to or drawn on. However, I would like to name a few of those who have, in the course of personal contact (and often unwittingly), made a contribution to my thinking in preparing this book. They include Jay Blumler, Ray Brown, Christopher Bryant, Michael Gurevitch, John Hall, Cees Hamelink, Thelma McCormack, Karl-Erik Rosengren and Sven Windahl. I am grateful to Thomas McQuail for some expert advice on modern music and to Anne McQuail for working facilities in preparing Chapter 5. A number of the ideas were developed in work with and for students at the Department of Mass Communication of the University of Amsterdam and I appreciate the stimulus received from that quarter.

Denis McQuail
Schoorl, NH
October 1982

1 WHAT IS MASS COMMUNICATION?

Ideas about mass communication: 'common-sense', 'working' and social-scientific theory

This book is written at two or more removes from the subject of mass communication. What it does is to present the author's ideas about the various theories and explanations that have formed around those social forms and processes known as press, radio, television, cinema, etc. Insofar as we know what these are, and it would be difficult to name anything more widely known, the question at the head of this chapter looks superfluous, if not silly. Yet beyond the level of identification and summary description it is not a very easy question to answer and there are many components and variants of the answers that have been given. The aim of the book is to give as full a version of the answers as is possible, without completely losing coherence and consistency. Some new ideas have been introduced in order to link and supplement the ideas of others. The result belongs to a certain category of theoretical knowledge which, as noted, stands at some distance from the media themselves and their activities. It is useful to consider the other possibilities of theoretical knowledge, since they will all enter into the story in one form or another, often disguised in some way or not clearly identified.

The first kind of knowledge might be called 'common-sense theory', since it refers to the ideas we all have about mass media by virtue of our direct experience and use of them as part of an audience or public. Any newspaper reader or television viewer has an implicit theory in the sense of a set of ideas about the medium in question, what it is, what it is good for, where it fits into daily life, how it should be 'read', what it connotes and how it relates to other essential aspects of social experience. Everyone carries quite an elaborate set of associations and ideas of this kind which enable him or her to act consistently and satisfactorily in relation to the media. Such common-sense theories are not usually articulated, but in them are grounded a number of basic definitions of what the media are and how they differ from each other. It is here also that we find one source of norms and standards governing media use and of expressions of public opinion about mass media which have some influence in media planning and the making of social policy for media. While it is not the aim of this book to try to report directly on

the substance of this kind of theory, it makes its appearance
inevitably by way of survey findings about attitudes to media,
reasons for media use and in the interpretations of observers.

Secondly, there is what might be called 'working theory', those
ideas held by the practitioners of the media about the purpose and
nature of their work and about the way in which certain effects are
to be achieved. Some of the ideas involved are matters of technique,
some are enshrined in traditions, professional practices, norms of
behaviour, rules of thumb, which shape the work of media
production and give it consistency over time. The theory is
'practical' because it helps to answer such questions as: 'What will
please the audience?' 'What will be effective?' 'What is newsworthy?' 'What are the responsibilities of the journalist or broad-
caster in a given case?' It may be pointed out that it is inappropriate
to call something theory which is rarely fully articulated or very
conscious. Nevertheless, it is unavoidable for us to refer to, and
draw upon, such ideas whether we call them theory or not, since
they emerge from research on the 'communicators', in however
mediated a form, and show through in the content of what they
produce. Elihu Katz (1977) has likened the task of the researcher in
this instance to that of the theorist of music or the philosopher who
can point to underlying regularities which the practising musician
or scientist may not, or does not need to, be aware of. What we call
'working theory' also contributes to ideas about what the media
ought to do. These are discussed in Chapter 3.

The third kind of theory is the most obvious, and the one to be
expected in a book of this nature — it is the deliberately reflective
knowledge of the professional social-scientific observer, who tries to
generalize from evidence and observation about the nature and
consequences of mass media. What the book offers as a whole is
drawn from each of these three sources, the first two kinds
appearing in indirect, disguised and partial ways as conclusions of
empirical research, the third as independently formed views of
individual thinkers or summaries of certain schools of thought.
While this may simply be a long way of saying that the sources are
theory and research, it is useful to recall where such evidence comes
from. One way to answer the question 'What is mass communication?' is to say 'What people think it is'. This is not a trivial point,
because the media, and each mass medium in its own place and time,
are very much constrained by a 'public definition' and a set of
expectations and norms which grow around them. Such definitions
are not given, in the first instance, by legislators or media theorists;
these only express a version of what everyone in society, but
especially the principal actors, the 'mass communicators', their

clients and the audience, have first established. The emergence of these 'definitions' is a very complex process and their precise form often hazy, but a brief review of their origins and character may help to make clear what is meant.

The rise of the media: the shaping of media definitions

The term 'communication revolution' has been applied to more than one development in the long history of media, from the invention of printing in the mid-fifteenth century to the current phase of innovation in computer-based audiovisual technology. Whenever a revolutionary claim is made it is usually followed by a reassessment which either points to more continuity than had been thought to exist or attributes the seeming effects to some other cause. There is no space here to relate the history of any one medium, never mind the several which have to be dealt with, but it will be useful to set out the approximate sequence of development, medium by medium, and try to indicate the major turning points, whether truly revolutionary or not, so that 'public definitions' of different media can be given a location in time and social context. These have tended to form early in the history of a given medium and to have been 'fixed' by circumstances surrounding its introduction, beyond what was strictly required by the intrinsic characteristics of the means of communication. However, the definitions have also, as time has passed, become more complex, acquired more 'options' and sometimes even become internally contradictory so that one person's image of a given medium has little in common with another's. In putting together a typology of different media, as a step towards typifying mass communication in general, we have to assume a more or less universal convergence on an original western European form. This does some violence to history, but is not completely unjustified: there is a striking degree of universality about the global phenomena we recognize as mass media, whatever the reasons for the convergence.

In the history of mass media we deal with four main elements: a technology; the political, social, economic and cultural situation of a society; a set of activities, functions or needs; people — especially as formed into groups, classes or interests. These have interacted in different ways and with different orders of primacy for different media, with sometimes one seeming to be the driving force or precipitating factor, sometimes another. The history of modern media begins with the *printed book* — certainly a kind of revolution yet initially only a technical device for reproducing the same or rather similar range of texts that was already being extensively copied. Only gradually does it lead to a change in content — more secular, practical and popular works, especially in the vernacular, political and religious pamphlets and tracts — which played a part in the transformation of the medieval world. Thus there occurred a revolution of society in which the book played an inseparable part.

It was almost two hundred years after the invention of printing before what we now recognize as a prototypical *newspaper* could be distinguished from the handbills, pamphlets and news books of the late sixteenth and seventeenth centuries. Its chief precursor seems, in fact, to have been the letter rather than the book — the news-letters circulating through the rudimentary postal service, concerned especially with transmitting news of events with a relevance for international trade and commerce. It was thus an extension into the public sphere of an activity which had long taken place in diplomacy and within or for large business houses. The early newspaper is marked by: regular appearance; commercial basis (openly for sale); multiple purpose (for information, record, advertising, diversion, gossip); a public character; normally a dis-connection from identifiable sources, except in the case of official newspapers. It is thus a form of service, seeming in retrospect to be a discontinuity and a new beginning in communication history. In a sense, it was more of an innovation than the printed book — the invention of a new literary, social and cultural form — even if it would not have been perceived as so distinctive at the time. Its distinctiveness, compared to other forms of cultural communica-tion, lies in its individualism, reality orientation, utility, secularity and suitability for the needs of a new class, the town-based bourgeoisie. Its novelty consisted not in its technology or manner of distribution but in its functions for a distinct class in a changing and more permissive social-political climate.

The later history of the newspaper can be told either as a story of continuous progress towards mass distribution, independence and authority in society or as a series of struggles, advances and reverses. We can only deal briefly with those aspects of history which enter into the modern definition of the newspaper. The most important are: the varying degrees of tension in relations with the state; the increasing popular reach; the rise of the late nineteenth century liberal newspaper; the political party press; the 'commer-cialization' of the press in the present century. National histories diverge too much to tell a single story but these five elements can be recognized in many countries. From its beginning, the newspaper has been an actual or potential adversary of established power, though more a threat in the perception of the state and vested

interests than in reality. Even so, powerful images in press history
refer to the punishment of printers, editors and journalists, the
struggle for freedom to publish, the activity of newspapers in the
fight for freedom, democracy and working class rights, the part
played by an underground press under foreign occupation or
dictatorial rule. There has also, in general terms, been a linear
progression historically, if not towards more freedom for
newspapers then at least in the methods used for control. In
countries not under authoritarian rule, the form of control has
passed from violence to legal constraint, to fiscal burden and now to
institutionalization within a market system.

The second feature of press history, the growing popular availability, is familiar enough and its significance is obvious. However,
there are disputes about its immediate causes — whether better
technology, industrialization, rising literacy, popular demand, or
low cost. In fact, there seem to be different answers for different
stages and majority penetration of daily newspapers did not arrive
in most countries until after the first world war. It is also important
not to confuse the great 'market penetration' of the mass press with
those moments in history when the newspaper was very significant
for popular and working class movements, even when expensive and
not easily accessible (Thompson, 1963; Harrison, 1974).

The reason for singling out the late nineteenth century newspaper
as a high, if not a turning, point in press history is that it has
seemed to contribute most to our modern understanding of what a
newspaper is or should be. The 'high bourgeois' phase of press
history, from about 1850 to the turn of the century, was the product
of several events and circumstances: the triumph of liberalism and
ending, except in more benighted quarters of Europe, of direct
censorship or fiscal constraint; the establishment of a relatively
progressive capitalist class and several emergent professions —
thus forging a business-professional establishment; many social and
technological changes favouring the operation of a national or
regional press of high information quality. The chief features of the
new 'elite' press which was established in this period were: formal
independence from the state and from open vested interests; an
acceptance into the structure of society as a major institution of
political and social life; a highly developed sense of social and ethical
responsibility; the rise of a journalistic profession dedicated to the
objective reporting of events; an adoption, at the same time, of the
role of opinion-giver or -former; frequently a tendency to identify
with the 'national interest'. Many current expectations about what
is a good or 'elite' newspaper reflect several of these ideas and they
also provide the basis for criticisms of press forms which deviate

from the ideal, either by being too partisan or too 'sensational'.
The fourth feature of press history, the growth of a party press, is
not universally in evidence. It is, for instance, now more or less
absent in North America and has had a rather feeble growth in
Britain and countries under British influence, despite the
favourable early history of the radical press (Harrison, 1974). There
is a difference between a partisan press and a party-aligned press
and the latter has often shared some of the features of the 'high
bourgeois' press as well as being historically contemporaneous. It is
usually professional, it is independent from the state, it is
informative, serious and opinion-forming. Its unique aspects are its
attachment to its readers through party, its sectionalism and its
mobilizing function for party ends.

Lastly, we must consider the rise of the mass newspaper, often
called the 'commercial' newspaper for two reasons: its operation as a
profitable business enterprise by monopolistic press concerns and
its heavy contribution from advertising revenue to operating costs.
The latter especially made it possible and desirable to establish a
mass readership. It has been argued that commercial aims and
underpinning have indirectly exerted considerable influence on
content, making sectors of the press implicitly favourable to
business, consumerism and free enterprise. Newspapers which are
part of large business empires, and not only the mass newspaper, do
often seem to display these characteristics (Tunstall, 1982). For our
purpose, it is more relevant to see, as a result of commercialization,
the emergence of a new kind of newspaper: lighter and more entertaining, more sensational in its attention to crime, violence,
scandals and stars, having a very large readership in which lower
income and education groups are over-represented. While this might
now appear to be the dominant newspaper form, it draws its status
as a *newspaper* from the 'high bourgeois' form and is otherwise
defined by its deviation from the latter.

It has been necessary to give somewhat undue space to a potted
newspaper history, just because it is long and complex. Much less
can be said here of the other main media: film, radio, television and
recorded music. *Film* began at the end of the nineteenth century as a
technological novelty, but what it offered was scarcely new in
content or function. It transferred to a new means of distribution an
older tradition of entertainment, offering: stories, spectacles, music,
drama, humour and technical tricks for popular consumption. It
was partly a response to the 'invention' of leisure — time out of
work — and an answer to the demand for economical and (usually)
respectable ways of enjoying free time for the whole family. Thus it
provided for the working class some of the cultural benefits already

enjoyed by their 'betters'. To judge from its phenomenal growth, the latent demand met by film must have been enormous 'and if we choose from the main formative elements named above, it would not be the technology or the social climate but the needs met by the film for a class (urban lower middle and working) which mattered most — the same elements, although a different need and a different class, which produced the newspaper.

The characterization of the film as old show business in a new form for an expanded market is not the whole story. There have been three other significant strands in film history and one, or perhaps two, major turning points. Firstly, the use of film for propaganda is noteworthy, especially when applied to national or societal purposes, based on a belief in its great reach, supposed realism, emotional impact and popularity. The practice of combining improving message with entertainment had been long established in literature and drama, but new elements in film were the capacity to reach so many so quickly and to be able to manipulate the seeming reality of the photographic message without loss of credibility. The two other strands in film history were the emergence of several schools of film art (Huaco, 1963) and the rise of the social documentary film movement. Each of these was deviant in, respectively, having a minority appeal and having an orientation to realism. Yet both have a link, partly fortuitous, with the 'film as propaganda' strand of history, in that both tended to develop at times of social crisis in several countries. It is also worth drawing attention to the thinly concealed ideological and implicitly propagandist elements in many popular entertainment films, a phenomenon which seems independent of the presence or absence of societal freedom. A word is due also about the use of film in education, more advocated than practised, based in part on the apparent capacity of film to keep attention and in part on some of its unique message-carrying capacity. In retrospect, despite the dominance of entertainment uses in film history, there seems to be unifying thread in its leaning towards didactic-propagandistic applications, in other words towards manipulation. It may be that the film is intrinsically susceptible to manipulative purpose because it requires a much more conscious and artificial construction (i.e. manipulation) than other media. In this respect, only writing is its competitor.

Of the two turning points noted above one, the coming of television, is more clearly consequential than the other. The latter development, well chronicled by Tunstall (1977), is the high degree of americanization of film industry and film culture in the years after the first world war, partly because of the war itself. The relative decline of nascent, but flourishing, European film industries has probably been responsible for a good many trends in the homogenization of culture and for the dominance of one main definition of what film is about and what the world of film connotes. Television clearly took away a large part of the film-viewing public, especially the general family audience, leaving a much smaller and younger film audience. It also took away or diverted the social documentary stream of film development and gave it a more congenial home. However, it did not do the same for the art film or for film aesthetics, although the art film has probably benefited from the 'demassification' and greater specialization of the film/cinema medium. One last consequence of this turning point is the reduced need for 'respectability'. The film was freer to cater to the demand for violent, horrific or pornographic content. Despite some increase in freedom of this kind, due mainly to changing social norms, the film has not been able to claim the full rights of political and artistic self-expression and many countries retain the apparatus of licensing, censorship and powers of control. A last concomitant, if not consequence, of film's subordination to television in audience appeal has been its wide integration with other media, especially book publishing, popular music and television itself. It has acquired a certain centrality (Jowett and Linton, 1980), despite its direct audience loss, as a showcase for other media and as a cultural source, out of which come books, strip cartoons, television stars and series, songs. Thus it now contributes as a mass culture creator, instead of merely drawing on other media as it mainly did in its golden days.

Radio and television have, respectively, a sixty- and thirty-year history as mass media behind them and both grew out of pre-existing technologies — telephone, telegraph, moving and still photography, sound recording. Despite their obvious differences and now wide discrepancies in content and use, radio and television can be treated together. The first point of importance is the extent to which radio seems to have been a technology looking for a use, rather than a response to a demand for a new kind of service or content. According to Raymond Williams (1975), 'Unlike all previous communications technologies, radio and television were systems primarily designed for transmission and reception as abstract processes, with little or no definition of preceding content'. Radio, certainly, was firstly a technology and only later a service and much the same was true of television, which began more as a toy and novelty than a serious or even popular contribution to social life. Both came to borrow from all existing media and all the most popular content of both is derivative — films, news and sports.

Perhaps the main genre innovation common to both radio and television has been the direct account or observation of events as they happen. However, since many events thought worthy of public notice are planned in advance, the addition of actuality to what writing and film already offered has been somewhat limited. A second main fact of importance in radio/television history has been its high degree of regulation, control or licensing by public authority — initially out of technical necessity, later from a mixture of democratic choice, state self-interest, economic convenience and sheer institutional custom. A third and related historical feature of radio/television has been its centre-periphery pattern of distribution and the association of national television with political life and power centres of society, as it has become established as both popular and political in its functions. Despite, or perhaps because of, this closeness to power, radio and television have hardly anywhere acquired the same freedom, as of right, to express views and act with political independence as the press enjoys. At this moment in a short history we seem to be moving towards a first major turning point for television, in which several of its established features are being challenged by technological developments — especially under threat are the dominant centre-periphery form of organization and the high degree of control and supervision of content. It is appropriate that a medium owing its existence to a technology should be challenged by a technology, but in the event it is not the new technology as such which challenges television, but its greater functionality — the promise of more uses and services for different groups without the existing constraints. New electronic means of distribution, involving cable and/or space satellite, are now being developed mainly to meet demands raised, but not satisfied, by television and film.

Public definitions of the media

Dimensions of media images
The main purpose behind this inadequate potted history, apart from localizing the subject in time, has been to point to the sources of the main component strands in the dominant definitions acquired by the media. These strands can now be extracted and summarized. The first concerns the circumstances and manner of *distribution and reception* of media — with the kind of act or experience involved for the user. The main points to bear in mind are: whether one chooses an individual unit of content or peruses a wide range of items (specialist shop versus supermarket model); whether

attention is individual or collective; whether or not the supply is managed and organized; whether the act of use or the content itself is constrained by limitations of time or place. The second strand is the *political* dimension which refers both to tendencies for external authority to limit and regulate the medium and also to any tendency from within the medium itself to be critical or non-conformist. These two characteristics do not necessarily go together. Connected with this dimension is the centrality of a medium or its typical content to the state and societal power in general.

The third strand to take into account is a complex one which might be labelled summarily as a dimension of *cultural and social values*. It interrelates three sub-dimensions: the continuum between reality and fiction or fantasy; the contrast of the moral with the non-moral and associations of serious purpose with those of 'fun' and leisure; a distinction between art and non-art. While these can apply independently, there is a tendency for reality (information and education), morality and art to be associated. All tend to be favoured by the 'dominant values' in most societies.

A fourth component is that of *social relationships*. Different media seem to favour certain kinds and degrees of relationship between sender and receiver or amongst receivers and these have entered into the image and reality of different media. One aspect has to do with conditions of use — media can tend to be solitary or social in the context of reception. Another has to do with the degree of involvement and attachment between receiver and sender — which can be either strong or weak. Thirdly, media and media experience tend to have a location in society which corresponds to a certain level of social life and experience. Concretely, media do, or can, connect with experience in the context of neighbourhood, local community, region or nation. They may also be international or without any clear location. The more local the connection, the closer the social relationship between receiver and source.

A fifth dimension is a mixed one, but can be labelled *organizational*, referring to three things in particular: firstly, the location or 'weighting' of the medium according to the three elements of content, production and distribution. Here the essential question is whether a medium is message-centred, production-centred or distribution-centred. Another component is the importance of technology — has it a high or a low technology image? Lastly, has a given medium a clear professional definition? Is there a core professional activity which comes easily to mind?

These summarily described dimensions (set out in Figure 1, below) structure the public definition of media and will be guidelines in the pages that follow. The aim is to arrive at a composite view of each medium in which dominant features of its institutional form, its own self-image and the experience of its audience play a part. In several cases, it will be evident that these 'images' of media are fragile or internally incoherent, even 'untrue' to a given reality. There are several reasons for these inevitable weaknesses, aside from faults in their construction and their somewhat impressionistic character. They are vulnerable to historical change; there are differences between national societies; they are always multifaceted and the reality they summarize is complex; a definition imposed 'from above', or inherited from the past, sometimes comes into conflict with an image formed in current use from 'below'. The book provides a good example, since it is strongly associated with the social 'top', with education, religion and the law, having an aura of the sacred and permanent. Yet for most people the book is a magazine or comic or an erotic, romantic or mystery story used for 'escape' and diversion. This problem is essentially unresolvable and in the characterization that follows some preference has been given, where there is a conflict, to the dominant image and definition rather than that which can be inferred from observing content and behaviour. The sources for what follows are numerous and not easy to document but they draw on the three kinds of knowledge described above — 'common-sense knowledge' and 'everyday experience'; the knowledge which media and their personnel have and disseminate about themselves; concepts and theories of the social sciences. In many cases it would be possible to support points by reference to survey evidence, content analysis or the facts of audience behaviour and structure, but, for reasons of space, this has not been systematically done.

The 'media definition' has already been described as an outcome of a mixture of circumstances, experience and impression. As a concept, its intellectual origins include: the Weberian 'ideal type', which involves the selection and accentuation of key features of reality to form a manageable construct; the functional approach, which leads to a characterization of activities according to purpose or effect; the literary, art-historical or cultural study method, which deals with genres and schools of content. The uses of such a concept have been as varied as these origins would lead one to expect, but something of the kind has been used especially imaginatively by McLuhan (1962 and 1964), Carey (e.g. 1969), Williams (1975) and Tunstall (1977).

The book
The book is experienced in use as a set of innumerable, separate

items of content available for free choice and use by individuals. The supply is not very evidently managed, although shops, libraries, schools and families play a part. The book is rather time- and place-free as to use and book content is also rather unconstrained as to historical time and geographical space. On the second main dimension, that of politics, the book has strong associations with freedom, although its potential for dissidence is liable to be limited; and it has some political 'aura' despite the relatively small number of books with any direct political relevance. Again, notwithstanding the main orientation of book content to entertainment and fantasy, the dominant associations of the book are with reality, morality, art and the serious, rather than the reverse. On the dimension of social relationships, reading is a solitary activity, but lending itself to high involvement and a sense of vicarious attachment to the writer, despite the frequent separation by space and time of author from reader. The book is not generally associated with neighbourhood or locality but with nation or beyond — it is often international or lacking any fixed social location. Organizationally, the image of the book is 'message-centred', 'low technology' and strongly associated with a single profession — that of writer, however mythical the profession may be.

The newspaper
The newspaper is individual and time- and place-free within limits, but differs on all other points of use from the book. Its content is not unitary but multiple (the supermarket model), it is historically very specific and perishable, its supply very much managed and organized by others (the press organization). Its position in relation to the dimension of freedom and control is similar to that of the book, but the newspaper is much more clearly central to state power because of the preponderance of politically relevant content. The dominant norm is that the newspaper should be free and its own self-image is potentially oppositional to authority, whatever the day-to-day reality. Its definition in terms of cultural and moral values is ambiguous to much the same degree as is the book, reflecting the two main forms of newspaper — the elite or party newspaper on the one hand and the popular, boulevard, press on the other. The former is oriented to reality, the moral and the serious, although it has no image as art. Even the popular newspaper pays lip service to its reality-orientation, without which it would have no claim to form opinion or to be a real *news*paper.

The social relationship definition of the newspaper deviates interestingly from that of the book. Newspaper reading is an individual, yet public, activity, taking place in cafes and public places as much if not more than in the home. Thus it is a kind of bridge between private and public. Otherwise it is variable, according to its several forms. It can be a basis for a strong attachment to locality, region and nation. Yet the dominant image is of a loose tie, consistent with the service, functional and 'secular' character of the modern newspaper. The newspaper is, like the book, message-centred, however different the content, and the currently advanced technology used in newspaper production has not really altered a 'low technology' image, probably formed a century or two ago. The professional status of the newspaper person is rather uncertain, but tends to focus on the idea of the fact-gathering reporter. The fuzziness of professional definition has some basis in reality and in the complexity of the newspaper world.

Film/cinema
In experience of use film/cinema is comparable to reading only in the sense that we choose individual units of content — film stories. Otherwise, the situation differs through the limited and other-determined supply, the collective or social nature of the film experience, the high degree of time/space binding. The repertoire of film may, however, have some features of literature in being often detached from its historical time and place. These elements of the film/cinema definition are undergoing quite rapid change with the spread of personal video and film libraries, and the large film component on television has already blurred the definition for the post-television generation(s). The public film has never really been entirely free from control, nor has it been regarded as much of a political threat to society. It is rather easy to control because of its elaborate production and distribution requirements. It seems sometimes to choose conformity, although perhaps no more than other media. It is not usually regarded as close to the political centre of society and its image tends to ignore or undervalue its political potential. On the dimension of cultural and moral values, film belongs predominantly in the sphere of fantasy, the non-moral, non-art and 'fun'. Its potential as documentary and connection with real experience, while evident from the range of content, tend to be subordinate to the general association with exotica and now, perhaps, erotica. The connotations of escape, glamour, stardom, formed very early in film history, still seem to predominate. As noted, film-going is usually a social or group activity and it is thought to favour a high degree of personal involvement in fictional situations and identification with stars and heroes. On the latter

point, there is some similarity to reading, but there is usually
missing a sense of contact with an author or a writer, partly due, no
doubt, to the 'star-system' and the collective nature of film-making.
On the other main sub-dimension of 'social relationship', it is clear
the film has no local associations, being either identifiable at the
national or international level or lacking any such location.
Organizationally, the emphasis is less on the message than on
production, which takes enormous capital and is often given much
publicity. Film, however complex technically, does not have a 'high
technology' image, but the world of film-making has elements of
mystery and remoteness.

Radio
Radio, although initially 'content-free', has acquired more than one
definition in its sixty-year existence as a mass medium, depending
mainly on its fortunes vis-à-vis television. In use, it has moved from
an individual to a family entertainer and back to an individual
instrument for certain functions, especially for the young. It has
also become more than ever defined as habitual background
accompaniment, a general activity, with relatively little weight
attached to specific units of content within it. In use it is relatively
time- and place-free but the content is both organized by others
(despite increasing channel choice) and 'timely' and thus perishable
— mainly news and music of the day. Its place on the political
spectrum is variable, but in its dominant use in most countries it is
not very political. Even so, it has some political uses and is often
subject to regulation in matters which touch on politics. One
subsidiary element in its image connects it with concepts of freedom
and constraint: it can cross frontiers more easily than other media,
be operated illegally, like the press, and is increasingly available for
short distance communication between individuals, without
regulation.
   In relation to cultural and moral values, radio occupies a mid-
point between the 'reality' and 'serious' pole and its opposite,
reflecting the more or less even balance between information and
entertainment in what it does. Its definition in respect of social
relationships has changed over time, as it has become less a mass
medium and more multi-channel and smaller in organizational scale.
Coupled with telephone, it has become increasingly interactive and
it can and does operate at every level of social organization, from
group to international contact. Looked at against the criteria of its
organizational image, it seems predominantly identifiable as a
means of distribution, as 'low technology', unmysterious and
lacking any real professional definition.

Television

Television shares some of these defining characteristics, but is sharply different at several points. In use it is still more a family than an individual resource and still very time- and space-bound. Here too, the situation is rapidly changing through the spread of video recorders and additional receivers. Politically, television is highly sensitive, close to centres of state and societal power, subject to scrutiny and regulation. There is virtually no record of television being used for political intervention or opposition and it must be the least revolutionary communication medium in history. Close supervision has left its mark on television's definition in respect of cultural and moral values. Like radio, it has a midway position, drawn in two directions — towards the real and the serious by some of its intrinsic properties and appointed social purpose, yet also drawn in the opposite direction by the diversion demands of its audiences and by much of the culture which it has picked up from cinema, theatre, show business, book fiction, the world of popular music and the sport industry. It is not generally credited with promoting strong or deep ties with its audience, although there is much identification and involvement with individual stars and personalities. In its social location, it is less localized and more international than radio, but more national than cinema. Organizationally, it still has a 'high technology' image. This will probably remain until home television-making is as familar as home movie-making. It is difficult to locate its 'organizational centre', since message, production and distribution seem to claim equal importance.

Recorded music

Recorded music is not always identified as a separate mass medium, but it has its own distribution system, a separate industry and some institutional autonomy. It also has an image that separates it from other media, however much clouded by the variety of types of music which are embraced. As to circumstances of distribution and use, it involves unitary content and is little constrained in space or time, but supply is largely managed by others. It is ambiguous only in having a dual image as both an individual and a group resource. In 'political' terms it is peripheral, rather open, if not often subject, to control, but still with an element of non-conformity in its image, perhaps through its association with youth and change. There is a clear polarity between the 'serious' and 'non-serious', but the weight of association is with the latter and whatever kind of music is involved, there is more of fantasy than reality. Recorded music also has an inconsistent image in respect of involvement, since it can invoke strong attachment and yet also serve as 'background'. Like film it is 'distant' or unlocated in social terms. Its organizational image is least easy to sketch, but message and production have more weight than distribution. Further, it seems to be acquiring a more 'technological' image as production values gain over those of message or artistic performance and as the technologies of distribution develop and diversify.

A summary profile of media images

The results of these brief sketches and speculative comments are set out in summary form in Figure 1. It should be stressed that no firm and universally valid 'location' can be found for any medium and the figure is intended only as an aid to presentation of what has been described and as a stimulus to further thought about the nature of media and their varying characteristics.

Figure 1
Images of the media:
locating media on the main dimensions
of their public definition

I CONDITIONS OF CONTENT, DISTRIBUTION AND USE

i Unitary content	Book Film Music		Press Radio TV	Multiple content
ii Use time- and space-free	Book Press Radio Music		Film TV	Use time- and space-bound
iii Supply not managed	Book	Music Radio TV	Film Press	Supply managed
iv Content time- and space-free	Book	Film Music	Press TV Radio	Content time- and space-bound

II POLITICAL

i Central to the state	Press TV	Book Film Radio	Music	Peripheral to the state
ii Control and conformity	TV	Film Radio Music	Press Book	Freedom and resistance

III SOCIAL AND CULTURAL VALUES

i Reality-oriented	Press Book TV Radio		Film Music	Fantasy-oriented
ii Moral/ Serious	Book	Press TV Radio Music	Film	Non-moral/ fun
iii Art	Book	Film Music TV Radio	Press	Non-art

IV SOCIAL RELATIONSHIPS

i Solitary	Book Press Radio	Music	Film TV	Group
ii Involvement high	Book TV Film	Music	Press Radio	Involvement low
iii Location close	Press Radio	Book TV	Film Music	Distant or unlocated

V ORGANIZATIONAL

i Message central	Book Film Music	Press central	Production Radio TV	Distribution central
ii Technology high	Film TV	Press Music	Book Radio	Technology low
iii Profession defined	Book	Press	Film Music TV Radio	Profession ill-defined

Characteristics of mass communication

The media institution

This sketch of the main mass media provides the material for formulating in a more abstract way the key features of mass communication as it has been perceived by social scientists. This calls for separate remarks about the media institution, the process which goes on within it, the idea of a mass and of mass behaviour, and, finally, mass culture, the typical content which is produced. The mass media institution is a distinct set of activities (sending and receiving messages), carried out by persons occupying certain roles (regulators, producers, distributors, audience members), according to certain rules and understandings (laws, professional codes and practices, audience expectations and habits). Of the features of this institution, the most important are the following. Firstly, it is concerned with producing and distributing 'knowledge' — information, ideas, culture. Secondly, it provides channels for relating certain people to other people — senders to receivers, audience members to other audience members, everyone to their society and to its other constituent institutions. These channels are not only the physical channels of the communication network, but also the channels of custom and understanding which define who should, or is likely to, listen to whom.

Thirdly, the media operate almost exclusively in the public sphere — they comprise an open institution in which all can participate as receivers and, under certain conditions, even as senders. The media institution also has a public character in that mass media deal with

matters on which public opinion exists or can properly be formed
(i.e. not with personal and private matters or those which are
essentially for expert or scientific judgement). Fourthly,
participation in the institution as audience member is essentially
voluntary, without compulsion or social obligation, more so than is
often the case with other institutions concerned with knowledge
distribution, such as education, religion or politics. Going with this
voluntary character is the association of media use with leisure and
free time and its dissociation from work and duty. Related also is
the formal powerlessness of the media institution — it can claim no
authority in society nor has it a form of organization linking 'higher'
(message producers) with 'lower' participants (audiences). Fifthly,
the institution is linked with industry and the market, through its
dependence on work, technology and the need for finance. Finally,
the institution is invariably linked in some way with state power,
through legal mechanisms and legitimating ideas which vary from
one society to another (see below, p. 84). Despite variations, the
media are everywhere expected to meet some collective
informational, educational and recreational needs as well as to
satisfy the immediate demands of individual customers.

Mass communication process
The communication process which takes place within the framework
of the institution can only be described by exaggerating certain of
its features and, especially, by contrasting it with face-to-face communication between persons. Thus the source is not a single person
but a formal organization, and the 'sender' is often a professional
communicator. The message is not unique, variable and
unpredictable, but often 'manufactured', standardized, always
'multiplied' in some way. It is also a product of work and a
commodity with an exchange value as well as being a symbolic
reference with a 'use value'. The relationship between sender and
receiver is one-directional and rarely interactional, it is necessarily
impersonal and often perhaps 'non-moral' and calculative, in the
sense that the sender can have no responsibility for specific
consequences on individuals. The impersonality comes partly from
the physical and social distance between sender and receiver, but
also from the impersonality of the role of being a public
communicator, often governed by norms of neutrality and
detachment. The social distance implies an asymmetrical relationship, since the sender, while having no formal power over the
receiver, does usually have more resources, prestige, expertise and
authority. The receiver is part of a large audience, sharing the

experience with others and reacting in predictable and patterned ways. Mass communication often involves simultaneous contact between one sender and many receivers, allowing an immediate and extensive influence and an immediate response by many at one time. While uniformity of impact cannot be assumed, there is likely to be much less variability of response than occurs with slow and sequential person-to-person diffusion of information.

The mass concept
A key concept already much used in this book is that of 'mass' and while its elucidation should shed some light on the concept of mass communication, it turns out to be so complex and even contradictory in its uses and connotations that it does little more than remind us of the ambivalence with which society has regarded the phenomena under discussion (see Williams, 1976). It is important to record, nevertheless, that in social thought it has had, and retains, both negative and positive meanings. Its negative meaning comes from its use to refer to the mob or multitude, especially the mass of the ignorant and unruly. Mass connotes a lack of culture, of intelligence and even of rationality. In its positive sense, especially in the socialist tradition, it connotes the strength and solidarity of ordinary working people when organized together for political ends. Apart from the common reference to large number, the element which reconciles these two contradictory uses is the circumstance that unruly mobs were often observed acting in opposition to injustice or tyranny or in pursuit of some libertarian end. The difference is thus primarily that of opinion. The relevance for mass communication comes mainly from the meaning of multiple or mass production and the large size of the public reached by the media. There is also, in one of its original meanings, the idea of an amorphous collectivity in which the components are hard to distinguish. The shorter *Oxford English Dictionary* gives one definition of 'mass' as an 'aggregate in which individuality is lost' and this definition is close to the meaning that sociologists have attached to the word, especially when applied to the audience.

Herbert Blumer (1939) made the original definition and he did so partly by using a set of contrasts with other kinds of collectivity encountered in social life, especially the 'group', 'crowd' and 'public'. In the small group, all members know each other, are aware of their common membership, share the same values, have a certain structure of relationships which is stable over time and interact to achieve some purpose. The crowd is larger, but still restricted within observable boundaries in a particular space. It is, however, temporary and rarely re-forms with the same composition. It may possess a high degree of identity and share the same mood, but there is usually no structure and order to its social or moral composition. Its members are equal, but fuse temporarily together as part of an ongoing event which has brought the crowd into being and sustains it. It can act, but its actions are often seen to have an affective and emotional, perhaps also irrational, character. The third collectivity named by Blumer, the public, is likely to be quite large, widely dispersed and enduring. It tends to form around an issue or cause in public life and its primary purpose is to advance an interest or opinion and to achieve political change. It is an essential component of participant democratic institutions, based on the ideal of rational discourse within an open political system and often comprising the 'informed' section of the population. The rise of the public is characteristic of modern liberal democracies and related to the rise of the 'bourgeois' or party newspaper described above.

The term 'mass' captures several features of the new audience for cinema and radio which were missing or not linked together by any of these three existing concepts. It was often very large — larger than most groups, crowds or publics. It was very widely dispersed and its members were usually unknown to each other or to whoever brought the audience into existence. It lacked self-awareness and self-identity and was incapable of acting together in an organized way to secure objectives. It was marked by a shifting composition within changing boundaries. It did not act for itself, but was rather 'acted upon'. It was heterogeneous, in consisting of large numbers from all social strata and demographic groups, but homogeneous in its behaviour of choosing a particular object of interest and in the perception of those who would like to 'manipulate' it. The audience for mass media is not the only social formation that can be characterized in this or a similar way, since the word is sometimes applied to the 'mass market' of consumers, or the 'mass electorate'. It is significant, however, that such entities also correspond with audiences and that mass media are used to direct or control 'consumer behaviour' and the 'political behaviour' of large numbers of voters. The extension of the idea of the mass to the idea of a mass society is discussed in Chapter 2.

Mass culture

In the discussion of mass media and mass communication, a further word is needed about the concept of mass culture, which has often been used to describe the typical content produced and disseminated by the media. It too has many shades of meaning and strong pejorative connotations, although these are not universally present. Again the point of view is all important. Conservative critics of democratic tendencies refer negatively to mass culture because it is seen as the culture of the uncultivated, those with low tastes, a response to their lack of discrimination or education. Critics of mass culture sympathetic to 'ordinary' people and democracy often may share much the same judgement about the culture itself — that it is standardized, unoriginal, lacking in the richness, ambiguity and stimulating power of art, often ugly and debased — but they do not blame the people who consume it, but those who cynically impose it on ordinary people for profit or manipulative purpose. (See references to the Frankfurt School below, pp. 62–3.) A third possibility is to refer to the 'culture of the masses' in a favourable way, as in the Soviet Union, where the 'mass' is the repository of what is good, but the culture referred to is in fact often very different from the 'mass culture' of capitalist society. Finally, 'mass culture' or 'popular culture' can be used as neutral or even favourable references to what is modern, topical, interesting and fashionable at the moment.

Attempts have been made to define mass culture, or the typical culture of mass media, in an objective way. Thus Wilensky (1964, p. 176) makes use of a contrast with the notion of 'high culture' which

will refer to two characteristics of the product: (1) it is created by or under the supervision of a cultural elite operating within some aesthetic, literary, or scientific tradition; [....] (2) critical standards independent of the consumer of the product are systematically applied to it. [....] 'Mass culture' will refer to cultural *products manufactured solely for the mass market.* Associated characteristics, not intrinsic to the definition, are *standardization* of product and *mass behaviour* in its use.

The comparison would be strengthened by including another cultural form — that of folk culture or culture which does come from the people and predates mass media and mass production of culture. Such culture was tending to be rediscovered in the nineteenth century at the very time that it was rapidly disappearing. It was originally made unself-consciously, using traditional designs, themes and materials, and was incorporated into everyday life. It has sometimes been despised by the elite because of its simplicity, lack of fashion, or association with peasant and 'lower class' life and official protection usually came rather too late to save it as a living tradition.

The urban working class who were the first 'customers' for the new mass culture were probably already cut off from the roots of the folk culture. The mass media must have both drawn on some popular culture streams and adapted them to the conditions of urban life, to provide some forms of culture, especially of a literary and musical kind, where there was none at all. We can conclude this discussion of mass culture by reference to another rather convincing attempt to give an objective meaning to the concept. Bauman (1972) describes it, not in evaluative or aesthetic terms, but as an inevitable outcome of some near universal processes of modern society: the rise of the market; the supremacy of large scale organization; and the availability of new technology for cultural production. To some extent, the debate about mass culture is simply part of the long process of coming to terms with the consequences, for old conceptions of art, of new possibilities of reproduction (Benjamin, 1977). Yet, despite the increase of relativism about cultural standards and the seeming irrelevance or illogicality of many objections to 'mass culture', what we continue to call culture remains an important element in conceptions of a good society or desirable way of life and mass media continue to provide channels for distributing it.

Limits to mass experience
This long discussion of characteristics of mass communication may have tended to mislead in several ways, especially in overemphasizing the 'massive' character of the media phenomenon and our experience of it, in giving a weight to some apparently negative aspects, in seeming to show the media as centrally responsible for many aspects of modern social life. More will be said later, but it is worth stressing here that we encounter the media mainly in ways which are not anomic, alienating or threatening. We attend by choice to what we like, with others in our familiar social circle, and are able to interact with them, if not with the distant senders. Within the general audience for mass media are numerous small, selective or local audiences and the possibilities for interaction with, or response to, media 'senders' are greater than the 'ideal type' of mass communication suggests. The experience of mass media does not necessarily reduce the quality of social life and may contribute to it, since around 'mass communication' there often develop related or fringe activities. Mass communication also develops out of and extends family, group and neighbourhood activities and interests. Where experience of mass media does seem to fit the ideal type described, when we are members of an enormous audience, the causes often lie not with the media but in social life itself which gives rise to some occasions in which society exhibits its unity and solidarity and its members unite in common interests and feelings.

If there is a trend to be observed it is away from 'massive' experience and 'massive' media, since new developments in distribution systems and the spread of individually-owned means of communication (cameras, recorders, computers) are likely to reduce the distance between senders and receivers and demystify as well as demassify the mass media.

Mass communication and social change

The problem of causation
Any description and definition of mass communication by way of a historical sketch inevitably raises the question of the relationship between the rise of mass communication and other changes in society. Insofar as an answer has been provided in this chapter, it has tended towards the portrayal of media as an outcome of changes in society, a response to certain demands, or an expression of a given set of historical circumstances. However, if one takes up the question directly, there are several possible answers and a number of theories which give different versions of the relationship. In essence, each theory offers an alternative way of relating three basic elements: technology of communication; form and content; changes in society (social structure, institutional arrangements, the distribution of public beliefs, values and opinions). In the following review an attempt is made to summarize the main alternative views about the interrelationship of these three elements. It should be borne in mind that they are not all mutually exclusive and no single theory can be expected to apply universally, given the variety of historical circumstances involved.

The complexity of terms and propositions, as well as the variety of time and place involved, makes it essential to simplify. To this end, a very basic typology for handling most of the key elements has been borrowed from Rosengren (1980). This involves the cross-tabulation of two basic propositions: 'Social structure influences culture' and its reverse, 'Culture influences social structure'. For our purposes, which are much the same as those of Rosengren, we can read social structure as social change and culture as mass communication. The scheme offers no separate place for the technology, but by implication it is an aspect of the cultural rather than the social. However, its introduction as a separate element is important for some variants of theory about media. The cross-tabulation yields four cells for which Rosengren has supplied labels as in Figure 2 and these terms can serve as a classification of the main theoretical approaches.

Figure 2
Types of relation between culture (media) and society

Culture influences		Social structure influences culture	
		YES	NO
Culture influences	YES	Interdependence	Idealism
Social structure	NO	Materialism	Autonomy

Interdependence
Under this heading can be placed the numerous accounts of the media which portray them as interactive with changes in society but do not single out one dominant direction of effect. Thus society produces the demands for information and entertainment to which media respond, the resources of money and time needed for the growth of media industries, the inventions on which they are based, the social-cultural climate in which they are free to operate. Mass communication in turn, and coterminously, stimulates change, accelerates the demands for its own services, contributes to the climate of cultural and political freedom in which media can themselves better operate, diffuses new ideas and innovations. Clark (1969) reports the views of the French sociologist, Gabriel Tarde, writing about 1900, that he

> envisaged a constant interweaving of influences between these two levels (the social structural and the technical): technological developments made newspapers possible, newspapers promote the formation of broader publics, and they, by broadening the loyalties of their members create an extensive network of overlapping and shifting groupings.

The two influences are so bound together that neither mass communication nor modern forms of society is conceivable without the other and each is a necessary but not a sufficient condition for the other. Much use has, for instance, been made of possession of mass media as an index of development or modernization, without reference to which is the cause of the other. In summarizing the interaction perspective, we can say that the media may equally be considered to mould, mirror and follow social change. This covers all possibilities except that of independence.

Idealism
Because of its many connotations and uses, the term is somewhat

misleading but translates into the proposition that media (i.e. culture) are primary moulders of society as well as reflectors of it. The main difficulty in using the term comes from the distinction between technology and content and some variants of theory which emphasize the technological (medium and channel) aspects might seem to be more 'materialist' than 'idealist'. However, we distinguish four main versions under this heading: individual value change; media as an 'engine of change'; technological determinism, cultivation theory.

Individual value change
The basic view is that media encourage and help to diffuse a personal value system which is favourable to innovation, mobility, achievement and consumption. While it can apply very widely, the theory has been formulated specifically for developing societies. Lerner (1958), for instance, held that media (of any kind, but especially 'western' media) could help to break down the 'traditionalism' which is an obstacle to 'modernity', by raising expectations and aspirations, widening horizons, enabling people to imagine and want a 'better alternative' for themselves and their families. The view is consistent with psycho-sociological explanations of development (e.g. Hagen, 1962; McLelland, 1961) and emphasizes spontaneous, demand-based change, rather than planned change from 'above'.

Media as an 'engine of change'
Here we have the straightforward alternative view that media can best be used in a planned way to bring about change by applying them in large scale programmes of development. Their task is to extend public education and promote innovation in agriculture, health practice, population control and other social and economic matters. A principal worker in this sphere and chronicler of the results is Everett Rogers (1962; 1973; 1976), although he has come, over time, to emphasize less the direct impact of media than their involvement with other networks and channels of influence. Nevertheless, the theory is widely applied and not irrelevant for developed countries where media are used in campaigns with social change as an objective, especially in the field of health and education. It goes with a general belief that education leads to social change. If one counts the adoption of new products as social change, then advertising also provides a striking example of applied cultural determinism.

Technological (medium) determinism

As noted above, the location of such theories under the heading of 'idealism' may be disputed, although technology in this context has usually acquired a cultural meaning and form before it is treated as an independent influence on further developments in society. The most complete and influential variant of media determinism is probably that of the Canadian economic historian, Harold Innis (1950; 1951), especially as elaborated by Marshall McLuhan. Innis attributed the characteristic features of successive ancient civilizations to the prevailing and dominant mode of communication, each of which will have its own 'bias' in terms of societal form. Thus he regarded the change from stone to papyrus as causing a shift from royal to priestly power. In ancient Greece, an oral tradition and a flexible alphabet favoured inventiveness and diversity and prevented the emergence of a priesthood with a monopoly over education. The foundation of the Roman empire was favoured by a written culture on which legal-bureaucratic institutions, capable of administering distant areas, could be based. Printing, in turn, challenged bureaucratic control and encouraged both nationalism and individualism. There are two main organizing principles in Innis' work. Firstly, as in the economic sphere, communication leads over time to monopolization by a group or class of the means of communication and knowledge. In turn this produces a disequilibrium which either impedes change and expansion or leads to competitive emergence of other forms of communication which tend to correct the disequilibrium. Secondly, the most important dimensions of empire are space and time and some means of communication are more suitable to one than the other. Thus empires can persist for long in time or extensively in space, depending on the available form of communication. McLuhan's (1962) developments of the theory offered valuable insights into the consequences of print media, but attempts to assess consequences of audiovisual media by a similar method of analysis have been obscure or unconvincing (McLuhan, 1964).

Other writers have cited more historically-bound examples of social effect from forms of communication and there is a large literature on the social consequences of printing (e.g. Eisenstein, 1978). An interpretation of political changes in the modern period, which gives an important place to communication technology, has been offered by Gouldner (1976). He identified the rise and, perhaps, fall of 'ideology' as a key aspect of change, defining ideology as a special form of rational discourse. He writes (p. 39):

> The culture of discourse that produces ideology was historically grounded in the

technology of a specific kind of mass (or public) media and its specific mode of production: privately owned, small scale, widely diffused, competitive and decentralized units ... Printing made it possible and necessary to mobilize political support among the masses. Printing could reach the great numbers concentrated in the growing urban areas.

He goes on to attribute the 'age of ideology' of the eighteenth and nineteenth centuries to the wide availability of print material, especially in the form of news which led to a need for processing and interpretation of information. Ideology was a response to the 'communication revolution' — an effort to 'supply meaning' to otherwise fragmented public knowledge. He then portrays the newer media of radio, film and television as having caused an 'attenuation of ideology' by a shift from a 'conceptual to an iconic symbolism', revealing a split between the 'cultural apparatus' (intelligentsia) which produces ideology and the 'consciousness industry' which controls the new mass public. This is the cause of the 'decline of ideology', with a further change in prospect as universal computer-based systems of communication develop.

This thesis draws in part on the numerous critiques of mass culture and the 'consciousness industry' (e.g. Morin, 1962) and clearly much of the thinking of the Frankfurt School (see pp. 62–3) belongs to the 'idealist' category of media theory, however modified by marxist emphasis on structural determinism. In such theory, there is a general agreement on the power of modern mass communication forms as applied to shape political and social reality, in particular to hold back change.

Cultivation theory
The term derives from a particular approach to the study of media effects developed by Gerbner (1967) (see below, pp. 204–5), out of his assessment of the major historical significance of the rise of mass media. In essence, he argues that this significance comes not from the formation of 'the mass' but from the 'creation of shared ways of selecting and viewing events', by delivering to them 'technologically produced and mediated message systems', thus common ways of seeing and understanding the world. He calls it the 'cultivation of dominant image patterns'. In effect, the media tend to offer uniform and relatively consensual versions of social reality and their audiences are 'acculturated' accordingly. Gerbner makes a prediction that media, especially television because of the systematic character of its message and its consistency over time, have powerful effects and he comes down firmly in favour of the media as moulders of society.

Cultural imperialism
The ideas underlying the thesis of 'cultural' or 'media' imperialism
are at the same time simple and complex. They have their origin in
early theory and evidence concerning the role of media in national
development (e.g. Lerner, 1958; Schramm, 1964) and in critical
reformulation by writers such as Schiller (1969), Wells (1972),
Mattelart (1979) and many others. The correlate of the view that
media can help in 'modernization' by introducing 'western' values is
that they do so at the cost of a breakdown of traditional values and
the loss of 'authentic' local cultures. In the simple view, it can be
argued that the values so introduced are those of capitalism and
that the process is 'imperialistic' in deliberately, or knowingly and
systematically, subordinating smaller and developing countries to
the interests of the dominant capitalist powers, especially the
United States. The complexities, which are well discussed in
Tunstall (1977), Boyd-Barrett (1977; 1982), or Golding (1977), arise
from the great variety of forms and mechanisms of intercultural
penetration, the strength and diversity of the forces sustaining
media penetration and the difficulty of finding alternatives. Even
so, there is a clear proposition which belongs at this point in our
review of theories that states that media exert an influence
(formulated as negative or regressive) on receiving cultures, by way
of actual media products, themes and genres and by professional
practices and values. The direction of effect is said to be favourable
to the adoption of social forms and personal behaviour consistent
with capitalism and to the political institutions and perceptions
which predominate in the 'capitalist' world. The thesis is, however,
incomplete without its 'materialist' component, which is briefly
discussed below under the heading of 'dependency'.

Materialist approaches
Again there is a potential gap between general term and specific
theory, but a unifying element is a clear decision in favour of culture
(including media) as a reflection and a dependent phenomenon of
social structure. Certain main variants worth identifying are: the
main sociological tradition; classical marxism; recent 'political-
economic' media theory; dependency theory of development.

      The central position of *traditional sociology* is that individual
behaviour is shaped by social forces arising from the structure of
relationships and meanings of a society. In general, culture is also
seen as dependent on the structure of society and insofar as mass
communication is a cultural phenomenon (and it is treated as such
here) it will be dependent on society and not itself a cause. There is

room for some discussion as to whether or not mass media have become an element of the social structure, but even if so (argue Murdock and Golding, 1978) the fundamental cause remains the division of political and economic power, in effect the class structure. The media can do little independently to change a social world so determined.

Two main schools of marxist thought can be distinguished under the 'materialist' heading, although all, strictly speaking, should belong here. There is no need to give a detailed account of *classical marxism*, since its message about the role of the media in social change is clear and generally known. Since change emerges from the dynamics of struggle between dominant and subordinate classes, the media as a form of property must be an instrument of the dominant, capitalist class of the modern period in Europe. The work of media belongs essentially to the sphere of superstructure (ideas, ideology, consciousness) and is determined essentially by economic forces. Media do play a part in change, having assisted in the gaining and consolidation of bourgeois power. Subsequently they have been and are being used to resist working class advance, although the instruments of communication are potentially available to this class to achieve change. The key is always owner-ship, whether by the capitalist class, the bourgeois state, the working class or the socialist state. In the post-revolution soviet state, the 'engine of change' theory has come to operate in relation to media formally controlled by the working class party. Political-economic theory (discussed in Chapter 2) has arisen out of marxist sociology and media critical theory. It does not fundamentally depart from the main lines of marxist thinking, but has a narrower historical range and concentrates on uncovering, by empirically grounded analysis, just how the economic forces in capitalist media favour resistance to fundamental social change. Those marxist approaches discussed under the heading of 'hegemonic' theory in the following chapter have an ambiguous position in the present context. Their basic thrust is to emphasize the role of ruling ideas and ideology in the forging of consciousness or 'false' consciousness. As theories of the 'superstructure', they emphasize the influence of culture, even if the culture itself is ultimately shaped by class relations. They might be better entered in the present scheme as 'interactive' approaches to the relation between media and change, but this would dilute their central logic.

This is not the place to expound the theory of *dependency* (see especially Frank, 1971), but a word needs to be said to remove the impression that the only place assigned to media in development is as changer of personal values or 'engine of change'. Dependency theory portrays the media as frequently part of the system of exploitation by foreign capital and acting to increase and reinforce the state of dependence. The related theory of 'media imperialism' (Boyd-Barrett, 1977) contains both 'materialist' and 'idealist' elements, since it points both to technological and economic dependence on the capitalist world and to cultural penetration by the values favourable to capitalism. The media thus act to hold back change, except within the framework of capitalist growth (seen as ultimately regressive). For media to have a positive role in change would require a major structural change giving ownership and real autonomy to the developing nation and especially to elements at the basis of society. Dependency theory is thus ultimately a theory of structure rather than culture in relation to mass media.

Autonomy

The view that culture and social structure do, or can, vary independently seems empty of predictive or explanatory value, yet is is an important intellectual starting point and may have considerable practical consequences. It tends to undermine both those critical media approaches which suggest that fundamental change in capitalist society is held back by the dominant ideology purveyed through the media and the view that for Third World countries to develop they need modern, secular and free media on the western model. It is always possible to find historical cases of disjunction between sudden or rapid social or political change and what the media are doing and it is also possible to point to wide variations in cultural (even mass mediated) forms in societies with much the same economic and political base. The notion of autonomy is also consistent with a view of culture as a somewhat arbitrary or chance outcome of history. In turn, it stands in opposition to many of the theories just discussed and to general ideas of social and cultural 'convergence'. Yet convergence theory tends to be self-fulfilling and the 'autonomy option' helps to protect the freedom of societies to make choices about their media and other cultural forms, to resist, for instance, the insistence on development of secular, 'modern', market-based media institutions. It may thus be liberating as well as intellectually justifiable, given the low explanatory power of all the other theories which try to connect media systematically to social change.

Conclusion

There is little point in trying to make a choice amongst the positions on grounds of evidence. According to Rosengren (1980, p. 254), surveying what scattered evidence he could find, research gives only 'inconclusive, partly even contradictory, evidence about the relationship between social structure, societal values as mediated by the media, and opinions among the public'. A strong possibility exists that each theory may hold under different conditions at some levels of analysis. Thus mass media may contribute concurrently to two conceptually opposed, but empirically reconcilable, kinds of societal change which have been signalled in sociology: one towards fragmentation and individualization of society (a 'centrifugal' effect) and another towards a new kind of integration (a 'centripetal' effect) which can be portrayed in a more positive light as inter-dependency, or more negatively as a mass society (see McCormack, 1961). Carey (1969) has summarized these alternative tendencies and suggests that the 'communication revolution' has supported both — facilitating differentiation and at the same time helping to forge a national consensus. Aside from the remarkable range of choice offered by different views of the part played by mass communication in social change, we may also be struck by the ambiguity of the role assigned to media since they are as often cast in 'regressive' as they are 'progressive' roles. A final point on which there can be little doubt is that the media, whether moulders or reflectors of change, are undoubtedly messengers *about* change, or seen as such by their producers and their audiences, and it is around this observation that the main perspectives on mass media can best be organized.

2 ALTERNATIVE APPROACHES TO MASS COMMUNICATION THEORY

A frame of reference: the mediation of social relations and experience

From the account of mass communication that has so far been given, it is clear that we are dealing with something very complex and with many elements, which is open to analysis from alternative points of view and according to differing concepts and methods. The task of analysis is only possible insofar as we accept that the mass media institution does have a number of constant features across cultures and even over time. In this chapter an attempt is made to characterize the main social-scientific perspectives, which are as often complementary as alternative, and to do this in relation to a 'map' which locates different theories and levels of theory about the mass communication process. To provide such a map it is necessary to start with a single frame of reference, which in turn requires us to make some choices and adopt some presuppositions. Principal among these will be that mass media institutions do have a key activity which is the production, reproduction and distribution of knowledge, in the widest sense of sets of symbols having a meaningful reference to the world of experience. This knowledge enables us to make sense of the world, shapes our perception of it and contributes to the store of knowledge of the past and the continuity of our present understanding.

We usually speak of knowledge as the outcome of a communication or learning process. Thus the direct product of the media is not knowledge itself but messages with a potential for knowledge-forming, messages which are more commonly known under the headings of information, culture, entertainment, propaganda, etc. Of course, mass media do not comprise the only institution with knowledge production as a core activity. Others, such as education, religion or science can be characterized in much the same way and other institutions, like politics and law, produce knowledge as an important subsidiary activity. It is often difficult to separate media, in their working, from these other institutions, since mass media often provide them with a channel for reaching the public. However, the media are distinctive in several ways in respect of knowledge production. They have a general 'carrier' function for knowledge of all kinds. They operate in the public sphere, accessible to the whole society and for all members. The conditions of participation in the 'system' of production and reception of knowledge are distinctive: it is voluntary, continuous, unspecific, open, low in cost, requiring little qualification or competence. In principle, at least, the relationship between sender and receiver is balanced, with the receiver having the power of choice and rejection, while in other institutional contexts knowledge is usually transmitted from a source with higher power or status.

In addition to an assumption about this core activity, the chosen frame of reference requires one other assumption, which is that the media institution is essentially *intermediate* and mediating, as the name implies. Such institutions are intermediate in several senses: often interposing between us (as receivers) and the world of experience which lies outside direct perception and contact; sometimes standing between ourselves and the other institutions with which we have dealings — church, state, law, industry, etc.; providing a link between these other institutions themselves. They are mediating in the sense of being channels for others to contact us (and even occasionally for us to contact others) and in the sense that our relationships with persons, objects, organizations and events are shaped by the knowledge that we acquire from mass media. We can know relatively little from direct experience even of our own society and our contact with government and political leaders is largely based on media-derived knowledge. In a similar way, our perception of groups in society to which we do not belong or cannot observe is partly shaped by mass media. It is rare, in any given case, to be entirely dependent on mass media for information and impressions but, in practice and for most people, alternative possibilities are not, or cannot be, used extensively.

The notion of mass media as occupying a place 'between' ourselves and other people and things in space and time is a metaphor which invites the use of other metaphors to characterize the part played by mass media and the possible consequences of that part. Firstly, this role has been referred to as one of *mediation*, but mediation has more than one connotation and it can be more or less actively exercised. In particular, it may imply for mass media one or more of the following functions: acting as neutral carrier; serving as an interactive link, with varying chances of participation; serving as a means of control, with or without consistent purpose and direction. Secondly, we can add further images that distinguish these functions internally and that have been used to characterize the mass media. Insofar as the media are a carrier they may be seen as a *window* on experience — enlarging our possibilities of vision of the social and physical world. But, alternatively, they may provide a *platform*, giving an opportunity for views to be transmitted (access) and chosen voices heard (Katz, 1971). In their capacity as an interactive link, the media can connect us with experience and with others and provide means of connecting us better with experience and with others.

The images that go with the notion of *control* are more varied. One is that of integration, connoting a low degree of purpose. Another is that of *signpost*, implying that the media direct attention purposefully to certain chosen aspects of reality. Further, we can think of media not as a window, but as a *filter*, since they give only restricted vision and the more systematic this filtering, the more likely it is that the resulting view will be a distorted version of reality. Beyond a certain level of distortion the appropriate image will not be that of filter but *screen* or barrier, cutting us off from genuine knowledge and from possibilities of understanding our experience.

While some of these images derive from external analysis of media activity, some can also be found in the media's own self-definition. They do often see themselves as reflecting society, making it more visible, allowing elements within it to speak to the whole society. They also accept some responsibility to engage actively in social interaction and at times to give direction or leadership and contribute to integration and coherence. Even the notion of filtering is recognized, since media apply themselves often to the task of selection and interpretation of what would otherwise be a confusing world of happenings. Not surprisingly, the media reject the negative connotations of filtering and control, and, as will be discussed in Chapter 4, there are quite sharp differences of view within media about the extent to which their activity, should be neutral and reflective or participant and directive.

Media theory map

The diagram that follows gives graphic expression to the metaphor of mediation. The media institution is placed in the space enclosed by two arcs, one representing what is more remote and powerful, the other locating what is close at hand in the way of things, experience and people. On the first arc are located the main institutions and power centres of society and, beyond these, the world which is relatively hidden or otherwise inaccessible. Social institutions handle the events and eventualities of this more distant reality and sometimes create them. On the second arc, we locate ourselves as members of families, associations, working organizations, communities, observing and experiencing the consequences of institutional activities and environmental changes. Here we also locate the audiences, whose composition is influenced by these other ties and experiences.

Figure 3
Media theory map:
mass communication and the mediation of social experience

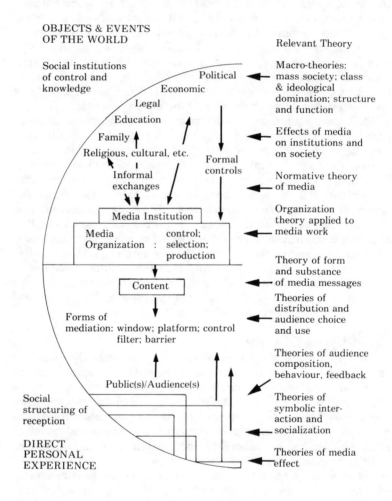

For purposes of the 'map', the media institution has been enlarged and detached from 'society' to show its main component activities and its connections 'back' to society and 'forward' or 'down' to the public. The label 'media institution' refers to the principles, rules, laws, conventions and instruments of control and regulation in the given society and is shown separately from the 'media organizations' which actually perform the production and distribution function. The separation is artificial, since the media institution is often only open to observation in practical activity, but it is useful for purposes of analysis.

The links between the media (in practice often actors in media organizations) and other institutions of society are of several kinds. Firstly there are general normative and philosophical principles concerning the proper relationship of 'press' to society, which, whether codified or not, are likely to be widely shared by 'elites', media and public. We refer to these as 'normative theories of the press' although they include such general ideological presuppositions as liberty, social responsibility, rationality (see Chapter 3). Secondly, there are formal ties in law that put some limits on media freedom and in some cases give positive direction to the media. Thirdly, there are economic links which connect media with financial and work institutions. There may also be formal ties with other social institutions. Fourthly, there are many informal links between media and society which go in both directions and have the character of exchanges. Many things are involved, but especially: attempts to gain access to or to influence the media; the search by the media for sources amongst societal elites and for information; mutual contacts within the same social milieu. Such informal contacts may either further the control of media by society or facilitate the task of the media in reflecting or revealing what is happening in society. Whichever of these applies, the inevitable result is to place the media 'nearer' to institutional sources and to centres of power in society than to their future audiences.

There are, of course, links between media organizations and the public, apart from that represented by the distribution of content. This content has to be shaped according to certain expectations about the interests and requirements of audiences. It is one aspect of media professional skill to be able to assess these, but there are several 'inputs' from the audience: individual personal contacts initiated by mass communicators; results of audience research; evidence of sales; letters and phone-calls from the public. In principle such linkages can be reciprocal and balanced but in the nature of things — the dispersal and lack of organization of the audience and the decision-making power of media organizations —

the contacts will be mostly controlled and directed by the media. In turn, this strengthens the probability, as the diagram implies, that the media are more dependent on, than in control of, institutions in society and the public is more dependent on, than in control of, the media. It should be borne in mind that several institutions, especially those of politics, seek, in various ways, to express or represent the interests of the public. This form of control is not very adequately illustrated, but its effectiveness will vary from one society to another.

The diagram indicates links in the sense of channels, relationships and contacts between the main elements of society, media and public. We should also recall the sets of ideas, norms, conventions and expectations which, although expressed in concrete form, tend to 'fix' the position of the media in this tripartite relationship. Mention has already been made of the general principles of social and political theory which govern the working of the media and of the fact that media personnel form their own view of their role in society and of their rights and responsibilities vis-à-vis sources and audiences. There are also the emerging definitions according to which the public orient themselves to media institutions. These are a mixture of attitudes and expectations based on past experience and individual wishes and needs. As noted in the previous chapter, they have historical roots, a certain continuity and stability and act as a constraint, in the short term at least, on what the media can attempt or achieve.

The diagram is intended to draw attention to certain other points. The composition of the media public is structured in terms of component social groups and categories and this structuring can be accounted for by different influences. One is the varying interest, relevance and accessibility of different kinds of content, so that selection will be related to differences of taste, life-cycle, education, general social circumstances. Secondly, there are economic influences on audience structure, arising from varying cost of media to the consumer and, more importantly, the financing of media by advertising which makes it essential for media to match messages with appropriate audiences, defined according to income and consumption pattern. Thirdly, there are certain differences in social structures of residence, class, religion, etc. that account for patterns of availability and media use. In practice, differences of cultural taste, of economic and social position, are too closely interrelated for the separate effect of any one to be clearly identified. The joining of the arcs on which social institutions and public, respectively, are located is also a reminder of the fact that there is a direct as well as a mediated contact between ourselves and the main institutions of society, however discontinuous and incomplete. We do also occasionally have personal experience of distant and less accessible events and objects in the world, whether by chance or choice. Thus the media do not monopolize all possibilities of acquiring knowledge and experience. But they do tend to serve as coordinator and common point of reference for the various pieces of separate experience and specialist knowledge, and for everything that we do learn or experience for ourselves they provide a massive supplement of vicarious experience and interpretation. Further, it is this supplement which is most widely shared and provides the common ground for social discourse.

Alternative perspectives: an introduction

The media theory map provides us with the terms and ideas for naming and comparing the main alternative approaches to the study of mass communication in the social sciences. We can broadly distinguish three kinds of approach, each with a link to different academic disciplines. Firstly, there are 'holistic' and usually 'top-down' approaches which presuppose a coherence or unity of the media 'system' and give more attention to 'society' as the source and determinant of this knowledge-producing and organizing institution. Such macro-approaches are more likely to be found in sociology and political science but they also draw on history, economics and philosophy. Secondly, there are approaches which focus primarily on the content of the media, on the universe of texts and meanings that is typically or most frequently offered by the media.

In this connection we think not only of content analysis but also of semiology, the science of signs, which has rapidly developed as a means of analysis and interpretation of media 'texts', including those which are pictorial or audiovisual, and which has helped to bring literary analysis closer to the social sciences. Another approach which combines the humanities and sociology has been labelled 'social-cultural' or, more loosely, cultural studies. Here the content is important, but its meaning is likely to be interpreted according to the social and cultural context of its reception and use. At this level of attention, we may also include those studies of media production and organization that are concerned to explain how and why particular configurations of content and media genres come into being and are sustained. The more sensitive practitioners of content analysis have from quite early days been inclined to draw attention to the context of production (e.g. Gerbner, 1964).

Thirdly, the complex of relationships and elements represented in the theory map has also been approached by way of the public, through studies of choice, preference, motivation and media use behaviour. Here we may also locate those many studies of reaction by, and effect on, the public. In general such approaches are pragmatic in conception, empirical in method and often practical or policy-oriented in purpose. They attract sociologists with a 'positivistic' leaning and psychologists who are, by the nature of their discipline, inclined to deal with individual behaviour and micro-social processes. A choice of audience as primary object of study may be associated with a presupposition that the interests, needs and wishes of the public largely determine the view of the world offered by the media and, indeed, the whole shape of media institutions themselves. More often, perhaps, there is no such presupposition, but rather the fact of availability of a certain media 'offer' is taken as a given. In the following pages the various approaches are described in somewhat more detail but according to this initial three-fold division of level of application.

Macro-approaches

Mass society theory
This is described first for reasons of historical primacy rather than its current importance and its elements are built around the concept of 'mass' which was described in Chapter 1 (pp. 35-6). There is an extensive literature to draw on, including Mills (1951; 1956), Kornhauser (1959; 1968), Bramson (1961), Bell (1961) and Giner (1976), but here we need point only to the consequences for the elements and relationships in our diagram. The theory emphasizes the interdependence of institutions that exercise power and thus the integration of the media into the sources of social power and authority. Content is likely to serve the interests of political and economic power holders and although the media cannot be expected to offer a critical or alternative definition of the world, their tendency will be to assist in the accommodation of the dependent public to their fate. People are likely to be offered some view of their place in the whole society, the means of relaxation and diversion from their problems, a culture which is in keeping with the rest of their existence. This latter is likely to be characterized by routine work and leisure, subjection to bureaucracies, isolation or family privatization, competitiveness and lower levels of solidarity and participation. Mass society theory gives a primacy to the media as

cause and maintainer of mass society and rests very much on the idea that the media offer a view of the world, a substitute or pseudo-environment which is a potent means of manipulation of people but also an aid to their psychic survival under difficult conditions. According to C. Wright Mills (1951, p. 333) 'Between consciousness and existence stand communications, which influence such consciousness as men have of their existence'.

This vision of mass society is pessimistic and not very open to empirical test, since it is already a world view and a total explanation of many of the phenomena in which we are interested. It is more a diagnosis for the sickness of our time, mixing elements of critical thought from the political left with a nostalgia for a golden age of community and democracy. As a theory of the media, it strongly invokes the images of control and filtering and portrays the direction of influence from above downwards.

Marxist approaches and critical theory

Starting point
The starting point for marxist media theory derives from the assertion by Marx in *The German Ideology* that 'the ideas of the ruling class are in every epoch the ruling ideas'. This statement and what follows is open to more than one interpretation, especially when it has to be applied to institutions which existed in rather limited forms in Marx's own time. Nevertheless, it suggests a clear prediction about the mass communication process as here portrayed, starting from the assumption of a fundamental class unity at the 'top' of society and a subordination of all significant social power to ruling class interests. The media, as a component institution of a predominant form of class society, will purvey a view of the world which accords with ruling class interests and is more or less consistent with the knowledge (or ideology) produced and disseminated by other institutions.

The general ideological tendency will be to inhibit the growth of opposed class forces or to misrepresent and delegitimate them. For the rest, the public will be provided with what it wants within the limits of what is safe for class dominance. From this perspective the study of mass communication is the attempt to uncover and unravel the complex mechanisms by which the production, distribution and consumption of ideological content is managed without recourse to the coercive use of state power in capitalist society. Inevitably such a large task has given rise to variants of marxist thought and analysis of which three are of special importance: political-economic theory, theory of media hegemony and Frankfurt School critical theory. It is also important to underline the existence of several critical approaches which it is not necessary or useful to label as 'marxist'. Marxists are not unique in noticing that societies are inegalitarian, that inequality is embodied into a class structure and that classes with more advantage seek to perpetuate their social and economic power. Sociology can provide the evidence for this and the tools for applying the evidence to the analysis of mass media (see Murdock and Golding, 1978). Even so, the ideas involved are not so very different from those described under other headings in this chapter or contained in the frame of reference with which the chapter began.

Political-economic media theory
Political-economic media theory is an old label that has been revived to identify an approach which focusses more on economic structure than on ideological content of media. It asserts the dependence of ideology on the economic base and directs research attention to the empirical analysis of the structure of ownership and to the way media market forces operate. From this point of view, the media institution has to be considered as part of the economic system, though with close links to the political system. The predominant character of the knowledge of and for society produced by the media can be largely accounted for by the exchange value of different kinds of content, under conditions of pressure to expand markets, and by the underlying economic interests of owners and decision makers (Garnham, 1979). These interests relate to the need for profit from media operations and to the profitability of other branches of commerce as a result of monopolistic tendencies and processes of vertical and horizontal integration (e.g. into oil, paper, telecommunications, leisure, tourism, etc.).

The consequences are to be observed in the reduction of independent media sources, concentration on the largest markets, avoidance of risk-taking, neglect of smaller and poorer sectors of the potential audience. The effects of economic forces are not random, but, according, for instance, to Murdock and Golding (1977, p. 37) work to consistently exclude

> those voices lacking economic power or resources . . . . the underlying logic of cost operates systematically, consolidating the position of groups already established in the main mass-media markets and excluding those groups who lack the capital base required for successful entry. Thus the voices which survive will largely belong to those least likely to criticise the prevailing distribution of wealth and power. Conversely, those most likely to challenge these arrangements are unable

to publicise their dissent or opposition because they cannot command resources needed for effective communication to a broad audience.

The main strength of the approach lies in its capacity for making empirically testable propositions about market determinations, although the latter are so numerous and complex that empirical demonstration is not easy. A weakness of the political-economic approach is that elements of media under public control are not so easy to account for in terms of the working of the free market. While the approach centres on media as an economic process leading to the commodity (content), there is an interesting variant of the political-economic approach which suggests that media really produce *audiences*, in the sense that they deliver audience attention to advertisers and shape the behaviour of media publics in certain distinctive ways (Smythe, 1977).

'Hegemony' theory

A second school of media analysis in the marxist tradition can, with caution (since it risks confusing the work of different theorists), be given the general label of 'hegemony' theory, using Gramsci's (1971) term for a ruling ideology. This has concentrated less on the economic and structural determinants of a class-biassed ideology and more on ideology itself, the forms of its expression, its ways of signification and the mechanisms by which it survives and flourishes with the apparent compliance of its victims (mainly the working class) and succeeds in invading and shaping their consciousness. The difference from the classic marxist and political-economic approach lies in the recognition of a greater degree of independence of ideology from the economic base. Ideology, in the form of a distorted definition of reality and a picture of class relationships or, in the words of Althusser (1971), 'the imaginary relationships of individuals to their real conditions of existence', is not dominant in the sense of being imposed by force by ruling classes, but is a pervasive and deliberate cultural influence which serves to interpret experience of reality in a covert but consistent manner. According to Hall (1982, p. 95)

That notion of dominance which meant the direct imposition of one framework, by overt force or ideological compulsion, on a subordinate class, was not sophisticated enough to match the complexities of the case. One had also to see that dominance was accomplished at the unconscious as well as the conscious level: to see it as a property of the system of relations involved, rather than as the overt and intentional biases of individuals in the very activity of regulation and exclusion which functioned through language and discourse.

The theoretical work of several marxist thinkers, especially Poulantzas (1975) and Althusser (1971), has contributed to the grounding of this approach, directing attention to the ways in which the relationships of capitalism have to be reproduced and legitimized according to the more or less voluntary consent of the working class itself. The tools for carrying out such work have largely been provided by developments in semiological and structural analysis which offer methods for the uncovering of covert meaning and underlying structures of meaning. The shift of theoretical attention from economic to ideological causes of the survival of capitalism has raised the priority of mass media, amongst other 'ideological state apparatuses' (Althusser's term) and led to some dissension within the marxist tradition from those who prefer to emphasize structural and economic determinants (see Williams, 1973).

The Frankfurt School
The work of the Frankfurt School, the third marxist stream, may now be of largely historical interest, but its intellectual inheritance is so important that it cannot be left out of this account. Those critical theorists who now follow what can be called a 'culturalist' approach owe a great deal to the work of members of the school, especially Adorno and Horkheimer (1972) and Marcuse (1964). The Frankfurt theorists began work in Weimar Germany and were dispersed with the coming of Nazi power, mainly to the United States (for a history, see Jay, 1973). They were concerned with the apparent failure of the revolutionary social change predicted by Marx and in explanation of this failure looked to the capacity of the superstructure, especially in the form of mass media, to subvert historical processes of economic change. In a sense, history seemed to have 'gone wrong', because dominant class ideologies had come to condition the economic base by a process of subversion and assimilation of the working class.

The universal, commercialized, mass culture was the chief means by which this success for monopoly capital had been achieved. The whole system of mass production of goods, services and ideas had more or less completely sold the system of capitalism, along with its devotion to technological rationality, consumerism, short-term gratification, and the myth of 'classlessness'. The *commodity* is the main ideological instrument of this process since it seems that fine art and even critical and oppositional culture can be marketed for profit at the cost of losing critical power. Frankfurt theory asserts the dependency of the person and the class on the definition of

images and terms of debate common to the system as a whole.
Marcuse gave the name 'one-dimensional' to the society that has
been created with the help of the 'culture industry'. The emphasis
that the school placed on the media as a powerful mechanism for
containment of change has survived and links it with the
'hegemonic' approach just described, but the 'negativism' of the
Frankfurt approach, and perhaps its cultural elitism, has been an
object of later criticism on the left. The affinity of general thrust
and of time with mass society theory should also be noticed.

The 'social-cultural' approach

The 'culturalist' or 'social-cultural' approach which is now
increasingly influential in the study of mass media owes a certain
debt to the Frankfurt School as well as to other traditions of
humanistic and literary analysis. It is marked by a more positive
approach to the products of mass culture and by the wish to
understand the meaning and place assigned to popular culture in
the experience of particular groups in society — the young, the
working class, ethnic minorities and other marginal categories. The
'cultural' approach seeks also to explain how mass culture plays a
part in integrating and subordinating potentially deviant or oppositional elements in society. It has led to much work on the products
and contexts of use of popular culture and the work carried out, in
particular at the Centre for Contemporary Cultural Studies in
Birmingham, has led to the identification of the 'Birmingham
School' as a locus for the approach. The person most associated with
the work of this 'school', Stuart Hall, has written of the cultural
studies approach that it

> stands opposed to the residual and merely reflective role assigned to the
> 'cultural'. In its different ways it conceptualises culture as inter-woven with all
> social practises; and those practises, in turn, as a common form of human activity
> . . . . It is opposed to the base-superstructure way of formulating the relationship
> between ideal and material forces, especially where the base is defined by the
> determination by the 'economic' in any simple sense . . . . It defines 'culture' as
> both the means and values which arise amongst distinctive social groups and
> classes, on the basis of their given historical conditions and relationships, through
> which they 'handle' and respond to the conditions of existence . . . . (quoted in
> Gurevitch et al., 1982, pp. 26-7).

In relation to our 'theory map', the political-economic approach
attends to the institutional causes, hegemonic theory to the
message, while the culturalist approach attends both to the
message and to the public, seeking, by a sensitive and critically-
directed understanding of the real experience of people, to account

for patterns of choice amongst media. The whole enterprise, in common with other marxist approaches, is also informed by an appreciation of the efforts of power holders, under given historical circumstances, to manage the crises to which they are subject (see Hall et al., 1978). While not all who work under the 'cultural studies' heading are marxists, there is a widely shared agreement that wider structures of society and particular historical circumstances are essential to an understanding of how media work.

Theory of media structure and function
Another theoretical approach that can encompass, by description at least, all the elements of the theory map is a version of general sociological theory which explains recurrent and institutionalized activities in terms of the 'needs' of the society (Merton, 1957). As applied to the media institution, the presumed 'needs' have mainly to do with continuity, order, integration, motivation, guidance, adaptation. Society is to be viewed as a system of linked working parts or subsystems, of which media comprise one, each making an essential contribution to the whole. In terms of our theory map, organized social life requires the continued maintenance of a more or less accurate, consistent and complete picture of the parts of society and the social environment. The emphasis is thus on the image of media as *connecting* in all the senses mentioned above, thus ensuring internal integration and order and the capacity to respond to contingencies on the basis of a common and reasonably accurate picture of reality. The mechanisms which produce this contribution from media to society are primarily the needs and demands of participants in society, whether as individual members, or collectivities. By responding to each separate demand in consistent ways, the media achieve unintended benefits for the society as a whole. Thus, structural-functional theory requires no assumption of ideological direction from the media (although it does assume ideological congruence) but depicts media as essentially self-directing and self-correcting, within certain politically negotiated institutional rules. It differs from marxist approaches in a number of ways, but especially in its apparent objectivity and universal application. While apolitical in formulation, it suits pluralist and voluntarist conceptions of the fundamental mechanisms of social life and has a conservative bias to the extent that the media are likely to be seen as a means of maintaining society as it is rather than as a potential source of change (see below, Chapter 3).

Normative theories of media
Here the reference is to alternative sets of ideas about how the

media *ought* to be related to their society, both to the 'top' or power structure and to their audiences. Such theories seek to deal with questions of regulation and control of media, assignment of purpose to them by the society, expectations of benefit for society, what they should seek to provide to their audiences. Normative theories provide the criteria by which media performance should be judged in a given society and, while there can be conflicts within a society over choice of normative theory, in general each media system, often within a national society, offers its own distinctive version or 'mix' of normative theory. The main alternative versions are outlined in Chapter 3.

Message-centred theory

Among the approaches which are important but have a more limited range of application to the elements included in the theory map, that which centres on the message itself, its internal structure and means of signification, its relation to the culture as a whole, is perhaps most in need of emphasis. While it seems to concern only one element in mass communication, it has implications for our knowledge of the originating society and directs our attention to the ways in which media messages are 'read' or 'decoded' by their audiences. It can be argued that the most concrete, least obscure and most open-to-study element in the process of mass communication is the 'text' itself. It is fixed, made public and produced systematically according to the rules of its own code or language and by its careful analysis we can hope to derive inferences about its originating culture, its meaning, purpose and probable use and effect. This study of media content provides a bridge between sociology and political science on the one hand and the humanities on the other and thus helps to link the methods and theory of the former with the long experience and, qualitatively, more sensitive character of the latter. Left aside here is what is later (Chapter 5) labelled 'traditional content analysis', not because it is unimportant, but only because it offers no new theoretical perspectives.

The origins of media study by way of the texts it produces are complex. They include structural linguistics and semiology (the general science of signs), but its current developments owe most to the work of Barthes (1972) and Eco (1977). The underlying theory holds that since the rules of a language (any mode of representation or 'encoding') are determined and limited by the inner structure of the originating culture, any given text offers a 'preferred reading'. Thus we can understand its meaning if we know the rules and are sufficiently familiar with the culture. Despite variations of approach we can name some key characteristics of this brand of theory. Firstly, the 'meaning' which can be read from careful study of media 'texts' is not necessarily that intended by the originator or that derived by the receiver. Rather it is assumed to be a given, objective meaning derived from the logic of the symbol system in which it is encoded. Secondly, the approach does not deal primarily with the overt, surface or literal meaning of a text, but with the latent, connotative meaning, which may or may not have been intended. Thirdly, the approach is not limited to the analysis of the written language, but extends to cover pictures, sounds, gestures and any devices consciously employed to carry meaning.

The wide currency of this perspective at the present time in media studies stems partly from the fact that it offers a method for the empirical analysis of ideology (see Fiske and Hartley, 1978). It also stems partly from its applicability to the non-verbal and partly from its capacity to connect long-standing traditions of cultural analysis with modern empirical sociology by providing the latter with a more qualitative tool of analysis and the former with a more systematic approach and both with some concepts which they can share. An important element in this bridge-building potential lies in the joining together of two kinds of cultural study — the one concerned with qualitative evaluation of cultural products according to aesthetic and moral criteria, the other with the objective analysis of culture in its social-anthropological sense, as a pattern of human activity and artefacts. In the study of the media, the 'message' provides the common object of study, with a use value, an exchange value and an aesthetic and moral value.

The logic of the present framework places research relating to communicators at this point in the discussion, although a focus on the message that results from mass media work is only one part of its significance. It is equally important for directing attention to constraints of institution and society within which the media operate. A central theme is the degree to which the specific organizational requirements lead to practices and routines which tend to the standardization and predictability of media content, reduce the scope for independent, original or critical media productions and may lead to a systematic distortion of the picture of the world offered to the public. Work carried out in this tradition, discussed more fully in Chapter 4, tends to emphasize the dependent nature of media and, consequently, the dependent situation of the audience.

Theory of audience and effect

Despite the enormous attention paid to media effects and the long pedigree of an approach that frames the central question about the media as one of effect, there is no unified body of effect theory. Each macro-approach tends to generate its own expectation, as we have seen in discussing the question of social change. We should nevertheless stress the importance of separate theories of effect for the whole frame of reference, since many, if not all, the other perspectives that have been named do rest heavily on the assumption that effects of certain kinds do occur regularly, predictably and, to some degree, demonstrably. Having spoken of the contributions of various scientific disciplines, it is worth recalling that the study of processes of media effect has always been multidisciplinary with a frequent cooperation between sociology and psychology, the former supplying general hypotheses, the latter supplying models of learning and attitude change, experimental methods and means of operationalization.

The divisions of effect theory are too numerous to summarize in advance of Chapter 7, which is itself little more than a summary, but attention should be drawn at this point to an important division between approaches that emphasize the source, sender and message and those that emphasize the receiver and active user of media. The situation represented in Figure 3 indicates some possibilities for receivers to react and interact. The entry 'symbolic interaction and socialization' is at least a reminder of a body of theory, dependent especially on the work of G.H. Mead (and later H. Blumer) and the phenomenologist, Alfred Schutz (discussed in McQuail, 1975), which emphasizes the intersubjectivity of all communication experience, including that of mass communication. The implication for effect theory is that meanings of messages and thus their consequences are open to some negotiation, depending on the situation and resources of the audience. An interesting attempt to develop a critical theory of mass communication based on these and related ideas can be found in Davis and Baran (1981),

Lastly, the study of the media audience has given rise to approaches to, and theories of, mass communication according to a basic distinction between 'marxists' and 'liberal pluralists', labels which seem largely to be accepted by both sets of protagonists. Each side is said to hold a fundamentally different political view of society. Thus, according to Gurevitch et al. (1982, p. 1) 'pluralists see society as a complex of competing groups and interests, none of them predominant all the time', while marxists 'view capitalist society as being one of class domination, the media are seen as part of an ideological arena in which various class views are fought out, although within the context of the dominance of certain classes; ultimate control is increasingly concentrated in monopoly capital'. Along with this distinction goes an implicit distinction between two models of the process by which the institutional power centres or 'top' of society are related, by way of mass media, to the various publics at the 'base'.

The two models are set side by side for comparison in Figure 4.

Figure 4
Mediation models compared

	Dominance	Pluralism
Societal source	Ruling class or dominant elite	Competing political, social, cultural interests and groups
Media	Under concentrated ownership and of uniform type	Many and independent of each other
Production	Standardized, routinized, controlled	Creative, free, original
Content and world view	Selective and coherent; decided from 'above'	Diverse and competing views; responsive to audience demand
Audience	Dependent, passive, organized on large scale	Fragmented, selective, reactive and active
Effects	Strong and confirmative of established social order	Numerous, without consistency or predictability of direction, but often 'no effect'

Both models are ideal-typical in the sense of accentuating and exaggerating certain features of media and it would obviously be possible to offer intermediate models in which features of both could be found together, as they almost certainly are in reality. Even so, for purposes of description, the polarization is useful and we can express the contrast in terms used in constructing the media theory map.

The 'dominance' model sees the mass media as subservient to other social institutions, which are themselves independent of each other only to a limited degree. The media organizations are likely to be owned or controlled by a small number of powerful interests and to be similar in kind and purpose. They would be characterized by a high degree of mass production and mass dissemination of content in which a limited and undifferentiated view of the world, shaped according to the perspective of ruling interests in the society, would be offered. This picture of the world in media content would be received by large audiences, conditioned or constrained to accept a certain kind of culture and information and without much capacity or inclination to make a critical response or to seek alternative sources. The effects would be strong and predictable in direction, both because of the near monopoly conditions of supply and the dependence and gullibility of the public. They would tend to reinforce both the hold of the media system over its public and that of dominant interests in society. The great power of the media posited in this model would be the power to head off change and challenge by continual legitimation of the present order, by filtering out of alternative voices, by reducing the critical capacity of the public and rewarding their compliance.

The 'pluralist' view is, in almost every respect, the reverse, since diversity and predictability are stressed at every stage, beginning with the concept of a society which is not dominated by any unified elite and is open to change and democratic control. The model stresses in particular the capacity of the differentiated public to make its alternative wishes known, to resist persuasion, to react, to use the media rather than be used by them. The media respond more to public demand than vice versa.

This contrast lies at the heart of media theory, deriving from a fundamental difference in perception of the context in which mass communication operates in liberal democracies and of the way in which media work. However, the contrast offered by the two models has a somewhat wider reference than merely to the difference between the self-designated critical researchers (not all marxist) and those who proclaim liberal values and see critical approaches as ideologically biassed. The 'dominance' model could stand not only for a view of commercial media systems, but also for a view of the media contained in mass society theory, or for certain western perceptions of the media in eastern Europe or under certain authoritarian regimes. The 'dominance' exercised by the media can thus have different causes. In the case of mass society it may be attributed not only to elite management, but also to the destruction of community by the forces of change. These forces have weakened the capacity of the community to resist authority and act auton-omously, so that it is more vulnerable to, and dependent upon, control from above. In the case of socialist society (as it is usually seen from outside), dominance is attributable not to commercial and class forces but to political dictatorship and outlawing of dissent as antisocial.

The pluralist model can also suit more than one perception of

media and more than one set of values. Firstly, it might represent
the libertarian ideal in which there is no control or direction, only
the 'hidden hand' of the market working to maximize the
satisfaction of changing needs and interests of the customers and
clients and eventually the whole society. Secondly, it might stand
for a social responsibility view of the media in a liberal democracy,
in which media institutions are inclined, and occasionally
encouraged, to satisfy the needs of divese competing interests and
to meet the wishes of the public within the limits of their own professional standards. Thirdly, the model tends to emphasize the
voluntarism and independence of the audience and could, with some
modification, accommodate the concept of 'emancipatory media'
developed by Enzensberger (1970). This concept stresses the
potential of media for encouraging interaction, self-expression and
self-realization, the raising of consciousness by a people or group
and self-mobilization. To correspond to this vision of a possible
media future, the directions indicated in the model and relations
between content and audience would need to be different, since
Enzensberger was indicating a high measure of de-institutionaliza-
tion, reduction of scale, multiple interaction and self-production of
content by means of technologies in the hands of individuals.
Perhaps the modification would be too great for the model to cope
with: we are now speaking of a version of relationships yet another
step further from the notion of dominant media, in which people
using small scale media prevail and large media institutions and
undifferentiated content can no longer be found.

3 MEDIA–SOCIETY LINKAGES: THEORIES OF FUNCTION AND PURPOSE

Introduction

A good deal has already been said about the link between media and society, especially in discussing alternative versions of the relationship between media and social change in Chapter 1. In the last chapter, the media institution was presented as having a connecting and mediating role in society by providing at least the materials by which individuals form a picture of social reality and of their society. We shall here look more closely at the nature of different forms of linkage, but especially at those which connect media 'back' to their sources in society and to other institutions. Two main questions are at issue: what do the media actually do for society, their clients (would-be communicators) and audiences? And what *ought* the media do? The second question can only be answered by reference to statements of value and principles from which expectations about media activity can be derived or which legitimate what is actually done and how it is done.

These questions cannot, on the whole, be answered as if they were matters of fact and record. The answers would fill many books and would have to be given separately for each society and each media system. However, one benefit of theory is its capacity for summarizing and rendering the essence of things and we can draw on two bodies of theory, one dealing with media functions (there is empirical evidence as well) and one with the matter of how the media ought to operate. The two kinds of theory have been referred to (by Peterson et al., 1965) as, respectively, 'objective' and 'normative' and the first-named at least does strive in the direction of objectivity.

On functional theory of mass media

The word 'function' has already been used a number of times in this book and a brief indication of its meaning has been given in the discussion of the structural-functional approach in sociology. The underlying thought is that the media exist to meet certain needs or requirements of society and that a function refers to the meeting of such a need. While seeming to be a simple proposition, this approach and the concept of function itself have given rise to great difficulties. The functional approach is very hard to express precisely or to apply empirically and the many hidden assumptions that it involves have led to much controversy. Since we shall retain the concept for reasons given below, a brief discussion of these difficulties is called for.

One persisting stumbling block has been the fact that the word 'function' has several meanings both in social-scientific usage and everyday language. It can mean a *consequence* or a *purpose*, or a *requirement* and it has other meanings — of correlation and of use. To take these first three, we might use the term 'information function' to refer to three quite different observations: the fact that people learn from the media; the fact that the media try to inform people; the fact that the media are supposed or expected to inform the people. There are even more ambiguities, but the meaning can obviously vary from one usage to another, depending on whose point of view one takes — that of sender or receiver or neutral observer. A further difficulty arises from the fact that media not only act on their own behalf but also for other groups or organizations, making it difficult to distinguish functions of media from those, for instance, of political parties or business interests which use the media.

More fundamentally, an agreed version of media functions would require an agreed version of society, since the same media activity (e.g. mass entertainment) can appear in a positive light in one social theory and negatively in another. Much has also been written about the circularity, and, consequently, conservatism of functionalism. Its starting point is an assumption that any recurrent and institutionalized activity serves some long term purpose and contributes to the normal working of society (Merton, 1957), yet beyond the fact of occurrence there is no independent way of verifying either the utility or indispensability of the activity. The conservatism stems from the consequent reification of the present — what exists and seems normal is taken as good and necessary. There is so little chance of proving long term effect from the media that whether they do good or harm can never really be empirically assessed.

Media function as purpose

Despite these difficulties and objections, we persist in using a functional approach for three reasons. One is that it offers a language for discussing the relation between mass media and society and a set of concepts which are very difficult to replace. Despite its lack of rigour, functional terminology has the advantage of being widely understood and shared by those on whom we need to call for evidence about mass media and it has a place in those different kinds of theory which were mentioned at the start of the book. Thus, to a certain extent at least, the functions of media are, or can be, spoken of by members of the audience, by the 'mass communicators' themselves and in documents, regulations and normative theories which express societal views and expectations about the media, as well as by sociologists. The second reason for retaining the approach and the terminology has to do with the limited purpose of this chapter. It seeks only to describe and not to explain, to provide a general map or guide to the main activities of mass media in terms of the working of society. As such it draws on the observations of previous theorists who have spoken of media functions and tries to incorporate them within a single framework. Thirdly, the description has a further purpose, which is to help give a more concrete point of reference to those normative theories discussed later in the chapter which do state purposes and give priorities to them and indicate how best they will be achieved.

For these reasons we cannot abandon something that is so widely used and still useful for our purpose, although we cannot claim to have escaped from the ultimate contradictions and aridities of the approach. In this spirit we adopt a view of media functions which emphasizes a purpose or motivation for using the media either as sender or receiver. This version has, consequently, two main components — a particular kind of media activity (a 'task' of the media) which can be more or less objectively named and a statement of purpose, value, utility or end provided by one or other of the users, or expected beneficiaries. Although there is an objective element in this version of media function, the construct as a whole is essentially subjective. We are speaking of ideas and beliefs, in effect about 'theories' in the various senses outlined at the start of this book. Thus what the audience member thinks he or she derives from media is part of 'common-sense theory' and what media practitioners think of as their purpose is part of 'practical theory', while sociologists or social theorists try to render what society expects or receives from the activities of the media.

In order to apply such an approach it is essential to identify the main alternative positions of those we expect to benefit from, or provide purpose to, the media. Three such positions have already been named: society, mass communicators and the audience. We need to add a fourth — the position of would-be users of the media for the specific ends of their own organization, interest or group. These are explicitly purposive communicators, called 'advocates' by Westley and MacLean (1957) to distinguish them from relatively non-purposive controllers of the media channels. They include party political campaigners, advertisers, educators, from outside the media. They are better conceived of not as individuals but as representatives of an institution or organized group which seeks benefit from using the media to reach a public. Less easy than identifying the main potential types of beneficiary from media is the discovery of their motivation and purpose. The perspectives involved are quite diverse and the entities involved do not normally make statements of purpose. Nevertheless, there is enough evidence to provide a general picture of the range of media functions, according to the chosen definition.

Media functions: a comparative framework

Sources of evidence
The sources are diverse and include a mixture of empirical evidence, theory and speculation. It is most difficult, perhaps, to give expression to media functions from the point of view of society, which cannot, strictly, speak for itself. Nevertheless, there are theories that attribute certain requirements to society, and actual societies (i.e. real political communities) do have appointed leaders who speak on their behalf. In addition, there are self-appointed voices purporting to represent the general interest of society. In many cases there are also legal documents and policy statements containing desiderata or criteria that give a good idea of the purposes assigned to the media, if only by implication in what is prohibited. The point of view of 'advocate' is less difficult to set down, although the diversity of potential advocates makes a general statement somewhat empty of meaning. There is a good deal of evidence from studies of campaigns about the range of purposes assigned to mass media and we also have some theory about the contribution of media to certain institutions, especially in the political sphere. For assessing media functions from the point of view of mass communicators, we have quite good material to draw on: many policy documents, regulations, licences and charters; increasingly, surveys of journalists and studies of media organizations. As to the functions for the audience, there is probably more direct empirical evidence here than for the other perspectives, deriving from the many studies of individual motive, expectation and satisfaction.

The perspective of society
The history and social theory of the press and later media are replete

with references to their social functions and the problem is less to find evidence and ideas than to provide an economical form of expression to capture what has been written. Democratic political theory probably offers the oldest and richest sources of ideas about the contribution of the press to society, and politics without the press is hard to conceive. The press has been seen as essential for: the formation of publics; the making of informed choices; the interaction between government and electors; the achievement by consent of common national purpose; the organization of parties. To judge from the account by Hanno Hardt (1979), Germany in the late nineteenth and early twentieth centuries was especially rich in reflections on the role of the press in society, especially in the works of Knies, Bucher, Tonnies and Weber. Among the functions named in this body of literature are: the function of 'binding society together'; giving leadership to the public; helping to establish the 'public sphere'; providing for the exchange of ideas between leaders and masses; satisfying needs for information; offering a means of expression to groups; providing a mirror of society; acting as an instrument of change; acting as the 'conscience of society'. These are not all equal statements of purpose but they all indicate an aspect of societal expectation.

Two ideas tend to dominate early theories about the societal functions of media: *change* and *integration*. Thus Gabriel Tarde, in Clark's (1969) account of his work, stressed the function of media in accelerating change by providing publicity for new ways of doing things and for new technologies. While change was positively valued by most late nineteenth-century social commentators, it appears in an ambivalent light in many of the works of the founding fathers of sociology. They saw change as not simply beneficial, but also damaging to old ways and destructive of community-based social order, leading to isolation, rootlessness and loss of control. Early sociologists did not include the press as a major cause of such change but later sociology, especially in the work of the Chicago School, which produced the modern concept of 'mass' (see pp. 35-6), did portray mass communication as both cause of disorderly change and as a potential solution to some problems of social order. The latter concerns us most here, especially as it appears in the work of Robert Park, who saw the newspaper as a means of assimilating immigrants into American society and of re-establishing in the city the lost sense of community: 'the motive, conscious or unconscious, of the writers and of the press in all this is to reproduce, as far as possible, in the city the conditions of life in the village' (quoted in Bramson, 1961, p. 101). Subsequent research on the local press, like that of Janowitz (1952), confirmed that such a process was at work and that local newspaper editors voiced a community-forming role. It has been a recurrent theme of later studies of local media (e.g. Jackson, 1971; Cox and Morgan, 1973; Murphy, 1976), although not always interpreted in a positive light.

At a more general level, McCormack (1961) has argued that the function fulfilled by the media in modern states is to integrate and socialize, but not because of the failure of other institutions. In her view, experience in a modern, changing society is necessarily segmented and the 'unique function of mass media is to provide both to industry and to society a coherence, a synthesis of experience, an awareness of the whole, which does not undermine the specialisation which reality requires.' This argument finds a place for media content which is not only informational, but also for entertainment and amusement that can provide a sense of wholeness, continuity and shared experience. Under the broad heading of integration, a subdivision can be made between 'functional' and 'normative' integration, the former referring to the interrelation and coordination of activities and relationships in a society, the latter to the maintenance of common values. The one deals mainly with problems of spatial separation, the other mainly with continuity over time.

The task of reaching an overall inventory of functions for society has been eased by the pioneering work of Harold Lasswell (1948), who presented a summary statement of the basic communication functions in the following form: surveillance of the environment; correlation of the parts of the society in responding to its environment; the transmission of the cultural heritage. These refer, respectively, to: the provision of information; the giving of comment and interpretation to help make sense of the fragments of information and also the formation of consensus; the expression of cultural values and symbols which are essential to the identity and continuity of society. Wright (1960) developed this basic scheme to describe many of the effects of the media and added 'entertainment' as a fourth key media function. This may be part of the transmitted culture but it has another aspect — that of providing reward, relaxation and reduction of tension, which makes it easier for people to cope with real life problems and for societies to avoid breakdown (Mendelsohn, 1966).

This overall view of media functions certainly seems to stress the societal perspective as overly, if not exclusively, concerned with order and control, and tends to support the contention that functional analysis is inherently conservative. However, the observation of these consensual tendencies is often a basis for radical critique and much the same set of propositions can be looked at in an alternative way. Peterson et al. (1965, p. 120) point out, for instance, that 'characteristically, they [the media] purvey the ethos of the social order in which they operate, yet they also provide the means for response and challenge to that order . . . . which of these tendencies is the stronger at a given moment depends on the stability or instability of the society's power structure'. Public policy for mass communication in several societies gives support to the view that media should contribute to change and diversity. There is also some evidence to suggest that media can help to forge minority identities or to engage creatively in situations of social conflict (McCormack, 1980).

While much more could be said about the social functions of media, we are at least in a position to identify them. Before doing so, however, one more item can be introduced which is strongly in evidence in some societies and present to some degree in all societies: the *mobilizing* role of the media. Nearly everywhere, the media are expected to advance national interests and to promote certain key values and behaviour patterns, but especially so in times of war or other crisis. And in certain developing societies and socialist states a mobilizing role is positively assigned to media.

This discussion has led to the specification of five basic ideas about media purpose for society, which can be listed as follows:

I *Information*
- providing information about events and conditions in society and the world
- indicating relations of power
- facilitating innovation, adaptation and progress

II *Correlation*
- explaining, interpreting and commenting on the meaning of events and information
- providing support for established authority and norms
- socializing
- coordinating separate activities
- consensus building
- setting orders of priority and signalling relative status

III *Continuity*
- expressing the dominant culture and recognizing subcultures and new cultural developments
- forging and maintaining commonality of values

IV *Entertainment*
- providing amusement, diversion, the means of relaxation
- reducing social tension

V *Mobilization*
- campaigning for societal objectives in the sphere of politics, war, economic development, work and sometimes religion

It should be emphasized that we cannot give any general rank order to these items, nor say anything about their relative frequency of occurrence. The correspondence between function (or purpose) and precise content is not exact, for one function overlaps with another, and some purposes extend more widely than others over the range of media activities. In general, entries I and V have to do with 'change' and II, III and IV are associated with 'integration'. To repeat an earlier point, we cannot easily distinguish between what the media do and what other institutions do, using the mass media, and it is partly for this reason that we need to look separately at media from the point of view of the institutional 'advocate'.

**The perspective of the 'advocate'
on media functions**
The range of functions, in the sense of purposeful media activities, varies a good deal from one institution to another. Without going into great detail, it is unnecessary to add any major new item to the existing set to take account of most purposeful uses of the media by such external agencies. We may note, however, that the societal level function of 'entertainment' is not widely a purposeful activity, except for the entertainment industry itself. We can, nevertheless, add certain glosses to the main headings to take account, in particular, of variant expressions of function for political and business communicators:

I *Information*
- informing about the aims and activities of the given organization
- informing about relevant external events and conditions
- allocating priorities according to the interests of the 'advocate'
- informative and attention-gaining aspects of advertising
- direct education and information campaigns

II *Interpretation*
- interpreting information and events according to the purpose of the 'advocate'
- opinion-forming, public relations, image-building
- criticism of competitors

III *Expression*
- giving voice to beliefs, values, ideologies, principles
- helping to develop a consciousness of belonging (e.g. to party, class or group)

IV *Mobilization*
- activating interest, involvement and support
- organizing and guiding the activities of members or followers
- attempts at persuasion and conversion (propaganda)
- fund-raising
- influence on consumer behaviour by advertising

Media perspectives on their own functions
Again diversity of purpose is prevalent, as between different media and between persons with different roles and different perceptions of their role. Some of the fundamental choices as to purpose and role in the organization and society are discussed in the next chapter and more information will be given there to document the alternatives named here. The basic question to be addressed is how media practitioners see their role in relation to society. The answers can still be largely accommodated within the same framework:

I *Information provision*
- collecting information of likely interest and relevance to the audience
- selecting, processing and disseminating this information
- educating the general public

II *Interpretation*
- expressing editorial opinion
- giving 'background' information and comment
- acting as critic or watchdog on holders of power
- expressing or reflecting public opinion
- providing a platform or forum for varied points of view

III *Cultural expression and continuity*
● expressing and reflecting the culture and values predominant at national, regional or local level
● voicing the culture and values of specific subgroups within the society

IV *Entertainment*
● pleasing the audience by amusement, diversion, etc.

V *Mobilization*
● advertising or propaganda on behalf of client 'advocates'
● actively campaigning for some cause
● increasing and organizing media use by audiences

This list omits certain organizational objectives, such as keeping in business, making profit, providing work, which are a condition for fulfilling other functions. They are important, even primary, goals for media organizations themselves, but they are not directed towards the society or its members outside the organization and are not content-specific. They are consequently not easy to place within the context of *media* functions.

**The audience perspective:
uses and gratifications of the media**
Again, the aim is only to state the range of purposes which the media are seen by their audiences to fulfill for themselves and the following list is a distillation of much work in the field of audience research (see below, pp. 163–4). Because of the shift from a sender to a receiver perspective, the framework adopted until now is no longer appropriate, although the component ideas are not dissimilar. The framework used here is adapted from a typology suggested by McQuail et al. (1972) to contain a number of their findings about audience uses of the media.

I *Information*
● finding out about relevant events and conditions in immediate surroundings, society and the world
● seeking advice on practical matters or opinion and decision choices
● satisfying curiosity and general interest

● learning, self-education
● gaining a sense of security through knowledge

II *Personal identity*
● finding reinforcement for personal values
● finding models of behaviour
● identifying with valued others (in the media)
● gaining insight into one's self

III *Integration and social interaction*
● gaining insight into circumstances of others: social empathy
● identifying with others and gaining a sense of belonging
● finding a basis for conversation and social interaction
● having a substitute for real-life companionship
● helping to carry out social roles
● enabling one to connect with family, friends and society

IV *Entertainment*
● escaping, or being diverted, from problems
● relaxing
● getting intrinsic cultural or aesthetic enjoyment
● filling time
● emotional release
● sexual arousal

It is even more difficult than usual to connect a motive, expectation or use with a specific type of content, since media use in general may be considered to supply at one time or another all the benefits named. It is also less easy to treat the items listed equally as statements of conscious motivation and purpose. A number of the ideas are often recognizable to a media user without being easily expressible. Yet, for each of the ideas named, there is sufficient empirical evidence to indicate that it is one element in the general pattern of motivation which supports audience behaviour. Consequently, they all fit our conception of media function and are relevant to an understanding of the part played by media in relating people to their society.

Functions and dysfunctions
Many of the connections and similarities between functions at different levels will already have been apparent, but it is useful to consider briefly the question of degree of correspondence. If the

functional description of media is at all valid there should be some measure of correspondence between the different perspectives. Thus, for purposes to be achieved at the level of society, it is necessary that the media and those who communicate through the media should set out to do certain things and that audiences should approach the media in a compatible way. In practice, societies will vary greatly according to whether there is an integrated and stable system for meeting different purposes. If, in a given case, there are sharp discrepancies between purposes at different levels they are likely to reflect a strain or conflict within the society and perhaps a failure by the media to meet certain demands.

The description of media functions has been confined to overt and positive (from the given viewpoint) uses or applications of media. There may also be latent or unacknowledged processes at work, most especially at the level of society, which change or conceal the true nature of media purpose. There may also be negative consequences, intended or not, which this formulation cannot cope with. Both latent and dysfunctional elements are allowed for in Wright's (1960; 1974) scheme, but they are bound to be hypothetical and we can as easily use the framework presented here as a source of speculation about concealed purposes or unintended effect. Thus informational purpose can lead to an intended or unintended 'disinformational' effect through bias in selection or misrepresentation. Interpretative activity may in practice be an excessive or partisan form of social control. Advancing cultural continuity may involve a suppression of new forms and of deviant cultural visions. Entertainment may mean systematic trivialization and consciousness control. Under totalitarian conditions, mobilization can be equated with brainwashing and coercion. This either demonstrates emptiness of the functional description or, alternatively, its great flexibility and convenience as a checklist of media activities and these possibilities are not mutually exclusive.

Normative theories of mass media in society

The question of links between mass media and society has already been approached in several different ways: as an aspect of the historical rise of mass media; by way of the portrayal of mass media as a mediating institution in society; just now through ideas about the functions of mass media in society. Here we turn to so-called 'normative theories', which mainly express ideas of how the media *ought to*, or can be *expected to*, operate under a prevailing set of conditions and values. For the most part each theory is connected with a particular form of political theory or set of political-economic circumstances and it would seem as if each kind of political system and even each society has its own separate press theory, even if it may not deviate far from a general type.

Despite this connection with the political system, it also seems that these theories are more implicit than explicit and often little codified. Hence the need for interpretation and reconstruction in assembling them and in the account that follows, economy dictates that only a brief summary of what are often complex bodies of ideas can be given. The first attempt at a comparative statement of major theories of the press dates from 1956 (Siebert et al.) and it remains the main source and point of reference for work of this kind. The four-fold division made by Siebert et al. has been retained, although supplemented by two further types, in recognition of more recent developments in thinking, if not in practice. It may be that the original 'four theories' are still adequate for classifying national media systems, but as the original authors were aware, it can often be that actual media systems are characterized by alternative, even inconsistent, philosophical principles. It is thus not inappropriate to add further theories to the original set, even if they may not correspond to complete media systems, since they have now become part of the discussion of press theory and provide some of the principles for current media policy and practice. In beginning with the four 'original' theories, it is not the intention to summarize the original versions, but to try to express the enduring core of truth that they contained.

Authoritarian theory

The term was given by Siebert and remains an appropriate one, since the theory identifies, first of all, the arrangements for the press which held in societies when and where the press first began, for the most part monarchies in which the press was subordinated to state power and the interests of a ruling class. The name can also refer to a much larger set of press arrangements, ranging from those in which neutrality is expected from the press in respect of government and state, to those in which the press is deliberately and directly used as a vehicle for repressive state power. Uniting all cases where the theory holds is the lack of any true independence for journalists and their subordination (ultimately by force) to government authority. Authoritarian theory justifies advance censorship and punishment for deviation from externally set guidelines which are especially likely to apply to political subject matter or any with clear ideological implications. The variety of forms in which authoritarian theory can be expressed or enforced is wide, including: legislation; direct state control of production; enforceable codes of conduct; use of taxation and other kinds of economic sanction; controlled import of foreign media; government right of appointment of editorial staff.

It is easy to identify authoritarian theory in pre-democratic societies and in societies that are openly dictatorial or repressive, for instance under conditions of military occupation or martial law. It is unlikely that under such conditions the media operate under any other principle. However, it would be a mistake to ignore the existence of authoritarian tendencies in relation to the media in societies that are not generally or openly totalitarian. There are cases and occasions when authoritarianism expresses the popular will and, in all societies, there are situations where press freedom may conflict with some interests of the state or society in general, for instance under conditions of terrorist insurgency or threat of war. It is also the case that elements of authoritarianism linger on in relation to some media rather than to others. Thus in many countries there are more controls on theatre, film, broadcasting and radio than on the newspaper and book press. In the case of broadcasting, in particular, the way is often kept open in the licensing arrangements for direct access or control under conditions of national need. We should not, in consequence, regard the theory as merely a historical survival or a relatively rare deviation from established norms. It still offers a justification for submitting the media to those who hold power in society, whether legitimately or not. The main principle of the theory can be briefly summarized:

- Media should do nothing which could undermine established authority

- Media should always (or ultimately) be subordinate to established authority

- Media should avoid offence to majority, or dominant, moral and political values

- Censorship can be justified to enforce these principles

- Unacceptable attacks on authority, deviations from official policy or offences against moral codes should be criminal offences

Free press theory

This relabelled version of Siebert et al.'s 'libertarian theory' has its origin in the emergence of the printed press from official control in the seventeenth century and is now widely regarded as the main legitimating principle for print media in liberal democracies. Perhaps because of its long history, great potency and high symbolic value, free press theory has attracted a very large literature (useful sources are: Smith, 1973; Curran and Seaton, 1981; Rivers et al., 1980). It is both a simple theory and one that contains or leads to some fundamental inconsistencies. In its most basic form it merely prescribes that an individual should be free to publish what he or she likes and is thus an extension of other rights — to hold opinions freely, to express them, to assemble and organize with others. The underlying principles and values are thus identical with those of the liberal democratic state, a belief in the supremacy of the individual, in reason, truth and progress, and, ultimately, the sovereignty of the popular will.

Complications and potential inconsistencies have arisen only when attempts have been made to account for press freedom as a fundamental right, to set limits to its application and to specify the institutional forms in which it can best find expression and protection in particular societies. As a statement of opposition to authoritarianism and as a pure expression of libertarianism, as from the pen of John Stuart Mill, few such problems arise. Even so, the motives for advancing it have always been somewhat mixed. It has been seen as an expression of opposition to colonialism (first in the American colonies); as a useful safety valve for dissent; as an argument for religious freedom; as a defence against misrule; as an end in itself; as a means of arriving at truth; as a concomitant and component of commercial freedom; as a practical necessity. A central and recurring element has been the claim that free and public expression is the best way to arrive at truth and expose error, hence the wide currency of Milton's eloquent denunciation of censorship in *Aereopagitica* and of John Stuart Mill's more liberal restatement two centuries later:

> the peculiar evil of silencing the expression of an opinion is, that it is robbing the human race, posterity as well as the existing generation, those who dissent from the opinion, even more than those who hold it. If the opinion is right, they are deprived of the opportunity of exchanging error for truth; if wrong, they lose what is almost as great a benefit, the clearer perception and livelier impression of truth, produced by its collision with error.

A free press has thus been seen as an essential component of a free and rational society. The nearest approximation to truth will emerge from the competitive exposure of alternative viewpoints and progress for society will depend on the choice of 'right' over 'wrong' solutions. Political theories of the enlightenment posited, in any case, a convergence between the good of society, the general welfare, and the good of individuals composing it, which only they could perceive and express. The advantage of a free press is that it allows this expression and enables 'society' to know what its members aspire to. Truth, welfare and freedom must go together and control of the press can only lead ultimately to irrationality or repression, even if it may seem justifiable in the short term. Aside from its various justifications, free press theory would seem to need no elaboration beyond such a simple statement as is contained in the First Amendment to the American constitution which states that 'Congress shall make no law . . . abridging the freedom of speech or of the press'. It is thus simply an absolute right of the citizen.

In practice the application of press freedom has been far from straightforward. The question of whether it is an end in itself, a means to an end, or an absolute right has never been settled and there are those, from the time of Milton to the present, who have argued that if freedom is abused to the extent of threatening good morals and the authority of the state it must be restrained. According to de Sola Pool (1973) 'No nation will indefinitely tolerate a freedom of the press that serves to divide the country and to open the floodgates of criticism against the freely chosen government that leads it'. For the most part, in societies which have recognized press freedom, the solution has been to free the press from advance censorship but to leave it answerable to the law for any consequences of its activities which infringe other individual rights or the legitimate claims of society. The protection (of their reputation, property, privacy and moral development) of individuals, of groups and minorities and the security or even dignity of the state have often taken precedence over the absolute value of freedom to publish.

Much difficulty has also arisen over the institutional forms in which press freedom has become embodied. In many contexts, press freedom has become identified with property rights and has been taken to mean the right to own and use means of publication without restraint or interference from government. The chief justification for this view, aside from the assumption that freedom in general means freedom from the government, has been through the transfer of the analogy of the 'free market of ideas' expressed above to the real free market in which communication is a good to be manufactured and sold. Freedom to publish is, accordingly, seen as a property right that will safeguard as much diversity as exists and is expressed by free consumers bringing their demands to the market place. Press freedom thus becomes identified with private ownership of the media and freedom from interference in the market. Not only have monopoly tendencies in press and other media made this a very doubtful proposition, but the extent of external financial interests in the press seems to many as potent a source of constraint on liberty of expression as any governmental activity. Moreover, under modern conditions, the notion that private ownership guarantees the individual the right to publish looks absurd.

Certain other problems and inconsistencies can also be noted. Firstly, it is very unclear to what extent the theory can be held to apply to public broadcasting, which now accounts for a large part of media activity in societies which remain attached to ideals of individual liberty and, indeed, how far it applies to other important spheres of communication activity where freedom may be equally important — as in education, culture and the arts. Secondly, the theory seems designed to protect opinion and belief and has much less to say on 'information'. Thirdly, the theory has been most frequently formulated to protect the owners of media and cannot give equal expression to the arguable rights of editors and journalists within the press, or the audiences, or other possible beneficiaries, or victims, of free expression. Fourthly, the theory proscribes compulsory control but provides no obvious way of handling the many pressures to which media are subject, especially, but not only, arising from market circumstances. Having said all this, the notion of a free press survives and can be expressed in the following principles:

● Publication should be free from any prior censorship by any third party

---

● The act of publication and distribution should be open to a person or group without permit or licence

---

● Attack on any government, official or political party (as distinct from attacks on private individuals or treason and breaches of security) should not be punishable, even after the event

---

● There should be no compulsion to publish anything

- Publication of 'error' is protected equally with that of truth, in matters of opinion and belief

- No restriction should be placed on the collection, by legal means, of information for publication

- There should be no restriction on export or import or sending or receiving 'messages' across national frontiers

Social responsibility theory
Social responsibility theory owes its origin to an American initiative — the Commission on Freedom of the Press (Hutchins, 1947). Its main impetus was a growing awareness that in some important respects the free market had failed to fulfill the promise of press freedom and to deliver expected benefits to society. In particular, the technological and commercial development of the press was said to have led to lower chances of access for individuals and diverse groups and lower standards of performance in meeting the informational, social and moral needs of society. It was also thought to have increased the power of a single class. At the same time, the rise of the new and seemingly powerful media of radio and film had demonstrated the need for some kinds of public control and means of accountability additional to those appropriate to the long established and professionally organized print media.

Social responsibility theory has a wide range of application, since it covers several kinds of private print media and public institutions of broadcasting, which are answerable through various kinds of democratic procedure to the society. The theory has thus to reconcile independence with obligation to society. Its main foundations are: an assumption that the media do serve essential functions in society, especially in relation to democratic politics; a view that the media should accept an obligation to fulfill these functions — mainly in the sphere of information, and the provision of a platform for diverse views; an emphasis on maximum independence of media, consistent with their obligations to society; an acceptance of the view that there are certain standards of performance in media work that can be stated and should be followed. In short, media ownership and control is to be viewed as a kind of public stewardship, not a private franchise, and there is a pronounced shift away from the relativism about ends character-istic of free press theory and from optimism that the 'free market place of ideas' will really deliver the individual and social benefits claimed on its behalf.

It can be seen that social responsibility theory has to try to reconcile three somewhat divergent principles: of individual freedom and choice; of media freedom; and of media obligation to society. There can be no single way of resolving the potential inconsistencies but the theory has favoured two main kinds of solution. One is the development of public, but independent, institutions for the management of broadcasting, a development which has in turn powerfully advanced the scope and political strength of the social responsibility concept. The second is the further development of professionalism as a means of achieving higher standards of performance, while maintaining self-regulation by the media themselves. The feature of new public institutions for broadcasting that contributes most to reconciling the principles identified above is the emphasis on neutrality and balance in relation to government and matters of societal controversy and the incorporation of mechanisms for making the relevant media responsive to the demands of their audiences and accountable to society for their activities. It happens also that professionalism encouraged by social responsibility theory involves an emphasis not only on high standards of performance but also on some of the virtues of 'balance' and impartiality which have been most developed in broadcast media. The influence of broadcasting as a practical expression of social responsibility theory on the privately owned press has been shown by the increasing willingness of governments to contemplate or carry out measures which do formally contravene free press principles. These include various forms of legal and fiscal intervention designed to achieve positive social aims or to limit the effects of market pressures and trends. They have made their appearance in several forms: codes or statutes to protect editorial and journalistic freedom; codes of journalistic practice; regulation of advertising; anti-monopoly legislation; establishment of press councils; periodic reviews by commissions of enquiry; parliamentary scrutiny; systems of press subsidy.

The main principles of social responsibility theory can now be stated as follows:

● Media should accept and fulfill certain obligations to society

---

● These obligations are mainly to be met by setting high or professional standards of informativeness, truth, accuracy, objectivity and balance

● In accepting and applying these obligations, media should be self-regulating within the framework of law and established institutions

● The media should avoid whatever might lead to crime, violence or civil disorder or give offence to ethnic or religious minorities

● The media as a whole should be pluralist and reflect the diversity of their society, giving access to various points of view and to rights of reply

● Society and the public, following the first named principle, have a right to expect high standards of performance and intervention can be justified to secure the, or a, public good

Soviet media theory

The Russian press and other media were completely reorganized after the Revolution of 1917 and furnished with a theory deriving from basic postulates of Marx and Engels and rules of application of Lenin. The theory so constituted and gradually furnished with institutional means has continued to provide the main framework for media practice, training and research and has provided the model for most media forms within the soviet sphere of influence (Zassoursky, 1974; Mickiewicz, 1981; Hopkins, 1970). The most important ideas are as follows. Firstly, the working class by definition holds power in a socialist society and, to keep power, has to control the means of 'mental production'. Thus all media should be subject to control by agencies of the working class — primarily the Communist Party. Secondly, socialist societies are, or aspire to be, classless societies and thus lacking in class conflict. The press should consequently not be structured along lines of political conflict. The range of legitimate diversity and debate does not extend to elements believed to be anachronistic, regressive or dangerous to the basic constitution of society along socialist lines. Thirdly, the press has a positive role to play in the formation of society and the movement towards communism and this suggests a number of important functions for the media in socialization, informal social control and mobilization towards planned social and economic goals. In particular, these functions relate to the furtherance of social and economic change. Fourthly, marxism presupposes objective laws of history and thus an objective reality that the press should reflect. This reduces the scope for personal interpretation and provides a set of news values divergent from those holding in liberal press systems. Finally, the general theory of the soviet state requires the media to submit to ultimate control by organs of the state and to be, in varying degrees, integrated with other instruments of political life.

Within these limits, the media are expected to be self-regulatory, to exercise a certain degree of responsibility, to develop and follow norms of professional conduct, and to be responsible to the needs and wishes of their audiences. Accountability to the public is achieved by research, by institutionalized forms of audience participation, by responding to letters and by taking some note of public demand. It is clear that, according to this body of theory, censorship and punishment for offences by the media against the state are justified, as they could not be under free press or social responsibility theory. There is, however, a distinction to be made between soviet theory and authoritarian theory. Under the former, the media are not subject to arbitrary and unpredictable interference; they are supposed to serve and be responsible to their publics; they are not usually monolithic (even if the forms of diversity are limited and not allowed to emerge freely); and they express a diversity of interests. The postulates of the theory can be summed as follows:

- Media should serve the interests of, and be in control of, the working class

- Media should not be privately owned

- Media should serve positive functions for society by: socialization to desired norms; education; information; motivation; mobilization

- Within their overall task for society, the media should respond to wishes and needs of their audiences

- Society has a right to use censorship and other legal measures to prevent, or punish after the event, anti-societal publication

- Media should provide a complete and objective view of society and the world, according to marxist-leninist principles

● Media should support progressive movements at home and
  abroad

Development media theory

It is not easy to give a short, general statement of an emerging body
of opinion and prescription appropriate to the media situation of
developing countries, because of the great variety of economic and
political conditions and the changing nature of situations. Nevertheless, it is necessary to make an attempt because of the (varying)
inapplicability of the four theories already discussed and the great
attention now focussed on matters to do with Third World
communication. No one source for what follows can be cited, but
perhaps the best single most recent source of ideas can be found in
the report of the Unesco International Commission for the study of
Communication Problems (McBride et al., 1980). The starting point
for a separate 'development theory' of mass media is the fact of
some common conditions of developing countries that limit the
application of other theories or that reduce their potential benefits.
One circumstance is the absence of some of the conditions necessary
for a developed mass communication system: the communication
infrastructure; the professional skills; the production and cultural
resources; the available audience. Another, correlative, factor is the
dependence on the developed world for what is missing in the way of
technology, skills and cultural products. Thirdly, there is the
(variable) devotion of these societies to economic, political and social
development as a primary national task, to which other institutions
should submit. Fourthly, it is increasingly the case that developing
countries are aware of their similar identity and interests in
international politics. Out of these conditions have come a set of
expectations and normative principles about mass media which
deviate from those that seem to apply in either the capitalist or
communist world. It is of course true that in many countries
accounted as 'developing', media are operated according to
principles deriving from the theories already mentioned —
authoritarian, libertarian and less often social responsibility or
soviet. Even so, there is enough coherence in an alternative to
deserve provisional statement, especially in view of the fact that
communication needs of developing countries have tended in the
past to be stated in terms of existing institutional arrangements,
with an especial emphasis on the positive role of commercial media
to stimulate development or on media campaigns to stimulate
economic change in the direction of the model of the industrial
society.

The normative elements of emerging development theory are shaped by the circumstances described above and have both negative and positive aspects. They are, especially, opposed to dependency and foreign domination and to arbitrary authoritarianism. They are *for* positive uses of the media in national development, for the autonomy and cultural identity of the particular national society. To a certain extent they favour democratic, grass roots involvement, thus participative communication models. This is partly an extension of other principles of autonomy and opposition to authoritarianism and partly a recognition of the need to achieve development objectives by cooperative means. The one thing which gives most unity to a development theory of the media is the acceptance of economic development itself (thus social change), and often the correlated 'nation-building', as an overriding objective. To this end, certain freedoms of the media and of journalists are subordinated to their responsibility for helping in this purpose. At the same time, collective ends, rather than individual freedoms, are emphasized. One relatively novel element in development media theory has been the emphasis on a 'right to communicate', based on Article 19 of the Universal Declaration of Human Rights: 'Everyone has the right to freedom of opinion and expression; this right includes freedom to hold opinions without interference and to seek, receive and impart information and ideas through any media regardless of frontiers'. While it is hard to find individual cases of national media systems that clearly exemplify development media theory, the main principles can be stated as follows:

● Media should accept and carry out positive development tasks in line with nationally established policy

● Freedom of the media should be open to restriction according to (1) economic priorities and (2) development needs of society

● Media should give priority in their content to the national culture and language

● Media should give priority in news and information to links with other developing countries which are close geographically, culturally or politically

● Journalists and other media workers have responsibilities as

well as freedoms in their information gathering and
dissemination tasks

● In the interest of development ends, the state has a right to
intervene in, or restrict, media operations and devices of
censorship, subsidy and direct control can be justified

Democratic-participant media theory
The last entry here and the most recent addition to the body of
normative theory of the media is the most difficult to formulate,
partly because it lacks full legitimation and incorporation into
media institutions and partly because some of its tenets are already
to be found in some of the other theories mentioned. Thus the case
for its independence as a theory may be questioned. Even so, it
merits separate identification, however provisional, and it represents something of a challenge to reigning theories. Like many
theories, it has arisen both as a reaction against other theory and
actual experience and as a positive move towards new forms of
media institution. Its location is mainly in developed liberal
societies but it joins with some elements present in development
media theory, especially its emphasis on the 'basis' of society, on the
value of horizontal rather than vertical communication. A primary
stimulus has been the reaction against the commercialization and
monopolization of privately owned media and against the
centralism and bureaucraticization of public broadcasting institutions, established according to the norm of social responsibility.
Thus, public broadcasting raised high expectations of media
systems that could assist in the long process of social improvement
and democratic change begun with the economic and political revo-
lutions of the nineteenth century. These expectations have been
disappointed by the tendency for some public broadcasting
organizations to be too paternalist, too elitist, too close to the
'establishment' of society, too responsive to political and economic
pressures, too monolithic, too professionalized.
   The term 'democratic-participant' also expresses a sense of
disillusionment with established political parties and with a system
of parliamentary democracy which has seemed to become detached
from its grass roots origins, to impede rather than facilitate
involvement in political and social life. There is some element here of
a continued reaction to a 'mass society' which is over-organized,
over-centralized and fails to offer realistic opportunities for
individual and minority expression. Free press theory is seen to fail

because of its subversion by the market and social responsibility theory to be inadequate because of its complicity in the bureaucratic state and in the self-serving of media organizations and professions. Self-regulation by the press and accountability of large broadcasting organizations have not prevented the growth of media institutions which dominate from the power centres of society or which fail in their task of meeting the needs that arise from the daily experience of citizens.

Thus the central point of a democratic-participant theory lies with the needs, interests and aspirations of the 'receiver' in a political society. It has to do with the right to relevant information, the right to answer back, the right to use the means of communication for interaction in small scale settings of community, interest group, subculture. The theory rejects the necessity of uniform, centralized, high cost, highly professionalized, state-controlled media. It favours multiplicity, smallness of scale, locality, deinstitutionalization, interchange of sender-receiver roles, horizontality of communication links at all levels of society, interaction. There is a mixture of theoretical elements, including libertarianism, utopianism, socialism, egalitarianism, localism. Media institutions constructed according to the theory would be involved more closely with social life than they are at present and more directly in control of their audiences, offering opportunities for access and participation on terms set by their users rather than by controllers. A summary statement of principles might appear as follows:

● Individual citizens and minority groups have rights of access to media (rights to communicate) and rights to be served by media according to their own determination of need

---

● The organization and content of media should not be subject to centralized political or state bureaucratic control

---

● Media should exist primarily for their audiences and not for media organizations, professionals or the clients of media

---

● Groups, organizations and local communities should have their own media

---

● Small scale, interactive and participative media forms are better than large scale, one-way, professionalized media

- Certain social needs relating to mass media are not adequately expressed through individual consumer demands, nor through the state and its major institutions

4 MEDIA INSTITUTION AND ORGANIZATION: PRODUCTION OF MEDIA CULTURE

Introduction

The last decade or so has seen much attention paid to the organizational setting of mass communication and out of a good deal of empirical research we can distill elements of theory about the general character of these organizations and about the options for behaviour open to personnel within them. The distinction between media institution and organization made in Chapter 2 (p. 55) is not always clear and when we speak of media institutions we cannot help also speaking of the organizations that carry out the 'institutionalized' activities. The media institution is likely to reflect the spirit of one of the main 'press theories' that have just been summarized, since the direction, inspiration and legitimation of media activity usually derives from such a theory or from a mixture of elements in these theories. The media organization is the specific setting in which mass media production takes place, with a more or less self-contained management system as in the case of a single newspaper, news agency, broadcasting company, publishing house, etc. Thus 'mass communicators' work in specific organizations which belong within a wider institution and they can be said to have occupational roles. Much of the theory concerning the 'mass communicator' is theory about this role, as it is shaped or constrained by the media institution. It is the latter which largely determines the nature of contacts with society and with audience, giving a meaning to such contacts and providing a pattern for their incidence and course. The media institution is not easy to study directly, except in its formal aspects and in its body of normative theory. For the most part it has to be seen in its consequences for the thinking, behaviour and products of those who work in media organizations. For this reason we shall concentrate here on theories about what happens in media organizations, after some further remarks on the context of their activities.

The diversity of institutional context of media production

Although the media institution has been referred to in the singular, it is doubtful whether it constitutes a unity or whether it can be clearly separated from other social institutions. These are important background considerations for the study of media organizations since they provide the key to some of the dilemmas, conflicts and options which are recurrently found in the work of mass communicators. As to diversity, we can point first to the very obvious differentiation by type of media: printed press; cinema film; radio; television; musical recording; and so forth. At the boundaries of such a classification scheme there are also other kinds of public performing arts and forms of communication, which use more limited forms of technology and reach smaller audiences more slowly, but which are related to the mass media through interchange of personnel and of content. The different media have their own definitions of purpose and, within each kind, there are further differences according to: function; intended public; type of content; type of work; relation to the society and state; economic basis. We are stretching the concept of a common institutional identity if we try to locate together, for example, a prestige national newspaper, a pornographic video show and a children's comic.

Secondly, in developed media systems, the constituent stages of any complete mass communication process have often become separated organizationally, even if certain kinds of integration remain or have increased. The early tendency towards division of labour has been modified by processes of vertical integration (bringing different stages under one organizational roof) and of horizontal integration, especially concentration of ownership across related fields of media and leisure activity (Murdock and Golding, 1977). Nevertheless, we can still find a good deal of diversity and fragmentation: the individual worker outside the media — author or freelancer; independent agencies mediating between organizations and individual 'out-workers' (e.g. literary agencies); organizations, such as news agencies, which service important sectors of the media; much remaining internal division of labour (e.g. between management, production and technical staff); distribution and publicity arrangements that involve other organizations for transport, display, advertising, transmission, retail sale, audience research, etc. These various aspects of separation often involve other kinds of institutional activity.

There are several other points where media activities overlap with those of other institutions: they may use the same forms of technology (there are many 'closed' uses of print, television, radio); they may be carried out on behalf of other institutions (e.g. advertising); they may duplicate or supplement the work of other institutions (e.g. in education and public information). In the first case, there will be an overlap of technique and profession with consequences for supply of material and organization of labour. As an example, the printing or film-making trades serve diverse institutional ends, in government, industry, education, etc. In the second kind of situation, instanced by the use of mass media for advertising, for government information, or political campaigning, the institutional requirements of the client may be more important for defining the media activity than are those of the media themselves. In this case, public definition, purpose, ethical rules and occupational rules may all be quite different from those which hold for autonomous mass media activity. In the third case, the situation of parallel or supplementary activity, where the media carry out purposes that belong to other social institutions as well, such as political information or adult education, a similar situation may arise, of displacement of the goals and rules of the media institution by those of, for instance, the political or educational system.

There are evidently a good many boundary problems in locating the media institution and there are many ties across the boundary to other institutions which have consequences for the degree of independence in society that the media can enjoy. We should, nevertheless, bear in mind that the social theories of the media, described at the end of the last chapter, do often help to define some basic activities and values at the core of the media institution and also give these some protection. These values and activities have essentially to do with: the (free) expression of opinion and belief; the dissemination of information about society and the world; the publication of original artistic and intellectual work. The unity of core ideas should not be overstated and we have already seen how much different media may vary and how much internal ambiguity and division exists in the public definition of any given medium. We can summarize the problem for theory by pointing to two central and recurrent issues. One has to do with the degree of freedom and constraint enjoyed by a medium in society and by media personnel within an organization. The other concerns the extent to which essentially idealistic and spiritual ends can and should be served as against material and utilitarian objectives, a dilemma faced by both the organization and those who work within it.

Ambiguity of organizational purpose

Research into mass media carried out under the auspices of organizational sociology has provided some pointers to the likely resolution of these two issues. A good deal of organizational theory has been concerned with charting the goals of different organizations or the alternative goals of the same one. Given the unclear boundaries and internal fragmentation of the media institution, this is a useful approach to our problem. One basic differentiation, developed by Etzioni (1961), distinguishes organizational goals as either coercive, utilitarian or normative. The term 'coercive' refers to the use of threat of force for achieving the ends of the organization, as with armies, prisons, etc. The utilitarian organization aims to produce or provide material goods or services and uses financial or material reward and legal contracts for this end (as with the business firm). The normative organization aims to advance some value or achieve a valued condition, based on the voluntary commitment of its participants, as with a religion or a scientific organization. The position of mass media organizations in respect of this typology is ambiguous. The media are never strictly coercive, although as instruments of social power or propaganda, under monopoly conditions, they may take on some coercive aspects, for instance by deliberately causing fear or alarm. The case of the media organization which is run as a business or public corporation, with paid employees and a public following based on the provision of some valued or useful service, is very common. Equally familiar, though nct so common perhaps, is the media organization operated for idealistic purpose with a personal commitment by staff and a moral commitment by the audience to the same purpose. Most media systems in liberal democracies show a mixture of 'utilitarian' and 'normative' components, with corresponding variations in audience commitment, although the modal case is the utilitarian one, given the nature of mass communication (open, voluntary) and the nature of the service provided (useful information, entertainment, etc.).

Another suggested basis for organizational classification distinguishes between type of beneficiary (Blau and Scott, 1963). Is it the society as a whole, a particular set of clients, the owners, the audience, or the employees of the organization, whose welfare or good is being served? Again, no single answer can be given for the media as a whole and particular organizations often have several actual or potential beneficiaries. Nevertheless, there is some reason to hold that the general public (not always the direct audience) should be the chief beneficiary. A common element in all the normative press theories discussed is that the media should meet the needs and interests of their audience in the first instance and the interests of clients and the state only secondarily. Since media depend on the voluntary choice of their audiences, this principle has a common-sense basis, but the view that the audience comes first is also often expressed by media personnel themselves.

In a study of newspaper journalists, Tunstall (1971) chose to state the goals of the newspaper in economic terms, distinguishing between revenue goals and non-revenue goals, the latter referring to purposes without a direct financial aspect: gaining prestige, exercising influence or power in society, achieving some moral end. Revenue goals are of two kinds — gaining income from sales and from advertisers. Different kinds of content and press policies go with variation of goals in these terms. While the audience appears to be subordinate in this typology, in practice the satisfaction of advertisers and the gaining of revenue from sales both depend on pleasing the audience, and non-revenue goals are often shaped by some conception of wider public interest. Furthermore, Tunstall indicates that in a case of conflict of goals within the newspaper, the audience revenue goal (increasing the circulation by pleasing the audience) provides the 'coalition-goal', on which most can agree.

The fact that mass media organizations have mixed goals is important for locating the media in their social context, understanding some of the pressures under which they are placed and helping to differentiate the main occupational choices available to employees. It is one essential aspect of a general ambiguity over social role which is discussed a little later. Some further light on this question is shed by the characterization of the newspaper as a 'hybrid organization' (Engwall, 1978), in the sense that it cannot be clearly placed on either of two key organizational dimensions (from Ellis and Child, 1973). These are the manufacture-service dimension and the dimension of variability of product and technology applied. The newspaper organization is both making a product and providing a service. It also uses a wide variety of productive technology, from the simple to the complex. In varying degrees, this holds true of other mass media organizations, certainly of broadcasting. In such an organization Engwall expects to, and does, find that several different 'work cultures' are flourishing, each justified according to a different goal or work task, namely: the news-oriented culture; the politically-oriented culture; the economically-oriented; the technically-oriented. The first two named tend to go together and are closer to the Etzioni label 'normative', while the second two are also related and can be thought of as essentially 'utilitarian'. Those holding to the news-oriented culture are likely to be journalists collecting and processing news, while the politically-oriented will generally comprise editorial staff and senior political correspondents. The economic and technically-oriented consist of those involved in financial management and in solving problems of production and they will have much in common with their counterparts in other business organizations.

Insofar as this situation can be generalized, it seems that media organizations are as likely to be internally divided as to purpose and orientation as they are different from each other. It is hard to think of another category of organization that is as likely to pursue simultaneously quite such diverse objectives and serve such divergent values. That this should happen without excessive conflict suggests some fairly stable forms of accommodation to the attendant problems. Such an accommodation may be essential in what Tunstall (1971) has characterized by the paradoxical label of 'non-routine bureaucracy'. It may also indicate the presence in media of an above-average degree of compromise, uncertainty and 'displacement of goals' by comparison with other types of complex organization.

The media occupational role

The evidence gathered from studies of members of media professions extends back over forty years, when, for instance, Rosten (1937 and 1941) wrote about Washington correspondents and Hollywood stars. It seems, on the whole, to fit rather well with the expectations already established in considering the nature of media organizations. In particular, we can see that media organizations offer alternatives for role definition which largely correspond to the differences of media goals and that internal mechanisms of control and socialization help to reduce conflict and tension of any potentially serious kind. We can also see that the position of a 'core member' of the media profession, such as the newspaper journalist, is characterized by two main kinds of ambiguity — the one having to do with his or her position in society and the other with the nature of the professional skill which he or she exercises. The potentially marginal position of the journalist in society may first have been recorded by Max Weber (1948), who said that 'the journalist belongs to a sort of pariah cast', sharing the fate of the artist in lacking a 'fixed social classification'. This is now much less true, to judge, for instance, from the findings of Johnstone et al. (1976) about American journalists. Nevertheless, it is still true that several media occupations, aside from management, are not fully bureaucratized, are difficult to place in the general scheme of status allocation, do not offer security, are not based on systematic training or documented skills, and are not well protected from various kinds of pressure and control.

Apt here is Schudson's (1978) characterization of journalism as an 'uninsulated profession'. Success also depends often on unaccountable ups and downs of public taste or on personal and unique qualities which cannot be imitated or transmitted. Apart from skills of performance and other artistic accomplishments, the essential media skill is hard to pin down and may variously be presented as an ability to: attract attention and arouse interest; assess public taste; be understood; 'communicate'; be liked; 'know the media business'. None of these seems comparable to the skills that underly other professions. Attempts to establish a claim to professional status for journalists have been made, largely resting on the skill of objective news reporting, but without complete success, since the concept of news objectivity is itself very vulnerable. It may be that the freedom, creativity and critical approach that many media personnel still cherish, despite the bureaucratic setting of their work, are ultimately incompatible with full professionalization.

It would, in any case, be very difficult, even allowing for the division of labour in any complex organization, to identify a general occupational type, or archetypal 'mass communicator'. We have to distinguish at least four main kinds of media occupation as follows: managers and controllers; creative workers such as writers, composers, performers, directors; journalists — reporters, editors, correspondents; technicians — design and video experts. The middle two categories are closest to the 'professional core' of media occupations, but in practice there is often no sharp line between categories and there is considerable movement between them, especially from technical to creative and from creative and journalist to management. But even the core professions appear to divide according to the way they see their professional task and studies of even apparently homogeneous professional groups reveal some basic lines of cleavage.

There is some general pattern to these divisions, a pattern which connects with a small number of basic oppositions of choice that are built into the media institutional pattern. These choices, in turn, may be thought to stem from the intermediary position of mass communication, as illustrated in Chapter 2, between, on the one hand, sources of social power (other institutions) which exert leverage and, on the other, the public who are supposed to be the beneficiaries of mass communication work. The main choices are as follows:

Figure 5
Media occupational role dilemmas

Playing an active, participant role in social and political life	vs	Adopting a neutral, informational position
Exercising a creative skill and doing independent original work	vs	Meeting the needs of the organization as determined by management
Achieving some communicative purpose with an audience or for society	vs	Satisfying known audience demands for a consumer product

The fundamental dilemma is one of freedom versus constraint in an institution whose own open or implicit ideology places a value on originality and freedom, yet whose organizational setting requires quite strict control. This dilemma is experienced in different ways in different contexts and the evidence from which to generalize is somewhat limited. However, there is evidence from newspaper and television journalism (e.g. Cohen, 1963; Johnstone et al., 1976; Sigal, 1973; Tuchman, 1978; Fjaestad and Holmlov, 1976; Altheide, 1974); from public service broadcasting (Burns, 1977; Schlesinger, 1978; Tracey, 1977; Blumler, 1969) and a small amount from the entertainment industry (e.g. Cantor, 1971). The critical distinction between the neutral and the participant role for journalism seems to have been first well explicated by Cohen (1963) when he (pp. 191ff.) distinguished two separate self-conceptions of the reporter's role: that of 'neutral reporter', covering the ideas of the press as informer, interpreter and instrument of government (lending itself as channel or mirror); and that of participant, the traditional 'fourth estate' notion covering the ideas of the press as representative of the public, critic of government, advocate of policy and even of policy maker. The weight of evidence (e.g. Johnstone et al., 1976) is that the 'neutral, informative' role is most preferred by journalists and it goes with the importance of 'objectivity' as a core value and element in the new professionalism (Lippman, 1922; Carey, 1969; Schudson, 1978; Tuchman, 1978; Roshco, 1975; Janowitz, 1975; Phillips, 1977). Much has been written about journalistic objectivity and there seems general agreement that it is both necessary and impossible. Rosten wrote in 1937 that 'objectivity in journalism is no more possible than objectivity in dreams'. However, it is now recognized to be not much more impossible than objectivity in social science and not dissimilar in being an approach or attitude rather than an achievement. There is an agreement that objectivity was a relatively late invention in the history of journalism and while some (e.g. Schudson, 1978) dispute the view that its cause lay in the new technology of the telegraph, as suggested by Shaw (1967), there is less dispute that it has a good deal to do with the practical and commercial need to serve large heterogeneous publics and to make the signalling of new events unproblematic (see below, p. 116). Edelstein (1966) sees objectivity as a device for minimizing conflict in a community and thus as a form of evasion.

Public broadcasting institutions, like the BBC, are under an especial pressure to meet requirements of neutrality and balance and the chief aim of BBC decision makers in news and actuality has been described as 'holding the middle ground' (Kumar, 1975), acting as a broker between disputants, rather than being a participant. The question as to whether this lends itself to supporting the established social order has often been discussed. Hall (1977) thinks it does. A more wide ranging investigation of the BBC by Burns (1977) reached a more cautious conclusion, but spoke nevertheless (p. 209) of a 'collusion thus forged with both the establishment and the "silent (and invisible, perhaps imaginary) majority"... against any disturbance of the peace'. At the heart of Burns' study is a very interesting discussion of 'professionalism' in broadcasting and of alternative orientations to the work task which forms one source of the statement of occupational dilemmas made above. Burns found in the BBC three main attitudes to the occupational task. One was a deep commitment to the traditional goals of public broadcasting as an instrument of cultural and social betterment and for the defence of 'standards'. The second was 'professionalism', sometimes 'television for television's sake', but always involving a deep commitment to the task and the craft of making 'good television'. This concept of media professionalism has several components — standing opposed to 'amateurism' and to external interference, resting on the judgement of work by fellow professionals and leading to some insulation from the pressures both of the public and management. It very likely has a much wider circulation than the specific context of the BBC or even television and some support is given to the view that media professions are somewhat marginal by Burns' observation that the word 'professional' has a much wider currency in television than it has in established professions, such as medicine or law. The third orientation noticed by Burns was a 'pragmatic' approach, representing the wish to maximize ratings and achieve management objectives. To judge from Altheide's (1974) study of American local television news organizations, this is much more likely to be found in commercial settings and at less elite levels of media news (cf. Gans, 1980). Its occurrence in British television has, however, also been confirmed by Blumler (1969) and Tracey (1977).

One of the few systematic studies of the occupations concerned with entertainment media production deals with producers of television films in Hollywood (Cantor, 1971) and distinguished three main types. Firstly, there were 'film-makers', mainly younger, well educated persons ambitious to become feature film directors and comparable to the 'professional' category which Burns singled out. Secondly, there was a group of writer-producers, with a main purpose of making stories with a worthwhile message and of communicating to the public. Thirdly, there were older, less well educated, career producers, whose main orientation was to the network and their career within it. The general pattern of choice of role definition that emerges from well-grounded theory and from some evidence seems to take the following shape:

Figure 6
Alternative communicator role orientations

Directions of orientation	Criteria of success
1 Society	External status Influence on affairs
2 Own media organization	Career advancement Achieve organization goals
3 Craft, profession	Professional approval Intrinsic satisfaction
4 Public	Popularity Communicate a message

These four orientations represent the main alternatives (not necessarily mutually exclusive) offered within an organization for handling the dilemmas signalled in Figure 5. They also indicate some of the conflicts that have been signalled in studies of media. For obvious reasons, those whose goal orientation is to the organization, like the older producers of Cantor (1971), the 'platonists' of Burns (1969) or the neutral, informative journalists of several research studies, rarely experience conflicts in their work. Less obviously, craft-oriented workers experience few conflicts, since only the media organization can provide the means of achieving the desired success and practising the craft. Where conflict occurs between organization and employee it seems most often to be where the wish to have influence in society or communicate a certain message conflicts with either the political interests and leaning of the organization or the economic interest of maximizing the audience.

Organizationally sanctioned alternative roles are not the only way in which freedom for the communicator is provided for. Elliott (1977) reminds us of some other features of the wider situation of media workers which give some scope for variation and personal freedom. Firstly, there is always some autonomy within the structure at a given level. Secondly, competition gives rise to some alternative employment possibilities, especially amongst more specialized and elite media. Thirdly, there is at times enough economic slack in the system and a need for 'overproduction', even of 'minority' content, for some degree of originality and non-conformity. Fourthly, private ownership and patronage may arbitrarily protect individuality as well as restrict it. Fifthly, novelty is itself protected by the values of the organization and the occupation and is even needed as risk-taking for the future of the organization. Finally, an active audience interest may support some otherwise unpromising initiatives. Between them, these factors help to sustain the possibility of communicator independence even under conditions of routinized work and external pressure.

Of the several kinds of conflict that can occur in media organizations, the most institutionally critical are those to do with content — what to leave in and what to leave out — referred to by Engwall (1978) as 'publication issues'. According to several accounts, such conflicts may ultimately be insoluble except by departure from the organization, but in the theory of media organizations, attention is drawn to several processes for modifying or avoiding this final solution. There is the fact of selective recruitment and organizations are known to recruit persons sympathetic to policy (Sigelman, 1973). There is often a process of 'in-house socialization' to policy, by informal hints, rewards and penalties (Breed, 1955). Thirdly, there is usually some institutionalized mechanism for handling potential conflict such as the editorial conference and the development of agreed norms. Finally, there is the possibility of appeal to the audience, mentioned above — the use of this as a 'coalition goal' (Tunstall, 1971). Ultimately, what can be expected to increase or please the public has an edge in any publication dispute.

Production process:
the antecedent phase

Media organizations are involved in four basic kinds of activity: originating new message productions and starting their circulation; channelling and selecting from existing communication flows; processing messages in transit, wherever originated, to fit distribution requirements; distribution itself. Certain recurrent problems are associated with these tasks: that of *selecting* systematically from available supplies and flows; that of maintaining *continuity* of supply for own distribution; that of *shaping* content to conform to operational criteria and technology; that of *matching* supply to audience demand. At the pre-production phase, the main questions we are concerned with have to do with selecting from potential contents in a situation characterized, paradoxically, by both oversupply and undersupply. The media are both sought out by would-be communicators and suppliers of content and also avoided by would-be non-communicators (those with potentially important information whose interests are not served by publicity, except on their own terms). A further aspect of undersupply has to do with differential cost. There are high costs associated with certain kinds of material — that which is scarce, difficult of access or simply expensive to buy (like the services of established performers).

The fact that media operate in an institutional conflict of this kind has been illuminated by Gerbner (1969), who notes that 'all mass production including that of messages is "managed"; selective suppression is the other side of the mass communication coin'. He identifies various 'power roles' bringing pressure to bear on mass communication, including clients (e.g. advertisers), competitors (other media), authorities (especially political and legal), experts, other institutions and of course patrons (the audience). He writes: 'While analytically distinct, obviously neither power roles nor types of leverage are in reality separate and isolated. On the contrary, they often combine, overlap and telescope ... the accumulation of power roles and possibilities of leverage gives certain institutions dominant positions in the mass communication of their societies'. Clearly, in the case of government and business, these can represent combinations of powerful leverage as well as being at the same time important *sources,* in the sense both of would-be communicators and would-be avoiders of attention for certain purposes. The media try to manage the supply of source material in competition with other would-be managers and, as it turns out, often in cooperation with these managers. As we have already noted, cooperation (e.g. with government or societal agencies) is an accepted part of the role of mass communication.

The variability of competence of the media organizations over the giving or withholding of access to other would-be communicators has been expressed by Elliott (1972) in the form of a typology which portrays an inverse relationship between the degree of freedom of access available to society and the degree of extensiveness of control and action by media personnel. The more extensive the scope of control by the media themselves (scope of production), the more limited the direct access by the society. The reference is to a varying degree of *intervention* or mediation by the media between the 'voice of society' or social reality on the one hand and the audience on the other.

Figure 7

Typology of production scope and directness of access by society

Scope of production	Production function	Directness of access by society	Type of access	Television example
Limited	1 Technical facilitation	Total	1 Direct	Party broadcast
	2 Facilitation & selection		2 Modified direct	Education
	3 Selection & presentation		3 Filtered	News
	4 Selection & presentation		4 Remade	Documentary
	5 Realization & creation		5 Advisory	Realistic social drama
	6 Imaginative creation	Zero	6 No control by society	Original TV drama
Extensive				

Source: P. Elliott, *The Making of a Television Series* (London, Constable, 1972).

This schema shows the variable degree to which social 'reality' is filtered by the media, with news and documentary falling at a midpoint on the scale, so that the scope of production for selection and shaping is more or less equal to the scope for society to claim direct access to the audience and, correlatively, equal to the scope for the audience to achieve a view of reality. In such 'actuality' material, there is an audience expectation of having a view of reality, but also a recognition of the right of the media to set criteria of selection and presentation. Apart from its other merits, this typology reminds us that news, on which so much study of media selection has been concentrated, is only one of several kinds of messages about reality that have to pass through the 'gates' of the media.

The concept of 'gatekeeper' has captured the imagination of many students of the news selecting process, since it was first used by White (1950) to describe the activity of the wire editor who must choose a small number of items from the large supply of news agency telegrams which may provide the bulk of news in many newspapers. The gatekeeping or news selecting activity has been a focus of interest mainly because of its potential for revealing the nature of 'news values' as applied by the media. The original issue was how far editors applied personal and arbitrary criteria and this issue has been fairly conclusively settled by evidence of strong consistency in the general pattern of selection (see Hirsch, 1977 for a summary view). The pattern can be partly explained in terms of certain needs of the organization and some persistent assumptions about the audiences, which vary from one media source to another (see below, p. 119). Here we are concerned with the gatekeeping role as an aspect of organizational behaviour and have to record some telling criticism of the concept. It tends, in particular, to give undue weight to the notion of news as a set of objective external views which come by reliable processes to the potential notice of media, so that free choice can be made of them according to some objective criteria. More likely, news is both 'supplied' by those with or without 'leverage', in the sense meant above, and also 'ordered' in advance. The media need certain kinds of news content more than other kinds and some 'suppliers' have more weight than others. The needs are met partly by the planned and organized work of specialized news agencies and partly by setting up linkages and relationships with valued or promising sources.

Two aspects are especially important — the routinization of supply and the risk of assimilation of news media to the purposes of others, despite the notional and valued independence of the media and their commitment to disinterested reporting. On the first matter, it was probably Walter Lippmann (1922) who first noticed the routinization of news gathering, the fact that news consists of events which 'obtrude' and that this is anticipated by looking for news at places where newsworthy events are likely to 'happen' or to show themselves — e.g. at courts, parliaments, airports, hospitals, etc. The second matter has been studied in contexts where news reporters depend on sources likely to have both inside information and interests in the amount or manner of its publication — sources such as politicians, the police, officials, etc. We can speak of a process of 'assimilation' (Gieber and Johnson, 1961) if the degree of collaboration which exists for mutual advantage between reporter and source reaches a point where it comes into conflict with the 'distributive' role normally associated with informers of the public. Although this type of relationship may be justified by its success in meeting the needs of the public as well as of the media organization, it may well conflict with expectations of critical independence from the media and lend itself to the suppression or manipulation of information (Whale, 1969; Tunstall, 1970; Murphy, 1976; Chibnall, 1977).

The news gatekeeper is only one amongst many who act as filtering and collecting agents to ensure the flow of sufficient and suitable 'raw material' for processing and distribution. Essentially similar are artistic and literary agencies, public relations consultants, publishers and their readers, radio disc jockeys, producers of films and plays. In their development into an industry, the media have caused secondary service industries to appear.

These are not so visible to the public eye and usually less accountable to the public according to general theories of the press or
specific media regulations. Notable in this aspect of media organizations is the interaction between media. Through processes of mutual
review and cross-reporting, gatekeepers in one medium act for
another — e.g. radio for music, newspapers for books, television for
films, etc. That this happens does not necessarily lead to collusion,
but it reinforces tendencies for different media organizations within
the same national system to cooperate and offer similar content,
with potentially negative consequences for the diversity of the view
of the world that the media allow to be seen.

   We can also see, in all media, a sequential gatekeeping activity,
from original idea or event through publication, with filtering at
several stages (Bass, 1969). The evidence is insufficient to be certain
about this, except perhaps in cases of news flow, but the probability
is that much the same criteria are applied at each stage, thus in the
process reinforcing any bias or tendency of content or form and
diminishing the chances of variety, uniqueness and unpredict-
ability. Here bias may mean no more than an accentuation of
content characteristics which, (1) lend themselves to easy
processing and, (2) are believed to meet the market criteria (audience
demand). However, the same characteristics are also likely to
reinforce existing elements of the given media culture (Elliott, 1972)
and to diminish potential conflicts of policy, in effect to reduce
certain kinds of controversiality.

The processing phase of media production

Mass communication is a form of mass production. Media organizations produce large numbers of standardized products — books,
newspapers, posters, records, tapes, films, etc. This is an aspect of
reproduction and multiple distribution, however, and does not
necessarily imply that the individual messages themselves must
have the characteristics of a mass produced item — standardized
form and relative cheapness. In principle, there is no reason why the
essential process of production needs to be influenced by a
technology designed first of all to aid distribution, and there is a
strong normative support for the idea that it should not be so
influenced — the norms of creativity, independence, originality. In
fact, many studies of media organizations have led to the conclusion
that the technology is not neutral and that organizational
adaptation to technology has indeed made a good deal of difference
to what is produced. Here we shall briefly review the main propositions about the course and nature of intervention in the 'processing'

of content, in the sense of activities designed to fit original content to forms suitable for reproduction and mass distribution, according to specifications and needs of the media organization. The main demands associated with media processing within organizations are to minimize cost, reduce conflict and ensure continuity and sufficiency of supply. Cost reduction exerts pressure according to different time schemes — in the long run it leads to the introduction of new technology, in the short run to maximizing output from existing staff resources and equipment and avoiding expensive or loss-making activities. The main pressures on media processors — to save time, use technology, save money, meet deadlines — are so interrelated that it is easier to see them in their joint consequences than in their separate operation. At the same time, media processing is not only subject to pressures of a fundamentally economic kind, but also to cultural pressures generated and maintained within the organization and, more widely, in the media organization. Thus media processing reflects the requirements of efficiency and also those to do with the satisfaction of norms of the occupational culture. We have evidence of both pressures and they have similar consequences for media content as eventually disseminated — especially in terms of greater uniformity and predictability.

The available evidence about media production is heavily weighted towards news and actuality and it is difficult to go beyond that sphere in this discussion. The expression 'manufacture of news' has been coined to express the reality of news processing and the contradiction inherent within it, since news is supposed to be reports of uncontrolled events, while manufacture implies planning, prediction and routine production. In reality, the contradiction is not so total, since news processing may also be seen as efforts to deal systematically with the unexpected and in so doing impose an order on it. Tuchman (1978) has illuminated two main aspects of news production in this connection. One has to do with the process of recognizing events as news and the need for caution, the other with ensuring the continued supply and efficient handling of news. On the first matter, she sees the essence of objectivity as a 'ritual' designed to protect the reporter and news organization, a ritual that involves the attribution of news to authoritative sources, the emphasis on factualness and verifiability. The second connects with remarks made above about gatekeeping. Tuchman points out that news organizations routinely establish a 'news net', distributed in space and time, to maximize the chance of capturing news events when and where they are likely to occur. As she observes, this increases the chance of actually reporting as news, events that fit

the predictions of the net and reduces the chance of events that do
not do so from being noticed, whatever their intrinsic significance.
Further, she reminds us that news people implicitly operate with a
typology of news which helps in planning their work. The main
types are 'hard news', dealing with events, and 'soft news', mainly
background or time-free news. There are other categories of: 'spot'
(very new, immediate, just breaking) news; 'developing' news; and
'continuing' news. There is also a time dimension, according to
which news can be classified as 'pre-scheduled', 'unscheduled' or
'non-scheduled'. The first refers to 'diary' events that are known
about in advance and for which coverage can be planned; the second
to news of events that happen unexpectedly and need to be
immediately disseminated — the most difficult for routine handling,
but not the largest category of news; the third relates to news
(usually soft) that is not tied to any particular time and can be
stored and released at the convenience of the news organization. The
typification of events in this way narrows the range of uncertainty,
but also encourages the tendency to rely on continuing news and
pre-scheduled or non-scheduled events, thus telling against uniqueness and novelty.

The extraordinary influence of time in the news operation has
been especially remarked in broadcasting and Schlesinger (1978)
refers to a 'stop-watch culture'. In his view it goes beyond what is
needed for practical purposes: 'It is a form of fetishism in which to
be obsessed about time is to be professional in a way which
newsmen have made peculiarly their own' (p. 105). Its consequence,
in his view, is to do some violence to history and reduce the
meaningfulness of news. Molotch and Lester (1974) see more significance in the time dimension of events than the needs of the
organization or inclinations of the profession. Time difference is also
related to possibilities for news management and intervention by
those with more social power. They suggest a four-fold category of
events of which the largest is that of 'routine events', the three
others being 'accidents', 'scandals' and 'serendipity'. Routine
events, however, are divided into: those where 'event promoters
have habitual *access* to the news assemblers'; those where 'event
promoters seek to *disrupt* the routine access of others in order to
make events of their own'; and those where 'the access is afforded
by the fact that the promoter and news assemblers are identical'.
The last category includes normal reporting and the 'pseudo-event'.

It should be clear from this discussion that some practices which
are essentially organizational and bureaucratic may tend to have
'ideological' consequences, to favour some kinds of content over
others. In his study of reporters and officials, Sigal (1973) points to

other aspects of this tendency — especially the importance of 'news pegs' or angles to which stories can be attached. The availability of such angles eases the search for news, validates its inclusion and gives continuity to stories. At the same time their use tends to make and reinforce stereotypes and biases the direction of attention in otherwise non-rational ways. We can add one more essentially 'ideological' factor — the value attached to scoops or exclusives, which also has an organizational function. To be first with a news report is intrinsically valued and solves one of the problems of giving priority to stories. The easiest way to achieve an exclusive is to sponsor the event itself and the practice of manufacturing pseudo-events for otherwise thin news times is a not infrequent media phenomenon (Boorstin, 1961) which brings bureaucracy and ideology together. Some kinds of content, especially those dependent on fashions and themes of known popular appeal (e.g. to do with royalty, sport, entertainment, personalities), lend themselves to production at will and may partake of the nature of pseudo-events.

Media organizations thus have preferences as to the form in which 'reality' should be processed and they act on material in ways which increase conformity to these preferences. The effect of technology, especially in audiovisual media, can be dealt with according to this proposition. Television is, not surprisingly, biassed towards transmitting what are believed to be interesting pictures — often meaning pictures with dramatic action or new pictures of established celebrities. It has to place equipment where it is likely to find such pictures (Whale, 1969; Halloran et al., 1970) and if good actuality is not available, it has to find suitable substitute illustration. Again, ideology (the value of 'good television') interacts with organization and resource deployment.

This brief account of some 'reality' processing tendencies in the media reminds us at least of the inherent tensions as well as interactions between bureaucratic and ideological factors. Bureaucracy favours predictability and uniformity (hence oldness and sameness) while (media) ideology stresses response to actuality, reality, novelty and originality. In the production of fiction there is little difficulty (although fiction has a varying relation to social reality) but in news and actuality the problem can only be resolved by greater expense and organizational flexibility.

The post-production phase

The discussion of organizations has followed a sequence from an origination in society, through the production process to distribution. As we have seen, the media organization is subject to external and internal pressures along this way. It is easy to lose sight of the fact that media production is for a purpose — to meet a public demand. Indeed, it may seem that in a given and familiar institutional context, a media organization, as long as it carries out its tasks as it has done in the past and done so efficiently, need not take too much notice of the last stage of mass communication — the reaction of the audience and the consequences of communication. The only necessary and sufficient condition is to observe figures for sales and ratings. The 'autism' of the media in an enclosed environment has been commented on by more than one student of the media and there is evidence not only of disinterest in, and ignorance of the audience, but even of positive hostility. Thus Altheide (1974, p. 59) comments that the pursuit of large audiences by the television station which he studied 'led to a cynical view of the audience, stupid, incompetent and unappreciative'. Burns (1977), Elliott (1972) and Schlesinger (1978) found something of the same in British television. According to Burns, there is a general tendency for service occupations to 'carry with them a countervailing and ordinarily concealed posture of invidious hostility' to the public they are supposed to serve. Schlesinger attributes this partly to the nature of professionalism (p. 111): 'a tension is set up between the professionalism of the communicator with its implied autonomy and the meeting of apparent audience demands and desires, with their implications for limiting autonomy'.

Apart from the proven success of existing activities and the seeming lack of available alternatives, there is an intrinsic difficulty for mass communicators to know their, usually large and disparate, audiences. The most common institutional device, that of reader and ·audience research, serves an important guidance purpose and relates media to the financial and political system, but seems to convey little that is very meaningful to the individual mass communicator (Burns, 1977; Gans, 1980). What we find, instead, is a tendency to use the various work-orientation alternatives mentioned above to guide the perception of, and attitude to, the public. The pragmatic are happy with the ratings, which also satisfy the organization. The craft-oriented are content with the judgements of their fellow-professionals. Those committed to the goals of the organization (carrying out a cultural mission, or political or commercial propaganda) are content with these goals as internally assessed. Those wishing to have influence in society look to their influential contacts in relevant social contexts. For everyone there are friends, relatives and casual contacts who can provide feedback of a comprehensible kind.

There remains an element of dissatisfaction and uncertainty for those who do want to communicate, who do want to change and influence the general public and use media for this purpose, or who direct themselves at minorities or for minority causes where impact matters. The most likely solution is for such communicators to construct for themselves an abstract image of the kind of people they would like to reach (see below, p.170). Nevertheless, mass communication seems unsatisfactory for people in this category and the organized process of mass communication under market conditions does not incorporate many satisfactory devices for relating the message to the active response of an audience. It produces audiences in the sense of spectators, who observe and applaud but do not interact with the senders (Elliott, 1972). Media organizations are to a large extent in the business of producing spectacles as a way of creating audiences and, incidentally, generating profit, employment and various kinds of satisfaction and service.

5 MEDIA CONTENT: ANALYSIS, REALITY REFLECTION AND THE NEWS GENRE

Purposes of content analysis

In a book about theories of mass communication, it may seem superfluous to give reasons for the analysis of media content. Nevertheless, it is clearly both desirable and necessary to be able to speak about the most visible evidence of the working of the media institutions. More to the point, there are several alternative ways of doing so and many themes and directions for the discussion of media content. Moreover, the choice of mode or method of analysis depends, as to suitability and effectiveness, on the chosen purpose or direction and it is useful to begin with a review of the main alternative purposes.

Content as sent and received:
media book-keeping

Here two questions are addressed, but involving essentially the same activity: how much of what sort of content is sent and how much of what sort is received by whom? For the answer, we need descriptions of content which are at the same time descriptions of audiences, since audiences are often defined by what they attend to and by little else (see Chapter 6). For the most part, the categories involved for such basic descriptions will be provided by the media institutions themselves and will be recognizable at a 'common-sense' level. The categories will be mutually exclusive sets of media output, varying only in degree of specification from whole media (e.g. all television or all newspapers) to content types (e.g. news, advertisements, fiction) to types within types (e.g. 'westerns', personal ads). For book-keeping purposes, no *analysis* of content is required. One undesirable consequence of the practice of describing audiences in terms of content is that value judgements about content (e.g. as 'trivial', 'escapist' or 'serious') tend to be transferred to the people concerned, as if such description was more than a very slight and unreliable indicator of 'taste', 'capacity' or 'cultural level'.

The search for effects

Media effect research always involves the attempt to relate message content to 'extra-media' data — aspects of audience or society that are considered to be dependent on media. The description or analysis of content has a dual role in this exercise — it may either give rise to expectations of effect, since content is usually attributed some purpose, direction or tendency, or it may take the form of post hoc analysis which could validate propositions about a media effect. For some kinds of effect analysis, for instance the study of 'displacement' effects on time use, a quantitative description of content in very gross terms may be sufficient (e.g. amount of time spent on viewing television). For other purposes, a more detailed analysis according to relevant categories is called for. The categories may be of several kinds, but usually relate, variously, to: units of information, facts or references; opinions and beliefs; theme and story types; values. Most effect analysis posits a correlation between the occurrence in content of elements so categorized and the occurrence of parallel elements in a population. The history of media effect research has seen a move from a stage at which content description was equated with a statement about effects, through one where *content as received* was regarded as an indicator of probable effect on the audience, to a stage where the link between content and receiver was understood to be mediated by many variables of content, perception and function. This trend in effect study, although logical and scientifically well founded, has led to a rather wide gap between content research and effect research. Further, more sophisticated effect studies tended to do without equally sophisticated content study. We now know much more about both, but the empirical, as opposed to the theoretical, links between the two bodies of knowledge have become attenuated.

Content as evidence of the communicators

It is much more defensible to use content as direct evidence about its *makers* than about its audience or about effect. At least it is something which is purposefully made and distributed by identifiable individuals and organizations. While it is rare to find the 'low taste' of media content to be attributed to the media producers, it is not uncommon for other aspects of content to be seen as evidence of the social outlook, class position or ideology of 'mass communicators', or of the way in which media organizations work in selecting, processing and choosing for distribution. The preceding chapter has provided some examples of this approach. As in the study of effects, the study of content has a dual role — either giving rise to hypotheses about how a given pattern of content has come into being or validating an analysis of media institution and organization. In some cases, content analysis may tell a good deal about the values, assumptions and social milieux of the makers, as in the case of Gans' (1980) analysis of newsmakers, or where the content comes from a specific identifiable source, such as a political party. Otherwise, content analysis sheds more light on organizational processes of 'gatekeeping' or shaping for certain 'target audiences'. For purposes of shedding light on the communicators, the requirements of a language of description may range from a simple classification (e.g. advertising versus editorial content of newspapers) to close dissection of values and ideology.

Media content as evidence of society

The uses to which content analysis has been put in the study of society and culture are numerous and varied. It happens to be one of the most voluminous and accessible sets of data which may indicate much about a society, and its accessibility extends over time and sometimes across national frontiers. As source material, mass media content has the apparent advantage of being 'non-reactive' to the investigator and not subject to decay. Media content also appears in forms which seem to be much more constant over time than other cultural phenomena. For these reasons it is valued by historians, sociologists and anthropologists. Among the many uses and schools of work, we can single out as most germane in the current context, the 'cultural indicators' approach, well described and exemplified by Rosengren (1980), which finds its model in existing 'economic' and 'social' indicator traditions and uses media content as its primary source. The central purpose of cultural indicator analysis is to test propositions about effects from media over time, but it is also a method for the study of social change in its own right and for the comparison of different national societies and cultures. While newly formulated, it follows a long tradition of work which has fruitfully related historical changes in society to dominant themes and images of content (e.g. Lowenthal, 1961; Johns-Heine and Gerth, 1949). It will be evident that types of classification for such purposes are likely to be both varied and complex and the current cultural indicators approach is highly eclectic.

Evaluation of media

The origin of content analysis may well be thought to lie in an evaluative purpose, since it was preceded and fed by traditions of literary and aesthetic criticism and of commentary and assessment of 'popular culture'. While such work is not without relevance to the study of media content, more germane to present purposes are evaluations that have been attempted within a social-scientific framework, seeking to provide objective assessments of media performance and tendency, according to certain stated criteria. There are various concerns underlying evaluation: (1), the regulation and control of media according to some moral criteria — for instance the portrayal of violence or sex; (2), the degree to which media conform to certain professional or institutional criteria — especially those having to do with such matters as diversity, balance, objectivity, informativeness, comprehensibility, accuracy, completeness, 'sensationalism', etc.; (3), the assessment of bias of ideological tendency, especially in contexts where media purport to be neutral and objective. The line between these different purposes is not a firm one and some are set by governments and regulatory bodies, some by the media themselves and some by external critics of the media. The aim of objective evaluation poses perhaps the most difficult challenge to content analysis, because of the intrinsic inconsistency between being objective and in making value judgements. Methods of evaluative research are, consequently, characterized by great diversity, improvization and provisionality.

Content study for content's sake
The heading may be misleading, but the reference is to that study of content which has no instrumental purposes, but seeks to reveal or illuminate intrinsic aspects of a given text, its meaning or form. A good part of linguistic and structuralist analysis belongs in this category, since it seeks to uncover the underlying structure of texts and the internal relationships of elements within them, rather than relations between text and creator, society or audience.

Conflicts and inconsistencies of purpose
It should be clear that these different purposes, besides leading to different kinds of investigative activity, are based on varied assumptions which cannot all be reconciled. One potential inconsistency has already been explored in discussing the link between media and social change (pp. 39–47): if the media are regarded as a *cause* of social and cultural phenomena, they cannot equally be regarded as a reflection and indicator, since the media should precede the 'effects'. The sharpest conflict is likely to exist between the common claim of the media that they give the public what it wants and the view that the media determine or shape culture and

social life. A second potential contradiction exists between the view that media content is a social and cultural indicator and the proposition that most salient aspects of media content are attributable to organizational structure and dynamics. The more that media content is thought to 'indicate' culture and society, the less we can expect it to be shaped by the specific features of the production process. There is also some divergence between a view of content as either the characteristic product of an organizational milieu or a historical time and the view underlying the last-named purpose of content study — the elucidation of language, code and structure of meaning. The question at issue is where the meaning of a text is to be found — is it inescapably embedded in the chosen language or form, is it in the purpose claimed by, or attributable to, the media producers, or is it in the varied and unpredictable response and interpretation of the receiver? The choice between these three as to prime location of meaning of content is a crucial one and a central issue for all students of content.

Modes of discussion
and methods of analysis

Common features of method

Modern methods for the analysis of mass media content have all been interposed between two pre-existing modes of discourse about content, which might be thought of as forming two poles of a 'dimension': at one end the 'unproblematic' description of content as a set of common-sense types or categories (books, news, plays, etc.); at the other end, forms of essentially subjective, moral and aesthetic evaluations of cultural production. Between these two are several approaches which vary in their degree of complexity, claimed 'objectivity', attention to surface or underlying features of content. They nevertheless share some general characteristics. Firstly, they claim some measure of scientific validity. They are methods which can, in principle, be replicated by different people and the 'findings' should be open to challenge according to some (not always the same) canons of scientific procedure. Secondly, they are meant to deal with regularity and recurrence in cultural artefacts rather than what is unique and non-reproducible. They are thus less appropriate for application to 'art' than to 'non-art', to the products of the 'cultural elite', than to those of the 'cultural industry'. Thirdly, they all avoid judgements of moral or aesthetic value. Fourthly, despite what has been said of content study for its own sake, they are all, in principle, instrumental. They *can* be used for other purposes, especially for answering questions about the links between content, creators, social context and receivers.

The variety of possibilities within these boundary conditions is wide and best dealt with by describing the two dominant versions of content study, one of which lies closest to the 'common-sense' pole of overt classification and the other nearer the pole of aesthetic and literary judgement. Beyond that, several variants and partial approaches can be distinguished.

Traditional content analysis

The label 'traditional' is given only because this is the earliest, most central and most widely practised method of analysis. Its use goes back to the early decades of the century (cf. Kingsbury and Hart, 1937), and the most commonly quoted definition was given by Berelson (1952) as 'a research technique for the objective, systematic and quantitative description of the manifest content of communication'. The basic approach for applying the technique is to: (1) choose a universe or sample of content; (2) establish a category frame of external referents relevant to the purpose of the inquiry (e.g. a set of political parties or countries); (3) choose a 'unit of analysis' from the content (word, sentence, item, story, picture, sequence, etc.); (4) match content to category frame by counting the frequency of the references to items in the category frame, per chosen unit of content; (5) express the result as an overall distribution of the total universe or sample in terms of the frequency of occurrence of the sought-for referents. The procedure is based on two main assumptions: that the link between the external object of reference and the reference to it in the text will be reasonably clear and unambiguous and that frequency of occurrence of chosen referents will validly express the predominant 'meaning' of the text in an objective way.

The approach is, in principle, no different from that adopted in surveys of people when one chooses a population (here a media type or subset), samples within it for respondents representative of the whole (here units of analysis — words, items, etc.), collects data from individuals according to variables (here the objects in the category system) and assigns values to these variables (here presence or absence, or frequency, of a given reference). As with the survey, such forms of content analysis are held to be reliable (reproducible) and not unique to the investigator. The method produces a statistical summary of a much larger field and it has been used for many purposes, but especially for extracting from content frequency distributions of references to things with a known frequency in 'social reality', for instance, occupations, crimes, strikes, demographic characteristics, political behaviours, opinions and so on. Hence the method lends itself well to purposes of comparing media with reality, the study of social and cultural indicators and certain kinds of effect research.

The approach has many limitations and pitfalls, which are of some theoretical as well as practical interest. The normal practice of constructing a category system before applying it involves the risk of an investigator imposing his or her meaning-system rather than 'taking' it from the content. Even when care is taken to avoid this, any such category system must be highly selective and hence distorting. The result of content analysis is a new text, the meaning of which may, or even must, diverge from the original source material. This result is also based on a form of 'reading' of content which no actual 'reader' would ever, under natural circumstances, undertake. In a certain sense, the new 'meaning' is neither that of the original sender, or of the text itself or of the audience, but a fourth construct, which has to be interpreted with care. Secondly, frequency of occurrence is not the only guide to salience or to meaning and much may depend on aspects of context of a reference, which are hard to capture, or on internal relationships between references in texts which are lost in the process of abstraction. The 'unit of analysis' convenient for sampling and frequency counts may not be a very meaningful division of content. Thirdly, there are a number of routine problems to do with reliability and with the assumption that overt meaning is really overt. The method tends to assume that training can eliminate from 'coders' of content those large variations of perception which ordinary audience members always exhibit and if no such assumption is made, the range of application of the method may be unduly narrowed.

The boundaries of the kind of content analysis described are, in fact, rather elastic and many variants can be accommodated within the same basic framework. The more one relaxes requirements of reliability, the easier it is to introduce categories and variables that will be of value in interpretation but 'low' in 'objectivity' and somewhat ambiguous. This is especially true of attempts to capture references to values, themes, settings, style and interpretive frameworks. A good many content analyses now display a hierarchy of reliability, extending from the relative 'hardness' of data about the 'topic' of a given unit of analysis to the relative 'softness' of giving values to some classifying variables of style, direction, or general theme. To this extent, the practice of content analysis, although continuing to be systematic, quantitative and descriptive, has tended to depart from Berelson's specification by being less concerned with 'manifest' content and more flexible about objectivity.

Structuralism and semiology

It is impossible in the space available to give a satisfactory account of this subject and one can do little more than apply one of structuralism's own methods and contrast it with 'traditional content analysis' in its pure form. There are several classic statements of the structuralist/semiological approach (e.g. Barthes, 1967; 1977; Eco, 1977) and now several useful introductions and commentaries (e.g. Hawkes, 1977; Fiske, 1982; Burgelin, 1972). A few explanatory words are, nevertheless, needed before making the promised comparison. As to the terms: structuralism is a development of the linguistics of de Saussure (1915) and combines some principles from structural anthropology with the latter. Structuralism differs from linguistics in two main ways: it is concerned not only with conventional verbal languages but also with any sign-system which has language-like properties, and it directs its attention less to the sign-system itself than to chosen texts and the meaning of texts in the light of the 'host' culture. It is thus concerned with the elucidation of cultural as well as linguistic meaning, an activity for which a knowledge of the sign-system is instrumental but insufficient. Semiology (or semiotics) is the 'general science of signs' (Peirce, 1931–35) and encompasses structuralism and other things besides, thus all things to do with signification, however loosely structured, diverse and fragmentary. The concepts of 'sign-system' and 'signification' common to linguistics, structuralism and semiology derive mainly from de Saussure. A sign is any 'sound-image' that acts as a 'signifier' of something 'signified' — an object or concept in the world of experience, about which we wish to communicate.

Fundamental here is the arbitrary nature of the link between the sound-image (signifier) and the thing signified. In principle, anything which can make a sense impression can act as a sign and this sense-impression has no necessary correspondence with the sense-impression made by the thing signified. The importance of this lies in the attention which is then directed to the whole *sign system* because it is from this and our knowledge of it that we derive, or transfer, meaning in communication. The separate signs gain their meaning from the systematic differences, contrasts and choices which are regulated in the linguistic or sign-system code and from the values (positive or negative valence) which are given by the rules of the culture and the sign-system. Semiology has sought to explore the nature of sign-systems which go beyond the rules of grammar and syntax and which regulate complex, latent and culturally dependent meanings of texts. This has led to a concern with *connotative* as well as denotative meaning — the associations and images invoked and expressed by certain usages and combinations of signs. In so doing it has been applied to the recognition of myths, which are pre-existing and value-laden sets of ideas derived from the culture and transmitted by communication.

The relevance of all this for the study of mass communication will be evident. Media content consists of a large number of 'texts', often of a standardized and repetitive kind, which are composed on the basis of certain stylized conventions and codes, often drawing on familiar or latent myths and images present in the culture of the makers and receivers of texts. The application of semiological analysis opens the possibility of revealing more of the underlying meaning of a text, taken as a whole, than would be possible by simply following the grammatical rules of the language or consulting the dictionary meaning of separate words. It has the especial advantage of being applicable to 'texts' which involve more than one sign system and signs (e.g. visual images and sounds) for which there is no established 'grammar' and no available dictionary. Much media content is of this kind. Such work presupposes a thorough knowledge of the originating culture and of the particular genre. According to Burgelin (1972, p. 317) 'the mass media clearly do not form a complete culture on their own...but simply a fraction of such a system which is, of necessity, the culture to which they belong'. Moreover, it follows from the theory summarized above that a text has its own immanent, intrinsic, more or less given, and thus objective, meaning, apart from the overt intention of sender or the selective interpretation of the receiver. As Burgelin also comments (p. 316) 'there is nobody, and nothing, outside the message which can supply us with the meaning of one of its elements'.

This body of theory supplies us with an approach, if not exactly a method, for helping to establish the 'cultural meaning' of media content and thus shedding light on some of the questions underlying the various purposes named above. It certainly offers a way of describing content: it can shed light on those who produce and transmit a set of messages; it is potentially as useful, perhaps more so, than conventional content analysis in predicting or explaining effects; it has an especial application in certain kinds of evaluative research, especially that which is directed at uncovering the latent ideology and 'bias' of media content.

But it has perhaps contributed most to an understanding of mass communication by revealing essential features of certain media 'genres' in film, television and print which show such a remarkable resilience and persistence over time and power to 'colonize' mass communication processes. Examples include: the dominant 'news' form; certain advertising forms; the western; the detective story or thriller. Not only do such genres comprise a large part of media output, they constrain would-be communicators and they remarkably survive cultural transplantation. It is fundamental to the semiological approach that to understand the meaning of signs we need to take account of the genre in which they appear.

The contrasts with traditional content analysis can now be summarized. Some are already self-evident. Firstly, structuralism is not quantitative, and is even antipathetic to counting as a way of arriving at significance, since meaning derives from relationships, oppositions and context rather than from quantity of references. Secondly, attention is directed to latent rather than to manifest content and latent meaning is regarded as actually more essential. Manifest meaning is much more open to alternative interpretation because it is 'further' from the structure of the text and consists of more random elements. Thirdly, structuralism is systematic in a different way than is content analysis — giving no weight to procedures of sampling and rejecting the notion that all 'units' of content should be treated equally and that the same procedure can be applied in the same way to different texts, as is often the case with content analysis. Fourthly, structuralism does not allow the assumption that the world of social and cultural 'reality', the message and the receiver, all involve the same basic system of meanings. Social reality consists of numerous more or less discrete universes of meaning, each requiring separate elucidation. The 'audience' also divides up into 'communities' each possessing some unique possibilities or tendencies for attributing meaning. Media content, as we have seen, is also composed on the basis of more than one code, language or sign-system. All this makes it impossible, even absurd, to assume that any category system of references can be constructed in which a given element is likely to mean precisely the same in the 'reality', in the content, to the audience member and to the media analyst. It follows from structuralist theory that it is very difficult to carry out research which relates or even compares findings in one of these 'spheres' with findings in another.

This comparison does not indicate the superiority of one approach over the other, since, despite the claim at the outset that these methods have something in common, there are few criteria which would be appropriate for a joint assessment. Structuralism does not offer a systematic method and is not accountable in its results according to normal standards of reliability. It is not a generalizing method in the same sense as is content analysis because it generalizes about form rather than substance. It offers no way of knowing whether or not its findings are 'representative'. Nor is it a summarizing method, like most descriptive social-science methods, including content analysis. Rather it produces a volume of 'findings' that is usually much larger than the text analyzed, even if the results may be regarded as broadly true of many other similar examples within the same genre.

Other variants and possibilities

In pursuit of one or more of the objectives stated at the outset, it has often been thought permissible and necessary to depart from the pure form of 'Berelsonian' or 'Barthian' analysis and a number of inquiries use combinations of both approaches, despite their divergent assumptions. A good example of such a hybrid approach is the work on British television news of the Glasgow Media Group (1977; 1980), which combines rigorous and detailed quantitative analysis of industrial news in relation to the industrial 'reality', together with an attempt to 'unpack' the cultural meaning of specific news stories and elucidate the many methods of signification which comprise the meaning system of television news. The school of 'cultural indicators' as represented by Gerbner and colleagues (see below, pp. 204–5) has also sought to arrive at the 'meaning structure' of dominant forms of television output by way of systematic quantitative analysis of overt elements of television representation.

In principle, any systematic attempt to characterize or typify bodies of content qualifies for inclusion within the range of approaches that has been identified between manifest categorization and critical or moral evaluation. There are also other methods which do not easily belong to either of the main approaches described. Three such approaches deserve recognition. One is the psycho-analytic approach favoured at an early stage of content study, which focusses on the motivation of 'characters' and the underlying meaning of dominant themes in the popular (or less so) culture of a given society or period (e.g. Kracauer, 1949; Wolfenstein and Leites, 1947; McGranahan and Wayne, 1948). Another longstanding approach has been concerned with form, style and word usage, especially in the service of evaluating media comprehensibility or readability, identifying authorship, or as a form of political intelligence (Lasswell et al., 1952). Thirdly, there is a possibility for a functional content analysis, as yet not widely developed, according to which media, and content within media, can be classified according to the dominant functions served for the audience. In this connection mention should be made of the study of political language (Bell, 1975; Edelman, 1967; Graber, 1976). Thus Graber names the following set of functions of political communication which could well serve as a category system for content analysis and, when applied, as a measure of purpose of one main kind of communicator: to arouse attention; to establish linkages and define situations; to make commitments; to create policy-relevant moods; to stimulate action (mobilize); to act directly (words as actions); to use words as symbolic rewards for actual or potential supporters.

Such possibilities are a reminder of the *relative* character of most analysis of content, in that there has invariably to be some outside point of reference or purpose according to which one chooses one form of classification rather than another. While structural analysis seems to avoid this form of relativism and Burgelin claims as much for it, it too can only supply meaning in terms of a much larger system of cultural meanings. The possibilities for speaking about content are thus extensive and without foreseeable limit and no one result will seem to serve all purposes. One recurrent problem with all methods and approaches is the gap that often exists between the outcome of such work and the perceptions of the creators and producers on the one hand and the audience on the other. The former tend to think of what is unique and distinctive in a given author or team, while the latter are inclined to think of content in terms of a mixture of conventional genre or type labels and a set of satisfactions which have been experienced or are expected. The version extracted by the content analyst is rarely easily accessible or communicable to the main participants in the mass communication enterprise and often remains a scientific or literary abstraction.

Media content and social reality

A unifying theme

The single theme which, more than any other, has seemed to guide studies of media content has been the relationship between media content and 'social reality'. This happens also to be the most critical issue posed by the framework outlined in Chapter 2 (Figure 3), since it concerns the manner in which the mediating role of mass communication is fulfilled. Moreover, each of the purposes stated at the outset of this chapter can also be relevantly framed in terms of this issue. How much of media output is realistic? Does content deviate from reality? What are the effects of such deviations? Does realism make a difference to the effect? Does media content reflect society? How should deviations from reality be evaluated? Whatever the scientific uncertainties that go with the concept of 'reality', it is a notion which is widely used in the practice of media production and present in the common-sense perception of media content by its audiences.

There are familiar conventions by which the reality claim or potential of content can be recognized and judged. The highest expectation of 'trueness to reality' is attached to 'news' and 'information'. Much fiction occupies an intermediate and variable position, but some is clearly marked as relating to the general reality of time and place, even if stories and characters are invented. The dominant mode of story-telling at the present time is 'realistic' or 'naturalistic'. There is also a set of contents which are generally regarded as fantasy or abstractions with corresponding expectations by their audiences. At the extreme, we find science fiction, supernatural, mythical and horror stories together with some abstract forms such as music and dance. Not only is the standard of assessment widely available, but it is also the case that a recurring conclusion of many and varied studies of content has been that media content, in whatever position along the continuum of reality expectation, tends to deviate away from 'reality', as conventionally understood, or as measured against other versions and indicators of how the social world is really composed. Clearly, a great part of media content is fictional or fantasy, making no claim to be 'about' reality. This would not, however, preclude a fairly high measure of 'realism', which is what content analysis often finds lacking.

A number of key points can be summarized from findings of research. Firstly, media content tends to overrepresent the societal 'top' — persons and occupations with higher income, status and power. This happens in news by giving more access to official sources, experts and leaders (e.g. Golding and Elliott, 1979) and in fiction by having more higher status characters and locations in urban middle class surroundings (DeFleur, 1964). At the same time, the media tend to deviate in the 'other direction' to represent a disproportionate number of deviants and troublemakers. Secondly, in the location of either news or fictional events portrayed there is a quantitative 'bias' towards some favoured countries and places — especially the United States, western Europe and leading international cities. The map of the media world is highly divergent from the real global map (Gerbner and Marvanyi, 1977). Thirdly, media content tends to employ stereotypes of minority and outgroups, such as women, ethnic groups, labour militants, the poor, immigrants (Tuchman et al., 1978; Hartman and Husband, 1974; Beharrell and Philo, 1977; Golding and Middleton, 1982; Berelson and Salter, 1946). While there is a realityꞏcomponent to these stereotypes, their narrowness, recurrence and exclusiveness must eventually be accounted as a limitation to, if not a deviation from, reality. Fourthly, the media tend to purvey many myths about situations and behaviour which, for similar reasons, are likely to distort some historical or human truth. This could be true of myths of war, or the American frontier, or espionage, or the police, or nationalism, or sexuality. Fifthly, media content, in its selection of events, concentrates on the dramatic and the violent. Thus violent crime against persons is given more weight than more common types of crime (Roshier, 1973; Graber, 1980) and is in any case misleadingly frequent, especially in television fiction (Gerbner and Gross, 1976). Finally, in reporting on industrial relations, strikes have much more prominence than other kinds of action (McQuail, 1977).

There are many other fragmentary examples and it is not uncommon to find these and other tendencies being interpreted as evidence that mass media tend to support the established order and consensual values. They positively evaluate and give privileged access to elite or official elements in society and symbolically punish or devalue deviants and outgroups, both in information and fictional content. Certainly, it is possible to interpret much accumulated evidence in this way although it is not in itself an explanation of why content should be so structured. It has also to be recognized that if the media, however indirectly, do end up supporting consensual values, they are in this one respect, at least, rather close to the reality of their societies which, by definition, are based on some form of consensus. However, there are alternative theories or explanations of why media content should be this way and they merit consideration. For the most part, these have already been discussed and need only brief treatment here.

Theories of reality-deviation

Functional theory
Functional theory offers several possibilities of accounting for the tendencies described, depending on whether we take the point of view of the society or of the individual. From the point of view of the society, media can contribute to continuity, social control, integration and motivation by symbolically rewarding those who conform to the social and economic values and succeed according to them

and by punishing those who do not conform, or who rebel. Hence the positive emphasis on the 'top' and on 'ingroups'. Further, the societal need for 'tension-management' is served by a diversionary emphasis on fantasy, unreality, dreams and 'escape'. From the individual point of view, the 'undue' emphasis on the elite and on the accepted values may also meet certain needs for models, objects of identification, value reinforcement, while diversion from reality also makes its burdens more acceptable. The empirical weakness of the functional explanation lies in the alternative view that much representation of crime tends to confirm its 'normality' and spread its incidence, while too much fantasy and lack of accurate information unfits a society collectively and individually from coping with its own real environment. There is a limit to the positive functions of ignorance.

Conspiracy or hegemony theory
Conspiracy or hegemony theory can, with little exercise of the imagination, be found to fit many of the findings about content into a theory of societal control by self-interested elites or classes. Their power is likely to be reinforced by public ignorance of social reality, emphasis on the legitimacy of the state and established class institutions, delegitimation of challenges to the social order and diversion of discontent and frustration towards the scapegoat deviants, militants and non-conformists. The weakness, noted already, is the lack of a good explanation of how ruling classes achieve such favourable tendencies in the media, and indeed the difficulty of establishing that they do so at all.

Organizational theory
Several lines of explanation may be subsumed under this heading. The political-economic approach can explain why economic and market forces lead to many of the deviations from reality already noted: the concentration on majority tastes of majority audiences; the lower diversity of media outlets and thus the narrower range of societal access; the value placed on mass production and repetition. In general, what is new, original, informative, diverse, will cost more and be less profitable. Secondly, many of the tendencies described in the preceding chapter would also be predictive of some consistent 'distortions' of reality. Objectivity requirements in news place a high value on higher status sources, as does the need to ensure a supply of news. The somewhat closed or insulated world of the media organization in itself limits the 'reality input' from society.

Several pressures in the media environment dictate a need to seek security and safety, and the freedom of media from pressure is greatest in matters of fiction and fantasy (the typology of societal access on page 113 is relevant here).

Thirdly, much media content is a reworking of themes and images from the past of a culture, often perpetuating elements of a pre-democratic past in which values of race, nation and social hierarchy have been embedded. The available cultural stock on which the media depend is inherently likely to lag behind contemporary reality. In sum, many features of media organization and production process militate against a close engagement with, and reflection of, reality and even against social representativeness. On its own, the organizational explanation is insufficient, however valid some of its components, since the media organizations described depend on their audiences, who have some opportunities to exert demands for alternatives or for 'truth'. One has either to attribute a considerable manipulative power to the media in the shaping of their own 'market', or to suppose that, on the whole, the audience does really prefer the degree of unreality which it is offered.

The news genre

The centrality of news
It is arguable that the newspaper is the archetype as well as the prototype of all modern mass media (Tunstall, 1977, p. 23) and certain, in any case, that the central ingredient of the newspaper and of those media modelled upon it, radio and television, is what we call news. It merits some special attention in a discussion of media content just because it is one of the few original contributions of mass media to the range of forms of human expression. It is also the core activity according to which a large part of the journalistic (and thus media) profession defines itself. According to Tuchman (1973-74), 'It would appear that news judgement is the sacred knowledge, the secret ability of the newsman, which differentiates him from other people'. Further, news provides the component which elevates or distinguishes something called a newspaper from other kinds of media, earns it the protection of free press theory or the sanctions of authoritarian theory, and by convention allows it to express opinion in the name of the public. Media institutions could barely exist without news and news could not exist without media institutions, since unlike almost all other forms of authorship or cultural creation, news-making is not something that can be done privately or even individually. The institution provides the

machinery for distribution and the guarantee of credibility and authority.

What is news?

While the question is one which journalists themselves find distinctly metaphysical and difficult to answer except in terms of their intuition, 'feel' and innate judgement, attempts to answer it by analysis of media have been revealing. It happens that the two 'founding fathers' of the sociology of news were both former or practising journalists and drew on their own experience in answering the question of the nature of the news. Walter Lippman (1922) focussed on the process of news gathering, which he saw as a search for the 'objective clear signal which signifies an event'. Hence, 'news is not a mirror of social conditions, but the report of an aspect that has obtruded itself'. Our attention is thus directed to what is noticeable (and worthy of notice) in a form suitable for planned and routine inclusion as a news report. It is for this reason that newspapers survey such places as police stations, law courts, hospitals, legislatures, where events are likely to be first signalled. The second early commentator on news, Robert Park (1940), paid much more attention to the essential properties of news. His starting point was to compare it with another 'form of knowledge', history, which is also a record of past events and to place news on a continuum that ranges from 'acquaintance with' to 'knowledge about'. News has its own location on such a continuum, being more than the first and less than the second. The result of Park's comparison of news with history can be distilled into a few main points:

● News is timely — about very recent or recurrent events

● News is unsystematic — it deals with discrete events and happenings and the world seen through news alone consists of unrelated happenings, which it is not the primary task of news itself to interpret

● News is perishable — it lives only when the events themselves are current and for purposes of record and later reference other forms of knowledge will replace news

● Events reported as news should be unusual or at least unexpected, qualities which are more important than their 'real significance'

- Apart from unexpectedness, news events are characterized by other 'news values' which are relative and involve judgements about likely audience interest

- News is mainly for orientation and attention-direction and not a substitute for knowledge

- News is predictable. This paradoxical and provocative point is explained by Park (p. 45) as follows:

> if it is the unexpected that happens it is not the wholly unexpected which gets into the news. The events that have made news in the past, as in the present, are actually the expected things . . . . it is on the whole the accidents and incidents that the public is prepared for . . . . the things that one fears and that one hopes for that make news.

The same point has subsequently been put more succinctly by Galtung and Ruge (1965) in the remark '"news" are actually "olds"'.

This assertion makes sense in the light of what has been said about strategies of news gathering and news production and we can add that readers will have from past experience an expectation about the *kind* of events they will find reported in the news and that newspapers will try to meet these expectations.

There have been other contributors to the general characterization of news, amongst them Warren Breed (1956) who listed the following terms descriptive of news: 'saleable', 'superficial', 'simple', 'objective', 'action-centred', 'interesting' (as distinct from significant), 'stylised', 'prudent'. He also suggested several dimensions along which an item of news might be placed: news versus truth; difficult versus routine (in terms of news gathering); information versus human interest. Further sources of variation in news have to do with its significance for future events, its relationship to editorial control, its function for the reader, its visibility to the public, its visibility to newsmen. According to Hall (1973), there are three basic 'rules of news visibility': (1), its link to an event or occurrence (the component of action); (2), its recency; and, (3), its newsworthiness or link to some important thing or person. Noteworthy, in Hall's view, is that news is itself responsible for creating over time the 'consensus' knowledge, by which newsworthiness is recognized by newspeople and accepted as such by the public. He writes: 'the ideological concepts embodied in photos and texts in a newspaper do not produce new knowledge about the world. They produce *recognition* of the world as we have already learnt to appropriate it'.

News and human interest

In Breed's characterization, news is at one point contrasted with 'human interest', implying that the former has to do with serious information, the latter with something else — perhaps entertaining, personalized, sensational. In practice it seems hard to separate the two and both have been elements in the newspaper since its earliest appearances.

A classic study by a pupil of Park, Helen McGill Hughes (1940), examined the relationship between the two forms of content and argued that the (American) newspaper had been 'transformed from a more or less sober record into a form of popular literature'. In her view, a human interest story is not intrinsically different from other news stories, but takes its character from the particular attitude which the writer adopts to the reader — it is a story which is intended to divert, but also one which is told, as it were, from the reader's point of view. It can, in consequence, be told only by a reporter who is 'able to see the world as his readers do'. Hence it is more akin to gossip or the folk tale.

The characteristics of news are derived to a larger extent than is sometimes recognized from much older traditions of story telling and it has been suggested by Darnton (1975) that our conceptions of news result from 'ancient ways of telling stories'. The tendency for news reports to be cast in the form of a narrative, with principal and minor actors, connected sequence, heroes and villains, beginnings, middle and end, signalling of dramatic turns, a reliance on familiar plots, has often been noted. In general the tendency for media to replace and incorporate earlier story-telling and moralizing forms has been termed the 'bardic function' by Fiske and Hartley (1978), a function which cuts across the line dividing 'reality' from 'fictional' content. While it may seem diversionary to pay much attention to elements of news which are subsidiary to informational purposes, it remains the case that much newspaper content is more akin to 'human interest' than 'news' about politics, economics and society (Curran et al., 1981). Human interest is vital to the economics of news and it helps us to understand the nature of 'news values'.

News values and the structure of news

One general conclusion from the many studies of news content is that news exhibits a rather stable and predictable overall pattern when measured as to quality and conventional categories of subject matter. There are variations from one country to another and one medium type to another and the pattern is naturally responsive to major events, such as war and world crisis. Nevertheless, the stability of news content is often quite remarkable and lends a good deal of support to those who argue that the content of news is very much determined by a variety of external political, ideological and cultural constraints and by internal organizational and technical requirements. Some of these matters have already been discussed and here we shall attend mainly to internal tendencies connected with the nature of news as it has been characterized above.

The single most valuable source in the quest for explanation has been the work of Galtung and Ruge (1965) who identified and interrelated the main factors influencing the *selection* of (foreign) news. In essence there are three types of factors: organizational; genre-related; socio-cultural. The organizational factors are the most universal and least escapable and they have some 'ideological' consequences. Thus news media prefer: 'big' (large scale or 'major') events; events which are clear and unambiguous; event which occur in a time scale which fits the normal production schedule (usually within 24 hours); events which are easiest to pick up and report and which are easily recognizable and of accepted relevance (cultural proximity). Amongst genre-related factors are: a preference for events which fit advance audience expectations (consonance with past news); a bias towards what is unexpected and novel within the limits of what is familiar; a wish to continue with events already established as newsworthy; a wish for balance among types of news events. Galtung and Ruge distinguish only socio-cultural influences that derive from 'north European' culture and especially news values favouring events which are about: elite persons; elite nations; negative happenings. Events with all these values are believed to produce most audience interest and these values are consistent with several of the organizational and genre-related selection require-ments. Thus 'bigness' goes with eliteness; personal actions fit the short time scale and are least ambiguous and most 'bounded'; negative events often fit the time schedule, are unambiguous and can be personalized (e.g. disasters, killings, crimes, etc.).

This framework has been found to apply fairly widely beyond the case from which it was first derived and beyond foreign news alone. It tells a certain amount about the kind of event that will tend to be reported and, by implication, about what will be neglected. Thus it is predictive of a pattern of one general kind of news 'bias'. News will not tend to deal with: distant and politically unimportant nations; non-elites; ideas; institutions and structures; long-term undramatic processes (e.g. social change itself); many kinds of 'good news'. The theory does not offer a complete explanation of all regularities of news composition and an alternative, less psychological and more structural, approach to explanation has been recommended by Rosengren (1974) who argues that several features of news flow can be accounted for by political and economic factors. He demonstrates that flows of trade between countries are good predictors of mutual news attention and one might expect that within countries the giving or withholding of attention might have as much to do with political and economic factors as with the news values of individual news selectors.

The question of news structure has sometimes tended to be argued in terms of 'bias', yet it need not be so, especially as the term has the connotation of a deliberate tendency to mislead. It is noteworthy that the characterization of news offered above does not place great emphasis on objectivity and its correlates, such as truth and accuracy. Indeed, since judgements of news value are agreed to be relative and based on a 'feel for the news' at the moment of time, there must be strong elements of subjectivity. Objectivity is no more than a mode of procedure, as noted above (p. 108), little different in journalism than in history or social science (Benet, 1970). Journalists do not usually claim to tell in the news what is objectively most important, significant or relevant for their audiences. In the dominant western liberal tradition, there are no criteria for objectivity in this sense, although Nordenstreng (1974) provides an interesting step in this direction. In the light of all the evidence about regularities of news content it is hard to resist Gerbner's (1964) conclusion that 'there is no fundamentally non-ideologically, a-political, non-partisan, news-gathering and reporting system'.

Despite the progress of media research and theory there remains a gap between two different conceptions of the news-making process in which the ideas discussed play a part and the gap tends to separate the 'common-sense' journalistic view from the position which derives from content and media organizational analysis. Four elements are related in a different sequence in the two views: events; criteria of news selection (news values); news interests of the public; news report. The 'view from the media' emphasizes the reality-responsive quality of news and the analytical viewpoint the structured and autistic nature of the news selection process. According to the former view, the sequence is as follows:

EVENTS⟶NEWS CRITERIA⟶NEWS REPORT⟶NEWS INTEREST

This sequence begins with the world of unpredictable happenings which 'obtrude' and break the normality and to which news media respond by applying criteria concerning relative significance for their public. They compile objective news reports of the chosen events and the public responds with attention and interest or not, a datum which feeds into subsequent selection behaviour. The alternative model of the sequence is:

NEWS INTEREST──►NEWS CRITERIA──►EVENTS──►NEWS REPORT

Here the starting point is experience of what gains the attention of the public, which contributes to a rather stable and enduring set of news criteria, including the organizational and genre requirements. News events are only recognized as newsworthy if they conform to these selection criteria. News reports are then written in conformity to news criteria, guided more by the news organization's own requirements and routine practices than by reference to the 'real world' of events or what audiences 'really' want or need. It is not necessary to make an absolute choice between the models, but they cannot both be true to what happens.

The form of the news report
A good deal of attention has recently been paid not only to the nature of news as a concept, and to the influences which shape its production, but also to the form in which it appears. Part of the claim that news is a particular cultural genre or type, in the same sense as the novel, feature film or opera, rests on observations about the constancy, predictability and universality of the news form. While much recent attention has been paid to television news (e.g. Glasgow Media Group, 1977; 1980; Frank, 1973; Altheide, 1974; Altheide and Snow, 1979; Schlesinger, 1978; Gans, 1980), there is a good deal of overlap between the main features of news in the newspaper and on television. This is not surprising, given the origin of television news, but the seemingly small difference that has been made by developments in visual reporting is rather remarkable. The elements of form shared by press and radio or television fall into three main categories: those to do with recurrence and regularity; those to do with indications of order and structure; and those relating to neutrality and facticity. It should be borne in mind that two levels of formation are involved — one on the level of the separate news item and the other the whole news 'packet' (newspaper page or news 'bulletin' on radio or television). While the media are comparable in this respect, the newspaper or page has to

be structured *spatially* and the television news *temporally*, giving rise to some obvious differences of device.

Several researchers have been struck by the great regularity of structure of the news vehicle (newspaper or bulletin) which seems only partly accountable in terms of the needs of the production process. Newspapers and bulletins are regular in appearance, but also length or duration and in the balance of types of content, when divided into 'topic categories', such as 'foreign', 'political', 'sport', 'economic', 'human interest', etc. (McQuail, 1977). In television news the average duration of items shows a high degree of constancy, so that the number of items does not vary much from one 'bulletin' to another and there is even a relationship between type of content and average duration (Glasgow Media Group, 1977). Some of these features of regularity are found to be much the same in different countries (Rositi, 1976). What is striking is the extent to which a presumably unpredictable universe of events seems open to incorporation, day after day, into much the same temporal or spatial frame. It is true that deviations occur, at times of crisis or exceptional event, but the news form is posited on the notion of normality and routine and might be thought to reinforce the notion of normality through its regularity.

The second main aspect of news form has to do with indications of order and devices for structuring the whole. Analyses of news content show two main devices for indicating the relative significance of events reported. One is relative primacy of items in the newspaper space or the time of the bulletin. According to what the Glasgow Media Group (1980) calls 'viewers' maxims' it will be understood that first appearing items are most 'important', and that, generally, items receiving more time are also more important. It is common knowledge that newspages, newspapers and news bulletins are put together with a view to their overall appearance or possible effect and are not a random set of items, even after allowance has been made for the principle of order of importance. However, it has not been easy to turn daily observation into systematic theory or general statement. Television news bulletins are generally constructed with a view to arousing initial interest, by highlighting some event, maintaining it by diversity and human interest and holding back some vital information to the end (sports results and weather forecast), sending the viewer away with a light touch at the close. The suspicion persists that there is more to the overall balance of items than the mechanics of keeping attention and the Glasgow Media Group argue that it has to do with an underlying 'primary framework' or .view of the world which is essentially ideological. Rositi's (1976) search for the latent organiza-

tion in the television news of four European countries led to rather
modest, but interesting results: 'perhaps the only latent organization to be found at the level of the entire news program is that
described as the movement from a fragmented image of society to
its recomposition through the homogeneity of interests and political
representation'. The regularities described characterize the
dominant 'western' news form and it is likely that media operating
under different 'press theories' will exert different kinds of
regularity.

Much news form is clearly devoted to the pursuit of objectivity in
the sense of facticity or factualness. The language of news is 'linear',
elaborating an event report along a single dimension with added
information, illustration, quotation, discussion. According to the
Glasgow Media Group (1980, p. 160) 'the language of news seems to
be in a form which would allow of a fairly simple test of its truth or
falsity. It has the appearance of being entirely *constative* (proposi-
tional and capable of being shown to be true or false) and not
performative'. Both terms are taken from Austin and have been
used by Morin (1976) in an attempt to describe the basic ambiguity
of the news discourse. According to her (structuralist) analysis of
the news form, an event has to be rendered into a 'story about an
event' and the process of doing so involves a negotiation between
two opposed modes — that of the 'performative', which is also the
interpretative and the 'fabulative' (story-telling) mode, and that of
the 'constative' which is also the 'demonstrative' and factual mode.
Thus pure facts have no meaning and pure performance stands far
from the irreversible, rationally-known, fact of history. In her view,
different kinds of story involve different combinations of both and
can be plotted against the two 'axes' of the television discourse.

There is little doubt of the vital nature of facticity to the news
genre. As Smith writes 'The whole idea of news is that it is beyond a
"plurality of viewpoints"' (1973, p. 174). In his view, without an
attribution of credibility by the audience, news could not be distinguished from entertainment or propaganda. This may point to
one reason why Gans' (1980) seemingly reasonable plea for 'multi-
perspectival news' is unlikely to receive universal acclaim and why
the secular trend in news development has been away from ideology
and towards neutrality. Much of what remains unsaid here about
the nature of the news form has to do with devices for maintaining
the claim to credibility, which involve, in television news, the
inclusion of film and tape containing direct evidence, illustration,
interview and discussion, part of which is directed toward establishing a 'balanced presentation', which in the news culture is
strongly related to credibility.

6 THE MEDIA AUDIENCE

Duality of the audience

The term 'media audience' has a universal currency and a rather simple surface meaning as the aggregate of persons forming the readers, listeners, viewers for different media or their component items of content. As such, there would seem little scope for alternative theories of the audience. Yet this seemingly simple phenomenon conceals different ways of looking at such aggregates and variations over time and between places in the reality and conception of the audience. The most crucial element giving rise to questions about the audience is its dual nature. It is a collectivity formed either in response to media content and defined by attention to that content or one that exists already in social life and is then 'catered for' by a particular media provision. Not infrequently, it is inextricably both at the same time. Thus fans of a particular writer, musical group or television series are its audience, but an audience which cannot easily be localized in time or place and may have no other existence as a social group. At the other extreme, the inhabitants of a small community may have their own local newspaper which serves their needs but which has played no part in bringing the community into being or defining its boundaries or determining its continuity. There are many empirical variants of the relationship between media as source and people as receivers which produce different kinds of audience and many questions in the study of audiences which have arisen from this diversity.

The issues to be dealt with in this chapter are all in one way or another connected with the fact that audiences are both a cause of, and a response to, a supply of messages. These issues have to do with the extent to which an audience is a social group, the degree and kinds of activity which audiences can and do exercise, the forces which contribute to the formation of audiences and the extent to which media 'manipulate' their audiences or are in turn responsive to them. We look first at the audience concept itself, since it can appear under different names or with different meanings for the same name. These different versions of the audience sometimes stand for different ways of perceiving the same thing and sometimes for different realities.

Alternative concepts of the audience

The rise of the audience
The historical origin of the audience phenomenon has played a large
part in shaping the various usages of the audience concept. The
original 'audience' was the set of spectators for drama, games and
spectacles, for 'performances' of all kinds which have taken different forms in different civilizations and stages of history. Despite
such variations, some central features of the pre-media audience
have persisted and still shape our understanding and expectation.
The audience was usually large, relative to total population and normal social gatherings. It was planned in advance and localized in
time and place, often with special provision to maximize the quality
of 'reception'. The settings for the audience (theatres, halls, chur-
ches) were often designed with indications of rank and status. The
audience was a public gathering, taking place within a given time-
span, brought together by individual voluntary acts of choice
according to some expectation of benefit to enjoy, admire, learn,
experience amusement, terror, pity or relief. It was also subject to
potential or actual control by authority and was thus an institutionalized form of collective behaviour. Many of these features have
persisted even if there have been changes in scale and in degree of
localization.

The first major historical addition to the audience idea follows the
invention of printing and is the development of a 'reading public' —
those who actually participate in private reading and provide the
following for particular authors and genres (including the
newspaper). This development brings with it a clearer social-
economic division (which would already have existed to some extent
between richer and poorer and urban and rural people). It also helps
to establish the very notion of a public as something existing within
the population as a whole and differentiated according to interests,
education and often religious and political aspirations, as societies
begin to experience social and political changes in the print era. The
second main development which is of relevance is the growing commercialization of most forms of performance and public communication, but especially of print media, leading to larger scale operation
and the separation out of advertising and 'media industries'.
Thirdly, electronic media help to further delocalize the 'audience'
and detach its members from each other and from the senders.
Finally, we may speak of an assertion or reassertion, under the influence of democratic political theories and the widening of mass
communication functions, of claims by, or on behalf of, the society
for control over media. The demands for access, participation and
media accountability and social responsibility reflect a society-wide

consciousness of the importance of media and have implications for the nature of media audiences. With these points in mind we can sketch the main variant conceptions that appear in the literature and in common usage.

The audience as aggregate of spectators, readers, listeners, viewers

This is the audience in its most recognizable form and the version employed in most research for the media themselves. Its focus is on number — the total number of persons reached by a given 'unit' of media content and the number of persons within this total of given demographic characteristics of interest to the sender. In practice, the application of the concept is not so uncomplicated and leads eventually to considerations beyond the purely quantitative. Clausse (1968) has indicated some of the complexities of distinguishing varying degrees of participation and involvement by audiences. The first and largest audience is the population which is available to receive a given 'offer' of communication. Thus all with television sets are in some sense the television audience. Secondly, there is the the audience which actually receives, in varying degrees, what is offered — the regular television viewers, newspaper buyers, etc. Thirdly, there is that part of the actual audience which registers reception of content and finally there is a still smaller part which 'internalizes' what is offered and received. Clausse puts this another way by pointing to a series of reductions, from the whole population of society, to the 'potential public' for a message, to the 'effective public' which actually attends, to the 'particular message public' within that and finally to the public actually 'affected' by the communication. In general, this concept of audience goes no further than the point of reception, or giving of attention, which can be recorded in various ways or estimated after the event, since the commercial or professional interest of the media senders is usually satisfied by such information. Elliott (1972) has made some critical remarks about the limiting effects of this concept of the audience as a body of spectators. The more the maximization of the number of spectators is taken as an end in itself, the less likely is there to be any concern with real communication in the sense of an 'ordered transfer of meaning'. In his view, mass communication is so preoccupied with such spectator counting that it is 'liable not to be communication at all' (p. 164).

The audience as mass

The meaning of the mass has already been discussed (pp. 35–6) as a

key element in the ideal type of mass communication and as
originally defined by Blumer (1939) and other sociologists (e.g.
Mills, 1956). We can recapitulate by saying that this view of the
audience emphasizes its large size, heterogeneity, dispersion,
anonymity, lack of social organization and fleeting and inconsistent
composition. The mass has no continuous existence except in the
minds of those who want to gain the attention of and manipulate as
many people as possible. According to Raymond Williams (1961,
p. 289) there are no masses, 'only ways of seeing people as masses'.
It has, even so, tended to become a standard by which media are
judged — the larger and more instantaneous the audience, the more
socially significant. It has also become a standard for judging the
audience — the more it approaches a mass, the lower must be its
culture and taste. The verbal accident which has equated mass with
the audience for mass media should not mislead us to favour this
conception.

The audience as a public
or social group

The key element in this version of the audience is the pre-existence
of an active, interactive and largely autonomous social group which
is served by particular media, but does not depend on the media for
its existence. The idea of a public has already been discussed as it
appears in sociology and liberal-democratic theory. It was, for
example, defined by Dewey (1927) as a 'political grouping of
individuals brought into being as a social unit through mutual
recognition of common problems for which common solutions
should be sought'. Such a grouping needs various means of
communication for its development and continuity but, according to
Mills (1956), the mass media had developed in such a way as to
hinder the formation of publics. Nevertheless, we can see continued
evidence of the existence of various audience formations with
characteristics of the public. Although rarely identified as such,
most societies have an 'informed public' — that section of the
audience which is most active in political and social life and draws
on many sources of information, especially the elite, opinion-
forming and specialist press. Secondly, many countries retain some
element of the party press or a press which does have political
connections with readership groups (Seymour-Ure, 1974). Here the
membership or supporters of a particular party form a public which
is also an audience. Thirdly, there are local or community audiences
for a local publication, of the kind described by Janowitz (1952). In
such cases the audience tends to coincide with the members,
especially the most active members, of a pre-existing community,

hence social group. Finally, there are numerous particular audiences formed on the basis of an issue, an interest, or an occupation which may have other forms of interaction and are not simply the creation of a media supply.

The examples cited relate mainly to the print media, but there is no reason in principle why audiovisual media should not come to serve publics in the sense used here. It happens, however, that in the rather short history of broadcasting, the dominant institutional arrangements have not favoured the separation out of distinct publics. There are exceptions, as in the Netherlands (van der Haak, 1977) and local radio (Brown, 1978) and local television distributed by cable make it increasingly possible for communities and neighbourhoods to provide audiences. In summary, one can say that an audience which is first a public or a social group will have a degree of self-consciousness, a common identity and possibilities for interaction internally and for influencing the communication supply.

The audience as market

While cultural developments led to the original audience and political developments to the concept of the public, it was economic developments in the last century that gave rise to the 'audience as market' concept. A media product is a commodity or service offered for sale to a given body of potential consumers, in competition with other media products. These potential or actual consumers can be referred to as a market and in the United States, where media are almost entirely commercial, it is customary, even in academic contexts, to refer to potential audiences as 'markets', sometimes indicating specific population areas, sometimes indicating aggregates of population characterized in some other way (e.g. young women, farmers or golfers). The audience so designated has a dual significance for media, first as set of potential consumers for the product, and second as an audience for advertising of a certain kind, which is the other main source of media revenue. Thus a market for a media product is also likely to be a market for other products, for which the media will be an advertising vehicle and a way of 'delivering' potential customers of other products. While it is necessary for commercially financed media to regard their audiences as markets in both senses and convenient sometimes to characterize given audiences in terms of life-style and consumption pattern, there are a number of consequences of this approach for ways of perceiving the audience.

Firstly, it specifies the link between media and their audiences as a consumer-producer relationship, hence 'calculative' from the point

of view of the consumer and manipulative from the point of view of
the sender — in any case it is not a moral or social relationship as in
the case of the public. Secondly, it gives little emphasis to the
internal social relationships of the audience: they are a set of
individual and equal consumers, sharing certain given demographic
or cultural features. The development of a social relations approach
to audience study and the relevance of 'opinion leadership' to
consumption decisions has modified this feature of 'market
thinking', but it still largely holds. Thirdly, the audience characteristics most relevant to this way of thinking are social-economic
and the social stratification of audiences has always claimed undue
attention. Fourthly, from a market perspective, the key fact about
audiences is their attention-giving behaviour, expressed mainly in
acts of purchase or viewing and listening choice. Such data provide
the main criteria for assessing the success or failure of media
content and lead to a lower emphasis on criteria of effective
communication or intrinsic quality. Finally, the market view is
inevitably the view 'from the media'. We never conceive of ourselves
as belonging to markets, rather we are placed in market categories
or identified as part of a 'target group' by others.

To summarize, we can define the audience as market as an
'aggregate of potential consumers with a known social-economic
profile at which a medium or message is directed'. There are
similarities with the mass concept, since the very largest market
(whole population) will have the features of a mass, but market
thinking pays much more attention to differentiation within the
total available audiences and is concerned with matching media
product to believed needs and interests of receivers. In market
thinking, there is also attention to cultural tastes and preferences as
well as to number or to purely social-economic criteria. Amongst the
audience concepts named, the widest gap lies between market and
public, since they diverge sharply in the way they attend to
audience origin, to the degree and kind of audience identity and
activity, and to the purpose and function of communication.

Sources of change
Between them, those four types exhaust the main possibilities for
defining the audience. They are all in some way dependent on a
given set of media possibilities and historical circumstances and
each is open to challenge because of changes that have occurred or
are occurring. Amongst the media changes, the most significant in
this respect are: (1) the multiplication of media items and channels,
individualization of use and a detachment from fixed and accountable systems of distribution; (2) the development of interactive

media based on computerized cable links. The consequence of the first is that it becomes increasingly difficult to predict who will provide the audience for a given 'item' or to know after the event who was in it. It is simply more difficult than in the early days of media to 'account' for the audience experience and to answer the question 'who receives what?'. The growth of 'interactive' media, still at a very early stage, is likely to further promote the fragmentation and specialization of media use, but also to give the 'audience' member a potentially more active role. Under pressure of current media changes, the whole concept of an audience as a group or set receiving much the same content at the same time and place is challenged and with it the original 'spectator' version of the audience.

Under conditions of great diversity of supply and flexibility of use by individuals, the concept of audience as mass seems even less realistic. There are fewer opportunities for an audience to form as a heterogeneous mass, although when it does happen, it is on a scale greater than ever before — as with world audiences for sporting events. The challenge to the audience as public has other sources and arises from two main tendencies: one within media themselves which, as they professionalize, have tended to weaken their direct links with political and social movements; the other, the trend to 'secularization' (decline in ideology) and growth in consumer-mindedness in many western societies in the last decade or two. Nevertheless, it is likely that the 'public' is only changing its manifestation, becoming more localized, issue- and interest-specific, less identified with either a 'single' informed elite public or the following of a major political party. If anything, the market concept is likely to become even more widely current under the conditions briefly described, since the application of yet more media innovations, the greater production of media content of all kinds and the increase of available time and money to spend on media, require yet more detailed specifications of target groups and the cultivation of more and more specialized 'markets'.

One conceptual development which is related to these changes is the appearance of the notion of a 'taste culture', which recognizes the importance of non-demographic factors and also the fleeting and overlapping nature of audiences. One definition of taste culture has been attributed by Lewis (1980) to Herbert Gans as an 'aggregate of similar content chosen by the same people'. The concept makes it easier to detach choice-making from social background and to regroup acts of choice according to similarity of content rather than to channel or medium location or to demographic variations. The concept is compatible with market thinking and challenges older conceptions of a socially and culturally stratified audience system. Thus taste cultures may be difficult to place in any hierarchical scheme and are a consequence in part of the genuine classlessness of some uses of leisure time and of media interests and in part of the success of the cultural industry in establishing a 'one-dimensional society' (Marcuse, 1964).

The social character of audience experience

Group properties of audiences

In order to answer the main questions about the audience posed at the start of this chapter, a somewhat arbitrary separation is made between whether audience experience is 'social' or whether audience behaviour is 'active'. In discussing alternative conceptions of the audience it has become clear that the solution to the first issue depends partly on how one chooses to regard the audience — whether as aggregate or social group — and partly on the facts of the case — some audiences do have a group character and some, strictly speaking, are no more than aggregates. In practice, there is a continuum, with 'mass' at one end and 'small close-knit group' at the other, along which actual audiences can be located. There is, however, more to be said before audiences can be identified in such a way and the purpose of the following discussion is to look at some of the theory and evidence that would be helpful in locating audiences according to the degree to which they exhibit group-like properties.

Much sociological effort has been devoted to studying the properties of groups and Ennis (1961) has provided a useful starting point for the study of audience as group by naming the main criteria which should be applied (drawing on Merton, 1957). He distinguished 'boundary' properties from those of 'internal structure'. It is the latter which are of most concern here, since the question of audience boundaries can usually be settled empirically and the main issues have already been discussed. If an audience corresponds more or less to an existing group — a public, a party membership, a minority, an association, a community, etc. — it inherits the characteristics of the group-like collectivity in question as to membership 'qualification', size, degree of engagement, stability over time, location in space, etc. This also reminds us that media audiences can acquire the boundary properties that groups have and may perhaps give rise to group formations. Audiences do sometimes correspond to the boundaries of a demographic group (e.g. age group) and may exhibit other group properties, such as feelings of identity with an age culture.

It is sometimes argued that, since local media use is correlated with attachment to a community, the introduction of new local media may help to strengthen the solidarity of the neighbourhood and give it some enduring identity. It is also clear that media often give rise to subsets of 'fans' who may become organized sufficiently to recognize and interact with each other. This leads us to consider the second set of properties, those to do with internal structure, and here Ennis names three in particular: the degree of social differentiation; the extent of interaction; the existence of systems of normative controls. With some 'stretching' these can still provide the headings for a discussion of the social character of the audience.

Social differentiation

Since we are dealing with the 'internal structure' of audiences at this point, it is not strictly relevant to discuss the question of the social stratification of different audiences and more is said below about audience composition. However, it is worth recalling that, within a given audience, there are almost always differences of interest, attention, perception and effect associated with social differentiation. Thus the behaviour of a given audience group is almost always patterned by the factors that more generally shape social behaviour. To that extent, audience behaviour is almost inevitably 'social'. More pertinent to the discussion, perhaps, is the evidence that has accumulated through studies of personal influence (Merton, 1949; Katz and Lazarsfeld, 1955) which shows that given audience groups can have an internal structure based on media use and content. Thus there is a recognized informal hierarchy separating those more expert on a certain content or subject from those less expert. This kind of social differentiation often reflects features of the rest of social life and is not directly caused by the media, though media use offers the occasion for its expression and perhaps reinforcement. While the social differentiation of audiences *may* correspond to the stratification pattern of society, it need not do so. Thus Katz and Lazarsfeld found such associations in the identification of opinion leaders for certain kinds of subject matter but not others. The development of 'taste-cultures', relatively free from class determination, may also tend to promote a dissociation between social stratification and audience composition.

Social interaction

Sociability
Of the several aspects to be considered, the most obvious is that of

the *sociability* of the behaviour itself, which varies according to the nature of the medium (see Chapter 1). It is some time since the concept of media use as solitary, atomized and alienated behaviour was tested against the evidence and found wanting. As Friedson (1953) remarked: 'mass communications have been absorbed into the social life of the local groups' and even the seemingly most private and individual act of media choice, going to a cinema, has been repeatedly shown to be, first, a social act with someone else and usually, secondarily, a communication act (Jowett and Linton, 1980). The most common medium for most people, television, is frequently watched in family group settings and is closely integrated into patterns of family interaction, just as music listening is often an integral part of youth peer group behaviour. It is true that some media, especially books and radio, provide opportunities for solitary enjoyment and are chosen for this reason at certain times (Brown, 1976), but it is rare for media use to be an obstacle to sociability. There is quite a lot of research to support the view that media use is either a means towards better social relations (e.g. Riley and Riley, 1951; Noble, 1975) or, where loneliness is enforced, a possible compensation or substitute.

Social uses
There is a good deal of evidence to support the view that media use is more *social* than otherwise and some recent research by James Lull (1982), based on participant observation of family media use, has confirmed, or added to, what had already been established. His work provides a useful framework and presents a 'social uses' typology with five main types: structural; relational; affiliation or avoidance; social learning; competence/dominance. The first of these, 'structural', refers to uses of media as background, providing companionship, regulating patterns of activity and talk. Mendelsohn (1964) had earlier described radio as 'bracketing' the day and creating 'moods'. The relational heading is similar to what had earlier been called the 'coin of exchange' function. The media provide common ground for talk, topics, illustrations — pegs on which to hang opinions. The 'affiliation' dimension refers to media as an aid to gaining or avoiding physical and verbal contact and also to the function of the media in increasing 'family solidarity', maintaining relationships and decreasing tension. 'Social learning' has mainly to do with various aspects of socialization. 'Competence/dominance' has to do with such things as role enactment and reinforcement, with validation of arguments, with being an 'opinion leader' or 'first with the news'.

Social isolation
A good deal of attention, especially in relation to children and young people, has been given to the potentially *isolating* effects of media use, a concern which has mainly expressed itself in anxiety over 'excessive' or 'addictive' use of media, especially television, although the same fears were once expressed about films. Very heavy attention to media, especially if one is alone, has often been interpreted as a form of self-isolation, even alienation, a withdrawal from reality. We shall return shortly to the subject of 'normative regulation', but here it should at least be noted that very high usage of media competes for time with normal social interaction. There are two relevant bodies of evidence; one suggesting that high use is correlated with poor social adjustment and other indications of problems (e.g. Maccoby, 1954; Horton and Wohl, 1956; Pearlin, 1959; Halloran et al., 1970; McLeod et al., 1965); another associating high media use (especially television) with other kinds of social marginality, such as sickness, old age, unemployment, poverty. Two main theses suggest either that media work against 'good' social adjustment and relationships, or that poor social circumstances are reflected in media use, either because the media offer some compensation or simply because they are a time-filler (Rosengren and Windahl, 1972). In the event, research has confirmed neither proposition in any general way. It is clear that high media use can go with and even promote good social contact (e.g. Hedinsson, 1981) and also that poor social circumstances may even deprive people of the small motivation needed to make extensive use of media (Meyersohn, 1968).

Audience–sender relationships
In speaking of social interaction within the audience, the obvious reference is to personal contacts between people, but the question of a certain kind of *social relation between audience and sender* can also belong here. At several points, reference has been made to the possibility for a relationship to be established or maintained between a sender and a public by way of the mass media. This can occur either when a sender is genuinely trying to communicate or when both sender and receiver are trying to achieve the same ends. It has, however, often been noted that individuals in audiences establish (mainly vicarious) relationships with mass communication, especially with characters, stars or personalities in fiction and entertainment. This has aptly been called 'para-social interaction' (Horton and Wohl, 1956) and its various forms have been described in different ways. Although difficult to study scientifically, the

phenomenon is very familiar — programme fans are physically affected by what happens to fictional characters and talk about them as if they were real. Realistic and long-running 'soap-operas' with fixed characters seem to lend themselves most to dissolving the line between fiction and reality. Noble (1975) has suggested two concepts for dealing with this kind of involvement: 'identification' and 'recognition'. He attributes the first to Schramm et al. (1961) who defined it as 'the experience of being able to put oneself so deeply into a TV character and feel oneself to be so like the character that one can feel the same emotions and experience the same events as the character is supposed to be feeling'. This concept implies some 'identity-loss', while 'recognition' does not, and even contributes to identity forming. Thus recognition is being able to interact with well known television characters as if they were similar to known people in real life. Noble writes (pp. 63-64) 'these characters serve as something akin to screen community with whom the viewer regularly talks and interacts . . . . this regularly appearing screen community serves for many as an extended kin grouping, whereby the viewer comes into contact with the wider society beyond his immediate family'. The emphasis is on the positive aspect of vicarious social interaction, rather than on its common association with social withdrawal and inadequacy.

Normative controls

The existence of systems of normative control in relation to mass media use seems at first sight counter to the view that media are voluntary, free-time, 'out of role' activities, more or less unrelated to social obligation. While media use is relatively uncontrolled compared to other types of institutional involvement, it follows from the fact of normative regulation of the institution by society that there should be discriminations and valuations made in relation to audience use. In practice, audience research continually uncovers the existence of value systems which regulate 'media behaviour' in several ways. Firstly, there are values governing content and often making fine distinctions, depending on context, between one type of content and another. Secondly, there are valuations of different media and time given to media as against other uses of time. Thirdly, there are expectations held by the audience about the obligations of media producers and distributors to provide certain services and meet certain obligations. Much the same set of values governs each of these aspects, although they are applied in different ways by different groups.

The values about content are rather familiar and stem from traditional judgements embedded in the culture and handed on mainly by the institutions of education, family and religion. They apply first to certain kinds of content, favouring the informational, educational, moral over entertainment, the immoral and the 'low-cultural'. One consequence is a carry-over to judgements about media, so that the media with stronger entertainment associations, such as television and film, carry a lower value than newspapers and books. Thus parents are more inclined to limit the use of television than newspaper or book reading, even though the last-named appears to have stronger connotations of 'escape' than do other media (Brown, 1976). It is mainly in the imposition of norms for media use in family contexts that we are aware of normative control of media (Geiger and Sokol, 1959; Hedinsson, 1981; Brown and Linné, 1976), but similar normative prescriptions have a much wider distribution. For instance, Steiner (1963) found a tendency for respondents to show a certain amount of guilt over high levels of television use and some kinds of content preference. In general, he attributes this to a legacy from the protestant ethic, which frowns on 'unproductive' uses of time. Among middle class audiences, especially, a sensitivity to this value persists. Steiner and others have found a tendency for this to show more in words than in behaviour and although it may be in decline, it seems likely that the broad value system remains and exerts some influence on actual behaviour as well as on reports of behaviour.

The question of audience attitudes to the media has been a rather frequent matter of investigation, usually in the context of intermedia comparisons (cf. Comstock et al., 1978, pp. 128-40). People voice complaints about media and they also appreciate them. Positive appreciation usually outweighs criticism, but the point here is that audiences feel it as a matter on which they should have opinions — the performance of the media is a matter for public opinion. Audiences expect to be informed and entertained and expect conformity to some norms of good taste and morality and perhaps also patriotism and other values. This takes us some way from the question of the audience as a group, but it is a reminder that the mass media are not protected from the application of normative judgements at whatever is the appropriate level of operation — be it that of the local community, the nation or even the international community.

One last aspect of the normative status of media should be raised and that has to do with the absolute level of attachment to media in

dependence of people on their media and Steiner (1963) reports that

many would feel quite lost without television. Although there is
little doubt that people often exhibit strong feelings of deprivation
when denied television or newspapers (Berelson, 1949), there is some
uncertainty about the strength of attachment at normal times.
Himmelweit and Swift (1976), for instance, on the basis of a
longtitudinal study of media use and preferences, conclude that 'the
media form part of the background rather than the foreground of
the leisure life and interests of adolescents and young men: they are
used far more than they are valued'. The truth is probably that
dependence, and hence valuation, varies a good deal according to
circumstances and that under some conditions, especially of confine-
ment to home and low income, the strength of attachment and level
of appreciation is indeed very high, whether for television, books or
radio.

How 'active' is audience experience?

This question arises in several contexts and involves various
concepts of 'activity'. It has to do, for instance, with the extent to
which the audience is selective, with the degree and kind of
motivation which leads to media use, with resistance to unwanted
influences, with the kind and amount of response which is made by
media audiences. There is some disagreement about the general
amount of selectivity in media use behaviour. On the one hand,
there is a strong indication from the constancy of audience ratings
and/or press readership figures than much media consumption is an
unchanging routine which barely responds to variations in what is
offered. This seems to be especially the case with television, where
there are many indications that people allocate a certain amount of
time to viewing in general, irrespective of what is on. A detailed
study of viewing patterns by Goodhart et al. (1975) came to the
conclusion that selectivity was extremely low, so low that even
consequent viewing of the next episode of a given series would only
encompass 55 percent of the first audience. Such patterns are thus
little more than chance. Audience sizes could be predicted (in
Britain) very well with knowledge only of channel and time of
output. Such findings conflict with what people often say about
their level of selectivity and with the known profiling of certain
kinds of content according to demographic variables such as education, income, sex. Yet, although such profiling of content is common
and also stable in different countries (Blumler, 1979), it is not
usually very strong in the case of television and, as between
different kinds of content within a given newspaper, it is also not
very much in evidence. There is a certain amount of evidence to

support the view that the media tend to shape tastes by what they offer (e.g. Himmelweit and Swift, 1976) and it may be especially true of media which seek large general audiences. The growth of taste cultures and the attempt to promote them tends to run counter to the assumption of audience unselectivity. But both are consistent with the idea of a passive audience.

The study of media audiences in the tradition labelled 'uses and gratifications' has set itself against the notion of a passive audience and depends on a number of assumptions, one of which is that the individual audience member is, in some measure, making a conscious and motivated selection amongst the various items of content. There are different versions of the approach, some more 'culturalist' and descriptive, and others more behaviourist and functionalist, and different formulations of the underlying theory (McQuail and Gurevitch, 1974). One much-quoted statement of the latter says that such studies 'are concerned with (1) the social and psychological origins of (2) needs, which generate (3) expectations of (4) the mass media or other sources, which lead to (5) differential patterns of mass media exposure (or engagement in other activities), resulting in (6) need gratifications and (7) other consequences . . .' (Katz et al., 1974, p. 20).

Thus the 'causes' of media use lie in social or psychological circumstances that are experienced as problems and the media are used for problem resolution (the meeting of needs). A number of the typical problems and needs have already been mentioned in this and earlier chapters — having to do with information, social contact, diversion, learning and social development. If media use is almost entirely unselective then, correspondingly, it does not carry a meaning attributed by the user and cannot in any significant degree be accounted as an instrument for problem-solving.

Much work has been done over a period of forty years to show that audiences can and do describe their media experience in functional (i.e. problem-solving or 'need-meeting') terms. There is a recurring pattern to the ideas which people produce about the utility of their media behaviour, the main elements having to do with: learning and information; self-insight and personal identity; social contact; diversion, entertainment, time-filling (see above, (pp. 82–3). It is clear that audience members do think about media and content as if they could be useful, and the ideas that are reproduced tend to be internally consistent and consistent with other kinds of reported behaviour. What is missing is extensive independent validation that much media use is prompted by consciously or unconsciously formed motives. This would confirm the view that the audience is indeed 'active' and that a causal process is at work, beginning in the experience of the viewer, listener or reader. There is so much 'noise' in the system, so much unmotivated and casual attention to media that the answer to the fundamental question is unlikely to be reached.

Research on audience motivation has, nevertheless, produced quite rich and varied accounts of the audience experience, beyond what is provided from descriptions of content and data about 'exposure'. It has been especially useful in comparing different media (e.g. Katz et al., 1973) and in the study of children's use of different media and kinds of content, as these develop over time (Wolfe and Fiske, 1949; Greenberg, 1974; Brown, 1976; Furu, 1971). A cogent critical discussion of the 'uses and gratifications' approach as a whole can be found either in Chaney (1972) or Elliott (1974). They raise doubts about the reliability and validity of some of the evidence on which the approach has been based and lean towards the view that most of the 'gratifications' identified are either indications of position in a social structure or 'needs' which the audience has acquired from the media.

It is relevant to the theme of the 'active audience', although too large a matter to deal with in detail here, to recall the expression 'obstinate audience' coined by Raymond Bauer (1964) to express the findings of much research that the audience actively resists attempts at influence and has a reciprocal 'transactional' relationship with media sources. One application of studies of audience motivation has been to examine the process of media effect, according to the notion that the degree and kind of effect will depend on the need of the receiver. There has been some success in this direction in the field of political communication (e.g. Blumler and McQuail, 1968; McLeod and Becker, 1974) and certainly audience attention to political communication is not independent of perceived utility.

Theories of audience composition

The description of audiences has been a perennial task of audience and market research and a by-product of almost all studies of media use and effect. There are much more data about the media audience than data of any other kind, yet they have been of little value in understanding the process of mass communication. Most such sets of data are time- and place-bound, although they do reveal the working of a small number of basic factors which seem to influence the size and composition of media audiences. The two most commonly recurring factors have to do with age and social class (or income and education), because both determine the availability of

free time and money for media use. Age influences availability and content choice. Thus, as young children, we are confined more or less to the range of family chosen media and watch more television. As we acquire freedom, we make more independent choices and go outside the home, leading to a pattern of radio listening and cinema going. With acquisition of our own family and work responsibilities, we return to a domestic context but with different interests, giving more time to newspaper reading and information generally. With more spare income after the growing up of our own children, media consumption diversifies and then contracts again with old age, leading to a return to more domestic media (television and books) and more 'serious' content choices. Social class position, as represented by income, governs the pattern of media use and, within this pattern, higher income tends to diminish the place of television because of wider non-media leisure choices. Higher education and professional work responsibility may also lead to different content choices — more informational content or content favoured by dominant educational and cultural values.

Such findings and others which relate, with less consistency, to differences of sex and locality help to describe and predict the overall shape of audiences and the underlying factors at work are not hard to recognize. However, there are differing explanations of the formation of audiences and the specific or typical patterns which are found and it is relevant to the purposes of this chapter to look at the various theories or part-theories that have been advanced. Those that follow are not all mutually exclusive and vary in their completeness and specificity. They tend to divide into three main groups, reflecting an emphasis on: 'media supply' as a determinant; on the conditions of distribution and possible reception; or on audience 'demand'.

Historical accident
The heading may be obscure and the theory itself vague, but the reference is to two main factors which account for a given overall audience structure. One factor is media history, since the media have grown on the basis of successive appeals to limited social groups and have gradually extended their reach, without closing some historic 'gaps' and having even institutionalized some of them. Thus the daily newspaper was developed primarily for a male, urban middle class readership, with functions in political and business life, and it still tends to have a greater appeal for the social groups for which it was originally intended. Television, on the other hand, borrowed from film and radio and established itself as a domestic and entertainment medium appealing most to those most

often at home, thus women and children and those with fewer resources. The second factor is the success of particular media, especially print media, in establishing and maintaining an identity or 'persona' to which a certain kind of audience has been drawn. This theory is likely to appeal to media themselves and is a distinctly 'supply-side' explanation. History plays a part here, in that at any given time the range of media will contain a number of titles or content forms which are retaining, or gradually losing, audiences composed according to some original specifications. Varying loyalty of audiences and varying economic fortunes both enter into the total, rather complex, explanation of audience pattern.

Market management
This is also a 'supply-side' theory, referring to the influence of advertising on media institutions. Commercial media have to match their product to a given market of consumers for the media product itself and for other goods for which it is an advertising vehicle. The readership 'profile' as well as size is thus of great importance to success or failure and market management aims to optimize the audience composition. The extent to which this has affected the structure of the British national press is well described by Hirsch and Gordon (1975) and we may well choose to see many features of audience composition as the outcome, whether successful or not, of attempts at media market management.

Giving the public what it wants
This might be termed an 'individual differences' theory and is one which also appeals to the media themselves. In essence it says only that observed patterns of audience composition are the result of large numbers of individual acts of choice, each guided by differences of taste, interest, intellectual capacity and opportunity. Under competitive conditions, laws of supply and demand should ensure that the public as a whole gets what it wants. This pragmatic and common-sense theory holds that different kinds of content, provided on the basis of research and experience, will tend to appeal to audiences of predictable size and composition.

Differential leisure resources
The stress here is less on content and active choice of content than on differential 'availability' for media reception of social groups. The opportunity to receive depends mainly on three things: amount

of free time; educational level; money. The general pattern of media use, as between social categories, can be seen as the complex outcome of each of these factors. Thus women and children and the old tend to have more time and less money available and consequently attend relatively more to media which are cheapest and most time demanding. Such simple associations are cut across by differences of income and education, both of which widen the range of content which is effectively accessible and also the number of alternatives to mass media for informational or diversionary purposes.

Functional theory
The essentials of this theory have already been outlined in discussing the motivations of audience members and the 'uses and gratifications' of media. The consequences for audience composition are clear enough, since we should expect that audiences will tend to seek, if not get, what they 'need' to solve problems or maximize their satisfactions. Insofar as 'problems' and 'needs' are rooted in social conditions or personality and life-circumstances, audience composition will reflect the connection between certain kinds of content and the recurring or typical needs of particular social groups. This is clearly a 'demand-side' theory and, of all those named here, the most open to operationalization and testing and with most potential for explanation. It is weakened, however, by the discovery that there is no 'one-to-one' relationship between content type and function, so that the same content can meet varied 'needs'. An extension of functional theory would be that the general shape of audience composition will reflect the overall distribution of needs and functions in the society (see Chapter 3), and will be a 'natural' or 'best' solution to the 'communication needs' of society. There is a risk here of assuming that what the audience gets is what it wants and also what it needs.

A social-cultural explanation
If we regard attention to mass media as part of a wider process of attention-giving, we should explain patterns of media use according to the same principles governing other communication (here attention-giving) behaviour. Individuals (and eventually groups or categories) have a more or less given social location and surrounding 'life space' (Kurt Lewin's term). They pay attention to things they encounter within this life space and develop a structure of attention-giving which is appropriate to their social location. In general, we

can expect attention to what is close, familiar, positive, unthreatening, equal or subordinate in social power and we can expect avoidance of objects with reverse characteristics. Such an explanation would, for example, predict working class avoidance of content which is unfamiliar, socially or physically remote, or likely to recall powerlessness in work contexts or intellectual inadequacy. There are other situations of varying dependency and powerlessness which might produce similar patterns of selection and avoidance. In general, this explanation emphasizes the location of media artefacts within a universe of socially defined objects. One acquires an orientation to such artefacts through experiences which are likely to be shared with others. The orientation thus becomes a collective phenomenon.

Concluding note

Underlying these different approaches lies an implicit division of factors into those that facilitate choice and those that constrain and suppress. Between media supply on the one hand and demand on the other are a set of 'filter conditions', some of which relate to individual differences, others to culture and social structure. While changes of media supply can have some effect on the pattern of demand and demand can also affect supply, many of the conditions are slow to change, hence the stability over time of patterns of media consumption.

The influence of the audience on content

A central issue in this chapter has been the varying dependency or activeness of the audience and there remains for consideration the matter of audience response or 'feedback'. While it is already evident that the competence and power of the audience to influence the producer/distributor depends very much on the character and setting of the audience in question, there are a number of general mechanisms by which senders and receivers are brought into a mutual relationship. These are described in the following paragraphs.

Critics and fans

The traditional concept of the audience or readership groups assumed two important elements of institutionalized response. One was the critical apparatus, operating on behalf of, mainly, middle class publics and in relation to the more elite kinds of content. The range of institutionalized critical attention has widened considerably to cover much television, popular music, films and reading, partly as an extension of the media's own requirements as an industry. At the same time, the gap between critics and fans, the other important element, has tended to narrow. Thus many different kinds of media and content have their more or less discriminating, enthusiastic and knowledgeable followers, whose role is not so different from that of the critic. This is a development which has been also encouraged by the media and plays a part in its self-publicity. While critics and fans certainly evaluate, it is less clear that they play much part in modifying performance or in shaping supply.

Institutionalized accountability
There are now numerous forms in which the claim of the audience, as an interest group in society, to influence media content has been recognized. The rise of public broadcasting has stimulated many such developments, since radio and television were often established as services with an assumption of accountability to the public as a whole. The range of instruments of control is large and varied and the main forms can only be named. These include: control through parliament; committees and commissions of inquiry; legal instruments of control; councils of readers, viewers or listeners; authorities which set and apply codes of standards in the public interest; press councils; systems of subsidy and support. Most such instruments and forms tend, in liberal democracies, to have a limiting rather than a positive role — they are more likely to restrict than prescribe.

The market
According to many proponents of media freedom, the main (and best) means of control and influence is the exercise of free choice under conditions of a free market.

Direct 'feedback'
The traditional form of response for the audience has been insti-tutionalized by the media themselves in the form of 'letters to the editor' and phone calls to radio and television stations. Although these have come to form an important component of media there is some doubt about their real value as feedback (Singer, 1973) and

they are very open to manipulation by the media themselves, with few widely held conventions about how letters should be treated and selected. For very large scale media, it is doubtful whether such direct response can either express the wishes of the audience or inform the media.

The use of 'audience images'

The problem for the media of addressing themselves effectively to chosen audiences, or any audiences, has already been raised (Chapter 4) and it arises again in the present context. There is a very indirect and inadequate form of influence on content through the practice by media sources of constructing 'images' of the audiences or anticipated audiences for which they shape their messages (Bauer, 1958). According to Gans (1957, p. 318) 'The audience participates in the making of a movie through the audience image held by the creator'. This construct may be based on personal experience, imagination or a stereotype, but it helps the creator to 'test' the product in the course of its formation. The existence of this tendency has been widely attested to and it has several times been concluded that such audience images are either shaped by professional self-interest or a very narrow range of social experience (Burns, 1977; Gans, 1980). Gans suggests, for instance, that newsmakers adopt an audience image that conforms largely to their own middle class social milieu. He notes also that four basic kinds of image are invoked: the interested (like themselves); the uninterested; the rejected (e.g. intellectual critics); the invented (any image which satisfies their own wishes).

Research

The many possibilities for research to influence the supply of media will have been illustrated at many points in this book and there is no need to review them here. Most relevant are those kinds of research which the media undertake to guide their own operations. Abraham Moles (1973) has given a useful guide to research as feedback and pointed out that possibilities for influence from research depend especially on the potential for quantification and on the time scale of application. Thus numerical findings which can be quickly applied are most likely to have some influence. However, we also have considerable evidence that media communicators tend to resist or reject the findings of research, either because these are not understood or because they are perceived as threatening. Thus any influence they have is likely to be with management. In the case of

research carried out outside media organizations there is unlikely to
be any direct influence on mass communicators or on management,
unless it is sponsored by powerful interests, clients or governments.
It is obviously possible for research to play a creative role in
matching the purposes of communicators to the needs, interests and
capacities of the public (cf. Belson, 1967; Katz, 1977) and clearly a
number of audience research departments attached to public service
broadcasting in several countries pursue this objective actively. Yet
it is also likely that, on balance, such research is used more for the
media than 'on behalf of' the public, let alone 'by' the public as a
means of influence. The last claim could not perhaps be made for
very much academic research, although this is more inclined to take
the 'side' of the public than of the media senders. In concluding this
section and the chapter, it is worth recording the existence of an
ambiguity about the desirability of audience influence. While one
norm supports responsiveness to and interaction with the audience,
another safeguards the autonomy of the communicator on grounds
of creativity, personal freedom and possibilities for change.

7 PROCESSES OF MEDIA EFFECTS

Introduction

The entire study of mass communication is based on the premise that there are effects from the media, yet it seems to be the issue on which there is least certainty and least agreement. This apparent uncertainty is the more surprising since everyday experience provides countless examples of small effects. We dress for the weather under the influence of a weather forecast, buy something because of an advertisement, go to a film mentioned in a newspaper, react in countless ways to television, radio or music. We live in a world where political and governmental processes are based on the assumption that we know what is going on from press and television or radio. There are few people who can trace no piece of information or opinion to a source in the media and much money and effort is spent in directing media to achieve such effects.

And yet it is true that much doubt exists about the degree, incidence and kind of effects and our knowledge is insufficient to make any but the most simple prediction about the occurrence of an effect in a given case. Even where we can make a prediction, it is usually based on experience and rule of thumb rather than on a precise knowledge of *how* a given effect has occurred or might occur. It is the availability of such pragmatic knowledge, based on experience, that enables the media and their clients to continue without too much self-questioning. There are many good reasons for scientific uncertainty and even common sense and 'practical knowledge' waver when faced with some of the possibilities of media effect in the contested areas of morals, opinion and deviant behaviour which attract most public notice. On many such matters there can be no question of the media being a primary cause and we have no real 'explanation' of patterns of thought, culture and behaviour with deep social and historical roots. Furthermore, it makes little sense to speak of 'the media' as if they were one thing, rather than an enormously diverse set of messages, images and ideas, most of which do not originate with the media themselves but come from society and are sent 'back' to society. It is thus not at all easy to name a case where the media can plausibly be regarded as the sole or indispensable cause of a given social effect. Despite the difficulties and the inevitable inconclusiveness, the question of

media effects has proved as fascinating and unavoidable for social
scientists as it has for the media themselves and the general public.
If we did not fundamentally believe them to have important long
term consequences, we could not devote so much time to their
study.

The natural history of media effect
research and theory

The development of thinking about media effects may be said to
have a 'natural history', since it has been strongly shaped by the circumstances of time and place and influenced by several 'environmental' factors: the interests of governments and lawmakers; the
needs of industry; the activities of pressure groups; the purposes of
political and commercial propagandists; the current concern of
public opinion; the fashions of social science. It is not surprising
that no straight path of cumulative development of knowledge can
easily be discerned. Even so, we can distinguish a number of stages
in the history of the field which indicate some measure of ordered
progression and of cumulation. In the first phase, which extends
from the turn of the century until the late 1930s, the media, where
they were well developed, were credited with considerable power to
shape opinion and belief, change habits of life, actively mould
behaviour more or less according to the will of those who could
control the media and their content (Bauer and Bauer, 1960). Such
views were not based on scientific investigation, but on observation
of the enormous popularity of the press and the new media of film
and radio and their intrusion into many aspects of everyday life.
These beliefs were shared and reinforced by advertisers and by
government propagandists during the first world war. In Europe
the use of media by dictatorial states in the interwar years appeared
to confirm what people were already inclined to believe — that the
media could be immensely powerful. It was in the context of such
beliefs, and with an inclination to accept them, that research of a
scientific kind, using the survey and experiment and drawing
largely on social psychology, was begun.

This second phase, opened perhaps by the series of Payne Fund
studies in the United States in the early 1930s (Blumer, 1933;
Blumer and Hauser, 1933; Peterson and Thurstone, 1933),
continued until the early 1960s. Many separate studies of the effects
ot types of content, particular films or programmes in whole
campaigns were carried out. The range was wide, but attention
concentrated on the possibilities of using film and other media for
active persuasion or information (e.g. Hovland et al., 1949;

Lazarsfeld et al., 1944; Star and Hughes, 1950) or for assessing, with a view to prevention, harmful effects in respect of delinquency, prejudice, aggression, sexual stimulation. What now seems like the end of an era was marked by some expression of disillusion with this kind of research (e.g. Berelson, 1959) and by a new statement of conventional wisdom which assigned a more modest role to media in causing any of their chosen or unintended effects. The still influential summary of early research by Joseph Klapper, published in 1960, set the seal on this stage of research by concluding that 'mass communication does not ordinarily serve as a necessary and sufficient cause of audience effects, but rather functions through a nexus of mediating factors' (p. 8). It was not that media had been shown to be, under all conditions, without effects but that they operated within a pre-existing structure of social relationships and in a given social and cultural context. These social and cultural factors have a primary role in shaping choice, attention and response by audiences. This new sobriety of assessment was slow to modify opinion outside the social-scientific community. It was particularly hard to accept for those who made a living out of advertising and propaganda and for those in the media who valued the myth of their own great potency. However, hardly had the 'no effect' conclusion been disseminated by social scientists than it was subject to a re-examination by those who doubted that the whole story had been written and who were reluctant to dismiss the possibility that media might indeed have important social effects (e.g. Lang and Lang, 1959; Key, 1961; Blumler, 1964; Halloran, 1965).

The third phase of theory and research, which is still with us, is one in which effects and potential effects are still being sought, without rejecting the conclusions of early research, but according to revised conceptions of the social and media processes likely to be involved. Early investigation had relied very heavily on a model in which correlations were sought between degree of 'exposure' to given content and measured change of, or variation in, attitude, opinion or information. The renewal of effects research was marked by a shift of attention towards: long term change; cognition rather than attitude and affect; the part played by intervening variables of context, disposition and motivation; collective phenomena such as climates of opinion, structures of belief, ideologies, cultural patterns and even institutional forms. Much of the chapter that follows is taken up with a review of these newer theories of effect and developments of the early model of direct effect. While there are many contributors to and causes of the revival of interest in effects, it was Noelle-Neumann (1973) who coined the slogan 'return to the concept of powerful mass media'. It is also not unimportant to note that the revival of (new) left thinking in the 1960s carried with it a tendency to credit the media with powerful legitimating and controlling effects.

Before leaving the historical aspect of research into media effects, it is worth reflecting on a suggestion by Carey (1978) that variations in belief in the power of mass communications may be accounted for by history itself:

> it can be argued that the basic reason behind the shift in the argument about the effects from a powerful to a limited to a more powerful model is that the social world was being transformed over this period . . . Powerful effects of communication were sensed in the thirties because the Depression and the political currents surrounding the war created a fertile seed for the production of certain kinds of effects. Similarly, the normalcy of the fifties and sixties led to a limited effects model. In the late sixties a period of war, political discord and inflation combined to expose the social structure in fundamental ways and to make it permeable by the media of communication.

We can only speculate about the reasons for this association in time, which indeed may be only coincidence. Even so, it is true that people often know about crises through the media and may associate the message with the medium; in times of change and uncertainty it is also highly probable that people are more dependent on media as source of information and guidance (Ball-Rokeach and DeFleur, 1976); media are more likely to be effective on matters outside immediate personal experience and the components of the current, as of past, world crises are of that kind; finally, under conditions of tension and uncertainty, government and business or other elites and interests are likely to try to use media for influence and control. All these are arguments for the view that the effect and power (potential effect) of media may indeed be greater under certain historical conditions.

Levels and kinds of effect

In speaking of 'media effects' we are necessarily referring to what has already occurred as a direct consequence of mass communication, whether intended or not. The expression 'media power', on the other hand, refers to a potential for the future or a statement of probability about effects, under given conditions. 'Media effectiveness' is a statement about the *efficiency* of media in achieving a given aim and can apply to past, present or future, but always denoting intention. Such distinctions can often be important for precision of speaking about the media, although it is hard to keep to a consistent usage. Even more essential for research and theory is to observe the distinction between 'level' of occurrence, distinguishing at least the levels of: individual; group or organization; social institution; whole society; and culture. Each or all can be affected by mass communication and effects at any one level always imply effects at other levels. It happens that most research has been carried out at the individual level, with consequent difficulties for drawing conclusions about effects at collective or higher levels, as recommended in the current research phase.

Perhaps the most confusing aspect of research on effects is the multiplicity and complexity of the phenomena involved. Broad distinctions are normally made between: effects which are cognitive (to do with knowledge and opinion); those which are affectual (relating to attitude and feelings); effects on behaviour. These distinctions have been treated in early research as distinct and following a logical order, from the first to the third (see below, p. 184). In fact it is no longer found easy to sustain the distinction between the three concepts or to believe in the unique logic of that particular order of occurrence. To add to the complexity, much of our evidence comes from replies to questionnaires which are themselves individual acts of verbal behaviour from which we hope to reconstruct collective phenomena, often with an inextricable mixture of cognitive and affectual elements.

A final word should be said at this point about another kind of differentiation — that of type and direction of effect. In his summary, Klapper (1960) distinguished between 'conversion', 'minor change' and 'reinforcement' — respectively: change according to the intention of the communicator; change in form or intensity; confirmation by the receiver of his or her own existing beliefs and opinions. This three-fold distinction needs to be widened to include other possibilities, especially at the supra-individual level, leading to the following:

media may : cause intended change (conversion)
　　　　　 : cause unintended change
　　　　　 : cause minor change (form or intensity)
　　　　　 : facilitate change (intended or not)
　　　　　 : reinforce what exists (no change)
　　　　　 : prevent change

The categories are mainly self-explanatory, but the facilitation of change refers to the mediating role of media in wider processes of change in society, as discussed in Chapter 1. Both of the last two named imply no effect, but involve different conceptions of media working. Reinforcement is an observable consequence of selective attention by the receiver to content which is congruent with existing views, aided perhaps by a generous supply of such content.

The second, 'preventing change', implies deliberate supply of one-sided or ideologically-shaped content in order to inhibit change in a conforming public. The 'no change' effect from the media, of which we have so much evidence, requires very close attention because of its long term consequences. It is indeed a somewhat misleading expression, since anything that alters the probability of opinion or belief distribution in the future is an intervention into social process and thus an effect.

Processes of media effects: a typology

In order to provide an outline of developments in theory and research we begin by interrelating two of the distinctions which have already been mentioned; between the intended and the unintended and between short term and long term. This device was suggested by Golding (1980) to help distinguish different concepts of news and its effects: thus deliberate short term effects may be considered as 'bias'; short term non-deliberate effects fall under the heading of 'unwitting bias'; deliberate and long term effects indicate 'policy'; while long term and non-deliberate effects of news are 'ideology'. Something of the same way of thinking helps us to map out, in terms of these two coordinates, the main kinds of effect process which have been dealt with in the literature. The result is given in Figure 8.

The main entries can be briefly described although their meaning will be made more explicit in the discussion of theory which follows:

Individual response: the process by which individuals change, or resist change, in response to messages designed to influence attitude, knowledge or behaviour.

Media campaign: signals the situation in which a number of media are used to achieve a persuasive or informational purpose with a chosen population, the most common examples being found in politics, advertising, fund-raising, public information for health and safety. Campaigns tend to have the following characteristics: they have specific and overt aims and a limited time-span and are thus open to assessment as to effectiveness; they have authoritative (legitimate) sponsorship and their purposes tend to be in line with consensual values and the aims of established institutions.

Individual reaction: unplanned or unpredictable consequences of exposure by a person to a media stimulus. These have mainly been noticed as imitation and learning, especially of aggressive or criminal acts, but also of 'pro-social' ideas and behaviour. Other types of effect include the displacement of other activities, the

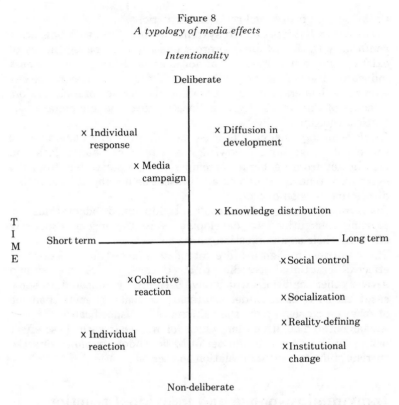

Figure 8
A typology of media effects

imitation of styles and fashions, the identification with heroes or stars, sexual arousal, reactions of fear, anxiety and disturbance.

Collective reaction: here some of the same individual effects are experienced simultaneously by many people, leading to joint action, usually of an unregulated and non-institutional kind. Effects from fear, anxiety and anger are the most potent, leading to panic or civil disturbance.

Diffusion in development: the planned diffusion of innovations for purposes of long term development, using a series of campaigns and other means of influence, especially the interpersonal network and authority structure of the community or society.

Knowledge distribution: the consequences of media activity in the sphere of news and information for the distribution of knowledge between social groups, the variable awareness of events, the priorities assigned to aspects of 'reality'.

Socialization: the informal contribution of media to the learning and adoption of established norms, values and expectations of behaviour in given social roles and situations.

Social control: refers here to systematic tendencies to propagate a conformity to the established order and reaffirm the legitimacy of existing authority, by way of ideology and the 'consciousness industry'. Depending on one's social theory, this can be placed either as a deliberate, or as an unintended extension of socialization. Because of this ambiguity, it is 'located' near the mid-point of the vertical coordinate.

Reality-defining: a similar process, but differing in its having more to do with cognitions (knowledge and opinion) than values and arising not from deliberate attempts to manipulate but from the systematic tendencies in media to present an incomplete and rather distinctive version of reality.

Institutional change: the result of unplanned adaptations by existing institutions to developments in the media, especially affecting their communication functions.

These entries in Figure 8 are intended to stand for processes of effect differentiated according to level, time-span, complexity and several other conditions which have been briefly indicated. In some cases, the same basic model is sufficient to deal with more than one of the processes since the difference of specification is not fundamental. The discussion which follows deals with these effect processes in terms of a number of basic models, summarizing the current state of theory in relation to each.

Individual response and individual reaction

The S-R model
These two entries in Figure 8 can be dealt with together since they share the same underlying model, that of stimulus response or conditioning. Its main features can be simply represented as follows:

Single message ⎯⎯⎯⎯▶ Individual receiver ⎯⎯⎯⎯▶ Reaction

It applies more or less equally to intended and to unintended effects although it does not show the difference between a response (implying some interaction with the receiver) and a reaction (which implies no choice or interaction on the part of the receiver). A more elaborated version of the basic process as it occurs in persuasion is indicated by McGuire (1973) in the form of six stages in sequence: presentation — attention — comprehension — yielding — retention

— overt behaviour. This elaboration is sufficient to show why stimulus-response theory has had to be modified to take account of selective attention, interpretation, response and recall. The model, in whatever form, is highly pragmatic, predicting, ceteris paribus, the occurrence of a response (verbal or behavioural act) according to the presence or absence of an appropriate stimulus (message). It presumes a more or less direct effect in line with the intention of the initiator or built into the message.

In discussions of media effect, this has been sometimes referred to as the 'bullet' or 'hypodermic' theory, terms which far exaggerate the probability of effect and the vulnerability of the receiver to influence. Much has been written of the inadequacy of such theory and DeFleur (1970) has shown how this model has had to be modified in the light of growing experience and research. Firstly, account has had to be taken of individual differences, since even where expected reactions have been observed, their incidence varies according to difference of personality, attitude, intelligence, interest, etc. As DeFleur writes, 'media messages contain particular stimulus attributes that have differential interaction with personality characteristics of audience members' (1970, p. 122). This is especially relevant, given the complexity of most media messages compared with the kind of stimulus used in most psychological experiments. Secondly, it became clear that response varies systematically according to social categories within which the receiver can be placed, thus according to age, occupation, life-style, gender, religion, etc. DeFleur notes, with some overstatement, that 'members of a particular category will select more or less the same communication content and will respond to it in roughly equal ways' (p. 123).

Mediating conditions

The revision of the S-R model involved the identification of the conditions which mediated effects. McGuire (1973) indicates the main kinds of variable as having to do with source, content, channel, receivers, destination. There is reason to believe that messages stemming from an authoritative and credible source will be relatively more effective, as will those from sources that are attractive or close (similar) to the receiver. As to content, effectiveness is associated with repetition, consistency and lack of alternatives (monopoly situation). In general, effect as intended is also likely to be greater on topics which are distant from, or less important for, the receiver. Variables of style, types of appeal (e.g. emotional or rational) and order and balance of argument have been found to play a part, but too variably to sustain any generalization. Channel factors offer least scope for generalization, but as between mass media, print and television have been shown to differ in certain effects, sometimes for self-evident reasons, sometimes because of the difference in type of audience attachment (see p. 161). As we have seen, a number of obvious receiver variables can be relevant to effect, but especial notice should perhaps be given to variables of motivation, interest and level of knowledge.

The degree of motivation or involvement has been singled out as of particular importance in the influence process and in determining the sequence in which different kinds of effect occur (Krugman, 1965). According to Ray (1973) the normal 'effect hierarchy' as found, for instance, in the work of Hovland et al. (1949) is a process leading from cognition (the most common effect) to affective response (like or dislike, opinion, attitude) to 'conative' effect (behaviour or action). Ray argues, with some supporting evidence, that this model is only normal under conditions of high involvement (high interest and attention). With low involvement (common in many television viewing situations and especially with advertising) the sequence may be from cognition directly to behaviour, with affective adjustment occurring later to bring attitude into line with behaviour (reduction of dissonance, Festinger, 1957). In itself, this formulation casts doubt on the logic and design of many studies of persuasive communication which assume attitude as a correlate and indicator of behaviour.

In any non-laboratory situation of mass communication, individual receivers will choose which stimulus to attend to or to avoid, will interpret its meaning variably and will react or not behaviourally, according to choice. This seriously undermines the validity of the conditioning model since the factors influencing selectivity are bound to be strongly related to the nature of the stimulus, working for or against the occurrence of an effect. Our attention should consequently be drawn away from the fact of experience of a stimulus and towards the mediating conditions described above, especially in their totality and mutual interaction. This approach to the effect problem is more or less what Klapper (1960, p. 5) recommends and describes as a 'phenomenistic' approach — one which sees 'media as influences working amid other influences in a total situation'.

Source–receiver relationships
There have been several attempts to develop theories which would account for different kinds of relationships at the individual level

between sender (or message sent) and receiver, in addition to the thought already expressed that trust in — and respect for — the source can be conducive to effect. One framework is suggested by French and Raven (1953), indicating five alternative forms of communication relationship in which social power may be exercised by a sender and influence accepted by a receiver. The underlying proposition is that influence through communication is a form of exercise of power which depends on certain assets or properties of the agent of influence (communicator). The first two types of power asset are classified as 'reward' and 'coercion' respectively. The former depends on there being a gratification for the recipient from a message (enjoyment, for instance, or useful advice), the latter depends on some negative consequence of non-compliance (uncommon in mass communication). A third is described as 'referent' and describes the attraction or prestige of the sender, such that the receiver identifies with the person and is willingly influenced, for affective reasons.

Fourthly, there is 'legitimate' power, according to which influence is accepted on the assumption that a sender had a right to be followed or obeyed. This is not very common in mass communication, but may occur where authoritative messages are transmitted from political sources or other relevant institutional leaders. Finally, there is 'expert power', which operates where superior knowledge is attributed to the source or sender and accepted by the receiver. This situation is not uncommon in the sphere of media information-giving and may apply to the influence of 'news' and the effects of experts used for comment or advice. This appears to be a further specification of the condition that messages from authoritative and respected sources are more effective than others, but these types of communicative power refer not just to a message or a source, but to a *relationship* between receiver and sender in which the former plays an active part and which gives rise to the necessary definitions of the situation. Such relationships are only established on a relatively long term basis and thus predate and survive any given instance of communication. One might add that more than one of these power sources is likely to be operative on any one given occasion.

Another rather similar attempt to account for the incidence of effects (especially on opinion) has been made by Kelman (1961). He names three processes of influence. One of these, 'compliance', refers to the acceptance of influence in expectation of some reward or to avoid punishment. Another, 'identification', occurs when an individual wishes to be more like the source and imitates or adopts behaviour accordingly (similar to 'referent' power). A third, 'internalization', is intended to describe influence which is guided by the receiver's own pre-existing needs and values. This last-named process may also be described as a 'functional' explanation of influence (or effect), since change is mainly explicable in terms of the receiver's own motives, needs and wishes.

Katz (1960) has recommended this approach to explaining the influence of mass communication in preference to what he considers to have been the dominant modes of explanation in the past. One of these he describes as based on an 'irrational model of man', which represents people as a prey to any form of powerful suggestion. An alternative view depends on a 'rational model', according to which people use their critical and reasoning faculty to arrive at opinions and acquire information. The former would be consistent with a view of the individual as sovereign against propaganda and deception. Katz finds both views mistaken and less likely than a 'functional' approach to account for communicative effect, thus giving most weight to the needs of receivers and to their motives for attending to communication. He suggests five main functions which attitude formation (and thus communication use) is likely to fulfill: instrumental; adjustive (maintaining cognitive balance) or utilitarian; ego-defensive; value-expressive; knowledge (giving meaning and experience).

Unintended reaction

These developments of theory take one a good way from the simple conditioning model and help to account for some of the complexities encountered in research into media effect. It is obvious that in situations of unintended effect, some individuals will be more prone than others to react or respond to stimuli, 'more at risk' when harmful effects are involved. An elaboration of the basic stimulus-response for the case of television viewing has been developed by Comstock et al. (1978) to help organize the results of research in this field. It rests on the presupposition that media experience is no different in essence from any other experience, act or observation which might have consequences for learning or behaviour.

The process depicted by the model takes the form of a sequence following the initial act of 'exposure' to a form of behaviour on television (TV act). This is the first and main 'input' to learning or imitating the behaviour concerned. Other relevant inputs are the degree of excitement and arousal (TV arousal) and the degree to which alternative behaviours (TV alternatives) are depicted: the more arousal and the fewer behaviours (or more repetition), the more likely is learning to take place. Two other conditions (inputs) have to

Figure 9
A simplified version of Comstock et al.'s (1978) model
of television effects on individual behaviour
(from McQuail and Windahl, 1982)

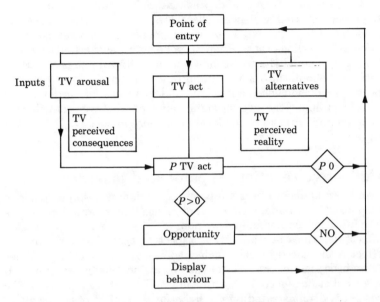

do with the portrayal of consequences (TV perceived consequences) and the degree of reality (TV perceived reality): the more that positive consequences seem to exceed negative ones and the more true to life the television behaviour, the more likely is learning *(P* TV act) to take place. All these inputs affect the probability of learning the action (the effect), but ultimately any resulting behaviour is conditional on there being an opportunity to put the act into practice. Apart from opportunity, the most important condition is 'arousal', since without arousal (connoting also interest and attention) there will be no learning. While full confirmation of this model from research is not yet available, it is quite an advance on the simple conditioning model and useful for directing attention to key aspects of a given case.

This model was intended to help organize research results, including those concerning the possible effects of the representation of violence in media. There is no space or need to summarize this field of study since it is periodically well reviewed (e.g. by Howitt and Cumberbatch, 1975) and since the underlying process of effect is much the same as for 'pro-social' effects. It is sufficient to note the following at this point: the balance of evidence supports the view that media *can* lead to violent behaviour and probably have done so (cf. Surgeon General, 1972); these effects occur mainly as a result of 'triggering' of aggressive acts, imitation, identification with aggressive heroes, 'desensitization', leading to a higher tolerance for real violence. There are also substantial areas of dispute: about the extent to which media provide release from aggressive feelings rather than provoke aggressive acts (Baker and Ball, 1969); about the applicability of laboratory findings to natural settings; about the relative importance of fictional vs. 'real life' portrayal of violence; about the independence of media as an influence; about the overall significance of whatever contribution media actually make to the level of violence in society.

Collective reaction — panic and disorder

Two main kinds of effect are here in question: widespread panic in response to alarming, incomplete or misleading information and the amplification or spreading of mob activity. The term 'contagion effect' describes one important aspect of both. The first kind of effect is instanced by the much-cited reaction to the Orson Welles radio broadcast of the 'War of the Worlds' in 1938 when simulated news bulletins reported a Martian invasion (Cantril et al., 1940). The second is demonstrated by the hypothesized effect of the media in stimulating civil disorder in some American cities in the late 1960s. In the first case there remains uncertainty about the real scale and character of the 'panic', but there is little doubt that the conditions for panic reaction to news could well arise given the increase of civil terrorism and the risk of nuclear attack or, more likely, of nuclear accident. Rosengren (1976) reports an instance of alarm spread by media about the latter. We are dealing here with a special case of rumour (see Shibutani, 1966), but the media contribute the element of reaching large numbers of separate people at the same moment with the same item of news. The other related conditions for panic response are anxiety, fear and uncertainty. Beyond this, precipitating features of panic seem to be: incompleteness or inaccuracy of information leading to the urgent search for information, usually through personal channels, thus giving further currency to the original message.

Because of the threat to the established order, non-institutionalized and violent collective behaviour have been extensively studied and the media have been implicated in the search for causes of such behaviour. It has been suggested that the media, variously, can provoke a riot, create a culture of rioting, provide lessons on 'how to riot', spread a disturbance from place to place. The evidence for or against these propositions is very fragmentary although it seems to be acknowledged that personal contact plays a larger part than media in any on-going riot situation. There is some evidence, even so, that the media can contribute by simply signalling the occurrence and location of a riot event (Singer, 1970), by publicizing incidents which are themselves causes of riot behaviour, or by giving advance publicity to the likely occurrence of rioting. While the media have not been shown to be a primary or main cause of rioting (Kerner, 1968), they may influence the timing or form of riot behaviour. Spilerman (1976) lends some support to this and other hypotheses, on the basis of rather negative evidence. After failing, through extensive research, to find a satisfactory structural explanation of many urban riots in the United States (i.e. explanations in terms of community conditions) he concluded that television and its network news structure was primarily responsible, especially by creating a 'black solidarity that would transcend the boundaries of community'. In treating together the topics of panic and rioting, it is worth noting that the most canvassed solution to the dangers just signalled, the control or silencing of news (Paletz and Dunn, 1969) might entail a local panic through lack of interpretation of observable neighbourhood disturbances.

An interesting variant of this theme of media effect arises in the case of media reporting (or not) of terrorism. Much violence or disorder is either planned or threatened for political objectives, by persons seeking, however indirectly, to use the media, giving rise to a complex interaction between the two. In an analysis of this problem, Schmid and De Graaf (1982) argue that violence is often a means of access to mass communication and even a message in itself. The media are inevitably implicated in this process because of the. weight they attach to reporting violence. An interesting example of possible effect is the sequence of aircraft hijacking crimes in 1971-72, which showed clear signs of being modelled on news reports. The same authors also show the existence of strong beliefs by police and a moderate belief by media personnel that live coverage of terrorist acts does encourage terrorism. More difficult to assess are the consequences of refusing such coverage. There has been other empirical support for the theory that press reports can 'trigger' individual but widespread actions of a pathological kind. Philips (1980) has reported empirical data showing that suicides, motor vehicle fatalities, commercial and non-commercial plane fatalities have a tendency to increase following press publicity for suicides or murder-suicides. On the basis of this evidence he argues for the need to develop a sociological theory of imitation and suggestion — the 'contagion' phenomenon mentioned at the outset.

The campaign

**General features of the campaign:
a model**
The defining characteristics of a campaign have already been
indicated, but we should pay special attention to the fact that
campaigns have typically dealt with well-institutionalized
behaviour that is likely to be in line with established norms and
values. They are often concerned with directing, reinforcing and
activating existing tendencies towards socially-approved objectives
like voting, buying goods, raising money for good causes, achieving
better health and safety, etc. The scope for novelty of effect or
major change is thus often intrinsically limited and the media are
employed to assist other institutional forces. Certainly most of the
research and theory available to us about campaigns has been
carried out in such circumstances and we know relatively little
about campaigns, insofar as they exist, to promote objectives that
are unusual or new. A second point to bear in mind is that
campaigns have to work ultimately through the individuals who
receive and respond to messages and thus many of the conditions of
effect which have been described also apply to campaigns. However,
the organized and large scale character of campaigns makes it
desirable to sketch a revised model of campaign influence, as in
Figure 10.

Figure 10
Model of campaign influence process

COLLECTIVE SOURCE	SEVERAL CHANNELS	MANY MESSAGES	FILTER CONDITIONS	VARIABLE PUBLIC REACH	EFFECTS:
			Attention Perception Group situation		Cognitive Affective Behavioural

The model draws attention to key features of the process. Firstly,
the originator of the campaign is almost always a collectivity and
not an individual — a political party, government, church, charity,
pressure group, business firm, etc. The known position in society of

the source will strongly affect its chances of success in a campaign. Secondly, the campaign usually consists of many messages distributed through several media and the chances of reach and effect will vary according to the established nature of the channels and the message content. Thirdly, there is a set of 'filter conditions' or potential barriers which facilitate or hinder the flow of messages to the whole or chosen public. Several of these have already been discussed and they are to some extent predictable in their operation, although only in very broad terms. Attention is named because without it there can be no effect — it will depend on the interest and relevance of content for the receivers, on their motives and pre-dispositions and on channel-related factors. Perception is named, since messages are open to alternative interpretations and the success of a campaign depends to some extent on its message being interpreted in the same way as intended. Research has indicated the occurrence of 'boomerang' effects, for instance in attempts to modify prejudice (e.g. Cooper and Jahoda, 1947; Vidmar and Rokeach, 1974), and it is a constant preoccupation of commercial and political campaigners to try to avoid counter-effects which will aid the 'opposition'.

Much has been written of the part played by the group in mediating the effects of campaigns (e.g. Katz and Lazarsfeld, 1955) and more is said below about 'personal influence'. Here we should only note that campaigns come usually from 'outside' the many groups to which people belong, according to age, life circumstances, work, neighbourhood, interest, religion, etc. Thus much of the history of media campaign research has been a struggle to come to terms with the fact that societies are not so conveniently 'atomized' and individuated as the first media campaigners had expected. Group allegiance or its absence has strong consequences for whether messages are noticed and then accepted or rejected. These 'filter conditions' together determine the structure of the public reached and the success of a campaign is ultimately dependent on a reasonable 'fit' between composition of the planned 'target' public and the actual public reached. Finally, the entry in the model for 'effects' reminds us of the enormous diversity of possible effects, some of which will be intended and others not, some short term and some long term. Again, a successful or 'effective' campaign will depend on some match between planned effects and those achieved. The criteria for effectiveness have thus to be set by the sender, but evaluation should also take account of side effects which have to be weighed in the overall balance.

The model is a reminder of the complexity of campaigns and the ease with which they can go wrong. There is a very large literature on political campaigns (well reviewed in Kraus and Davis, 1976) and on other kinds of campaign (Rice and Paisley, 1981) but no way of summarizing the results except to remark that some do seem to succeed (Mendelsohn, 1973) and some to fail (Hyman and Sheatsley, 1947), with partial failures and partial successes accounting for most cases in the research literature and probably in the reality. While success or failure can usually be accounted for in terms of the various conditions which have been named, it is worth adding a few extra remarks.

Firstly, in many areas of social life, especially in politics and commerce, the campaign has become deeply institutionalized and has acquired something of a ritual character. The question then arises, not whether campaigns produce this or that marginal advantage, but whether it would be possible not to campaign (or to advertise) without disastrous effect. Secondly, campaigners do not usually control the reality of a situation or reports about it and circumstances may intervene to destroy or invalidate the message of a campaign. However, the more power to manipulate the reality (e.g. government by policy making or information giving), the more control over the outcome of a campaign. Thirdly, most campaigns that have been studied take place under conditions of competition (counter-campaigning or with alternative courses argued). Rather too much of the theory that we have has been influenced by these circumstances and we know relatively little about campaigning for objectives that are not contested, under conditions which make it difficult to avoid otherwise trusted media sources. These are not very widely occurring circumstances, but they can occur, especially outside the 'western, industrialized' context, and evidence about them could modify existing theory.

Finally, it is worth emphasizing that campaigns do ultimately depend rather heavily on the relationship between sender and receiver and there are several ways in which relations favourable to successful campaigning are forged. Several aspects have been discussed in the context of individual level effects, but attention should be paid to the authority and credibility of media and sources. Especially important are moral or affective ties between audiences and media and audience belief in the objectivity and disinterest of sources. There is, however, some inherent conflict between objectivity and what is by definition a partisan activity. This has two consequences: the fact that other media may work against campaigns, and that an aim of many campaigners is to ensure either publicity or favourable coverage in the 'objective' media, especially in news. The capacity to do this is not unrelated to general power position in the society.

Personal influence in campaign situations

In the study of mass media effects the concept of 'personal influence' has acquired such a high status that it has, in a recent critical discussion (Gitlin, 1978), been referred to as the 'dominant paradigm'. While, in principle, the concept is relevant to any effect regardless of intention or time-span, it is appropriate to deal with it in relation to the campaign, partly because it originated in the study of campaigns and partly because the circumstances of medium term and deliberate attempts at persuasion and information are most conducive to the intervention of personal contacts as relevant and accountable sources of influence. The underlying idea of personal influence is a simple one expressed in the words of its originators (Lazarsfeld et al., 1944, p. 151) as follows: 'ideas often flow from radio and print to the opinion leaders and from them to the less active sections of the population'. Thus two elements are involved: the notion of a population stratified according to interest and activity in relation to media and the topics dealt with by mass media (in brief 'opinion leaders' and 'others'); the notion of a 'two-step flow' of influence rather than a direct contact between 'stimulus' and 'respondent'. The original evidence for these ideas was presented in a study of the 1940 US presidential election campaign and by Katz and Lazarsfeld (1955). Since that time many students of campaigns have tried to incorporate the role of personal influence as a 'variable' in their research and more sophisticated campaign managers have tried to apply the ideas for the more successful management of the commercial, political or social campaign purpose.

Not only has the 'personal influence' hypothesis had a strong effect on research and campaigning, it has also played an important part in mass communication theory, and even media ideology. It has been invoked to explain the paucity of evidence of direct media effect and to counter the view, advanced first by mass society theorists and later by proponents of ideological determinism, that the media are powerful and rather inescapable shapers of knowledge, opinion and belief in modern societies. The 'ideological component' of personal influence theory lies in the supposition that individuals are 'protected' by the strength of personal ties and by the group structure within which they acquire knowledge and form judgements. Much research and thought devoted to the question have gradually led to a lower degree of emphasis on the simple proposition as expressed above (Robinson, 1976).

Firstly, subsequent research, while confirming the importance of conversation and personal contact as accompaniment and perhaps modifier of media influence, has not clearly demonstrated that personal influence always acts as a strong independent or 'counter-active' source of influence on the matters normally affected by mass media. Some of the evidence originally advanced by the proponents of the concept has also been re-examined, with differing conclusions (Gitlin, 1978). Secondly, it has become clear that the division between 'leaders' and 'followers' is variable from topic to topic, that the roles are interchangeable and there are many who cannot be classified as either one or the other. Thirdly, it seems probable that the flow is as likely to be multi-step as two-step. Finally, it seems clear that direct effects from the media can occur without 'intervention' from opinion leaders and highly probable that personal influence is as likely to reinforce the effects of media as to counteract them. Despite these qualifications and comments on the personal influence thesis, there are circumstances where inter-personal influence can be stronger than the media: the overthrow of the Shah of Iran seems to provide a well documented case in point (Teheranian, 1979).

Diffusion in a development context

It is not easy to find documented cases of media applied consciously to long term change. Most evidence relates to the many attempts since the second world war to harness media to campaigns for technical advance or for health and educational purposes in the Third World, though often following models developed in the United States (Katz et al., 1963). Although early theory of media and development (e.g. Lerner, 1958) portrayed the influence of media as 'modernizing' simply by virtue of bringing western ideas and appetites (see above, p. 41), the mainstream view of media effect has been as a mass educator in alliance with officials, experts and local leaders, applied to specific objectives of change.

A principal chronicler of, and worker in, this tradition has been Everett Rogers (1962; Rogers and Shoemaker, 1973) whose model of information diffusion envisaged four stages: information; persuasion; decision or adoption; confirmation. This sequence is close to McGuire's stages of persuasion (see above, p. 182). However, the role of the media is concentrated on the first (information and awareness) stage, after which personal contacts, organized expertise and advice, and actual experience take over in the adoption process. The diffusionist school of thought tends to emphasize organization and planning, linearity of effect, hierarchy (of status and expertise), social structure (thus personal experience), reinforcement and feedback. Rogers (1976) has himself signalled the 'passing' of this 'dominant paradigm', its weakness lying in these same characteristics and its overreliance on 'manipulation' from above. The alternative theories of development allot to mass media a rather small role, with benefits depending on their remaining close to the basis of the society and to its native culture.

Distribution of knowledge

As we enter a new 'area' of our media effect typology (Figure 8) we have to deal with a set of topics and concepts which are difficult to locate in terms of the two main variables of time and purposiveness. They are, however, united by a concern with cognition: each has to do with information or knowledge in the conventional sense. One has to do with a major media activity, news provision. Another deals with differential attention to issues and objects in the world: 'agenda-setting'. A third covers the general distribution of opinion and information in society, potentially leading to the 'knowledge gap' as an effect. These different kinds of media effect are included under the rather neutral label 'distribution of knowledge', since the media do actually distribute and the result can be expressed as a distribution in the statistical sense. Alternative terms such as 'control' or 'management' of information would imply a consciously directed effort. This would accord with some general theories of media but not with others and the evidence for 'manipulation' in this field is not conclusive (Weaver, 1981). The kinds of effect dealt with here cannot be accommodated within any of the models so far presented, but they can be considered as falling within the scope of the model which follows (Figure 11).

News diffusion

The diffusion of news in the sense of its take-up and incorporation into what people 'know' is mainly a short or medium term matter, but with long term and often systematic consequences. It is also open to alternative formulations as to purpose: the media do intend in general that their audiences will learn about events but they do not try to teach people what is in the news. The question of how much people understand and remember from the news has only recently begun to receive much serious attention (e.g. Findahl and Höijer, 1981) and most research has so far concentrated on 'diffusion' — the spread of news as measured by the capacity to recall certain named events. Four main variables have been at the centre of interest here: the extent to which people know about a given event; the relative importance or salience of the event concerned; the volume of information about it which is transmitted;

the extent to which knowledge of an event comes first from news or from personal contact. The possible interactions between these four are complex, but one model of the interaction is expressed by the J-curved relationship between the proportion who are aware of an event and the proportion who heard of the same event from an inter-personal source (Greenberg, 1964).

The J-shape expresses the following findings: when an event is known about by virtually everyone (such as the assassination of Kennedy in 1963), a very high proportion (over 50 per cent) will have been told by a personal contact (associated conditions here being high event salience and rapid diffusion). When events are known by decreasing proportions of the population, the percentage of personal contact origination falls and that of media source rises (associated conditions are lower salience and slower diffusion rates). However, there is a category of events which is known about ultimately by rather small proportions of a whole population. These comprise minorities for whom the event or topic is highly salient and the proportion of knowledge from personal contact rises again in relation to media sources, because personal contact networks are activated.

Theory about news diffusion is still held back by the bias of research towards a certain class of events, especially 'hard news', with a high measure of unexpectedness (Rosengren, 1973). In order to have a fuller picture of processes of news diffusion we would need more evidence about 'soft news' and more about routine or anticipated events. We are also limited by the difficulty of estimating event importance independently of amount of attention by the media, bearing in mind the differing interests of different sectors of the society. We can, nevertheless, reach a truistic conclusion that news learning does occur and much of it is a result of direct contact with media.

Agenda-setting

This term was coined by McCombs and Shaw (1972) to describe in more general terms a phenomenon that had long been noticed and studied in the context of election campaigns. An example would be a situation in which politicians seek to convince voters as to what, from their party standpoint, are the most important issues. This is an essential part of advocacy and attempts at opinion shaping. As a hypothesis, it seems to have escaped the general conclusion that persuasive campaigns have small or no effects. As Trenaman and McQuail (1961) pointed out: 'The evidence strongly suggests that people think *about* what they are told...but at no level do they think what they are told'. The evidence at that time and since collected consists of data showing a correspondence between the order of importance given in the media to 'issues' and the order of significance attached to the same issues by the public and the politicians. This is the essence of the agenda-setting hypothesis, but such evidence is insufficient to show a causal connection between the various issue 'agendas'. For that we need a combination of party programmes, evidence of opinion change over time in a given section of the public, preferably with panel data, a content analysis showing media attention to different issues in the relevant period and some indication of relevant media use by the public concerned. Such data have rarely if ever been produced at the same time in support of the hypothesis of agenda-setting and the further one moves from the general notion that media direct attention and shape cognitions and towards precise cases, the more uncertain it becomes whether such an effect actually occurs.

Recent assessments (e.g. Kraus and Davis, 1976; Becker, 1982) tend to leave agenda-setting with the status of a plausible but unproven idea. The doubts stem not only from the strict methodological demands, but also from theoretical ambiguities. The hypothesis presupposes a process of influence from the priorities of political or other interest groups, to the news priorities of media, in which news values and audience interests play a strong part, and from there to the opinions of the public. There are certainly alternative models of this relationship, of which the main one would reverse the flow and state that underlying concerns of the public will shape both issue definition by political elites and those of the media, a process which is fundamental to political theory and to the logic of free media. It is likely that the media do contribute to a convergence of the three 'agendas' but that is a different matter from setting any particular one of them.

Knowledge gaps

It has been a longstanding assumption that the press, and later broadcasting, have added so greatly to the flow of public information that they will have helped to modify differences of knowledge resulting from inequalities of education and social position. There is some evidence from political campaign studies to show that 'gap-closing' between social groups can occur in the short term (e.g. Blumler and McQuail, 1968). However, there has long been evidence of the reverse effect, showing that an attentive minority gains much more information than the rest, thus widening the gap between certain sectors of the public. Tichenor et al. (1970)

wrote of the 'knowledge gap hypothesis' that it 'does not hold that lower status population segments remain completely uninformed (or that the poorer in knowledge get poorer in an absolute sense). Instead the proposition is that growth of knowledge is relatively greater among the higher status segments'. There is certainly a class bias in attention to 'information-rich' sources and strong correlations are persistently found between social class, attention to these sources and being able to answer information questions on political, social, or economic matters.

There are two aspects to the knowledge gap hypothesis, one concerning the general distribution of aggregate information in society between social classes, the other relating to specific subjects or topics on which some are better informed than others. As to the first 'gap', it is likely to have roots in fundamental social inequalities which the media alone cannot modify. As to the second, there are many possibilities for opening and closing gaps and it is likely that the media do close some and open others. A number of factors can be named as relevant to the direction of media effect. Donohue et al. (1975) put special emphasis on the fact that media do operate to close gaps on issues which are of wide concern to small communities, especially under conditions of conflict, which promote attention and learning.

Novak (1977) has given particular attention to the broad issue of the incidence and consequences of information gaps associated with divisions of social and economic power. At the same time, he directs attention to practical solutions which would be helpful to specific groups with identifiable 'information needs' and known 'communication potential', the latter referring to the various resources which help people to achieve goals through communication activity. Useful in Novak's contribution is the emphasis not only on form, presentation and manner of distribution in the 'gap-closing' enterprise but also on the kind of information involved, since not all information is equally useful to all groups. In general, motivation and perceived utility of information influence information seeking and learning and these factors come more from the social context than from the media. It has, however, been argued that different media may work in different ways and that print media are more likely to lead to a widening of gaps than is television (Robinson, 1972) because these are the favoured sources for the favoured classes. The suggestion that television can have a reverse effect (benefiting the less privileged) is based on the fact that it tends to reach a higher proportion of a given population with much the same news and information and is widely regarded as trustworthy. However, much depends on the institutional forms within which developments in television are changing its early status as a limited channel and common information resource and it may become a very differentiated source of specialized information, with the same characteristics as print media.

Long-term change, planned and unplanned: a model

We enter an area where there is much theory and speculation but little firm evidence of confirmed relationships between the mass media and the phenomena under discussion: systems of values, beliefs, opinions, social attitudes. The reasons for this uncertainty are familiar: the matters are too large and complex to investigate reliably or fully; they involve broad historical and ideological judgements; the direction of influence between media and social phenomena can nearly always be two-way and is often unclear. Where evidence exists, it does little more than illustrate and add to the plausibility of a theory and it may be difficult ever to expect more. Nevertheless, we are dealing with one of the most interesting and important aspects of the working of mass communication and can at least try to develop an intelligent way of talking about what might happen.

Each of the effect processes to be discussed can occur in western liberal societies without intention being present in any significant, visible, or well-organized manner. Yet we should also recognize that these same processes are central to normative and ideological control, to the composition and maintenance of public belief systems, climates of opinion, value patterns and forms of collective awareness posited by many social theorists. It is hard to conceive of a society without such phenomena, however difficult they are to specify and quantify. Thus something of the sort is happening and the media are implicated. More important than determining the

Figure 11
Process model of social control and consciousness-forming

SOURCE →	CONTENT →	FIRST EFFECT	SECOND EFFECT →	THIRD EFFECT
Unspecified multiple sources: media in general	Messages with stable and systematic structure	Available stock of knowledge, values, opinions, culture	Differential selection and response	Socialization Reality definition Distribution of knowledge Social control

precise degree of intention is the question of direction. Do the processes favour conservation or change, and in either eventuality, in whose interest? Without some attention to this question, however provisional and beyond the scope of 'media theory' alone to answer, the discussion of these matters is rather pointless.

The model given in Figure 11 indicates some features common to various kinds of (variably) unplanned and long term effects which have been attributed to mass media, irrespective of purpose or direction.

Firstly, the outcomes of the various processes all posit some pattern and consistency over time in media output. Secondly they presuppose an initial cognitive effect, of the kind partly discussed. Thus the media provide materials for recognizing and interpreting reality beyond what is available from personal experience. What is termed in the model the 'second effect' refers to the encounter between what is made available and people in audiences. Here the set of 'filter conditions' signalled in the case of the campaign operate in much the same way, but especially those which have to do with social group and cultural environment. Beyond this, the processes listed as 'third effects' need to be discussed separately, having already paid attention to 'knowledge distribution'.

Socialization

That the media play a part in the early socialization of children and the long term socialization of adults is widely accepted, although in the nature of the case it is almost impossible to prove. This is partly because it is such a long term process and partly because any effect from media interacts with other social background influences and variable modes of socialization within families (Hedinsson, 1981). Nevertheless, certain basic assumptions about the potential social-ization effects from media are present in policies for control of the media, decisions by media themselves and the norms and expecta-tions which parents apply or hold in relation to the media use of their own children. An anomalous, but not contradictory, strand in the assumption of media as a socialization agent is the high attention given to media as potentially de-socializing — challenging and disturbing the setting of values by parents, educators and other agents of social control.

The logic underlying the proposition that media do socialize or de-socialize involves a view of socialization as the teaching of established norms and values by way of symbolic reward and punishment for different kinds of behaviour. An alternative view is that it is a learning process whereby we all learn how to behave in certain situations and learn the expectations which go with a given role or status in society. Thus the media are continually offering pictures of life and models of behaviour in advance of actual experience. Studies of children's use of media (e.g. Wolfe and Fiske, 1949; Himmelweit et al., 1958; Brown, 1976; Noble, 1975) confirm a tendency for children to find lessons about life and to connect these with their own experience. Studies of content also draw attention to the systematic presentation of images of social life which could strongly shape children's expectations and aspirations (e.g. DeFleur, 1964; Tuchman et al., 1978). These studies focus especially on occupation and sex roles, but there is also an extensive literature on political socialization (e.g. Dawson and Prewitt, 1969; Dennis, 1973).

McCron (1976) points to a basic divergence of theory, one strand emphasizing the consensual nature of social norms and values and another viewing media along with other agencies of social control as tending to impose on subordinate groups the values of dominant classes. The latter perspective emphasizes the central conflicts of society and the possibility of change through resistance and renegotiation of meanings. In this view, the media are neither 'pro-social' nor 'anti-social' but tending to favour the values of an established order and probably of a dominant class. In whichever formulation, the general theory that media have a socialization effect is hard to doubt, but only indirectly founded on empirical evidence, mainly concerning content and use.

Reality defining

That media offer many representations of the reality of society has already been argued and some aspects of the nature of this 'reality' have been discussed. One possible effect has been discussed under the heading of 'agenda-setting'. If the media can convey an impression about priorities and direct attention selectively amongst issues and problems they can do much more. The step from such a ranking process to wider opinion-forming is not a large one, and the theory of media socialization contains such an element. The basic process at work may be described by the general term 'defining the situation' and its importance rests on the familiar sociological dictum of W.I. Thomas that 'if men define situations as real they are real in their consequences'.

The spiral of silence: opinion formation

In the sphere of opinion-forming one interesting theory has been developed by Noelle-Neumann (1974), starting from the basic assumption that most people have a natural fear of isolation and in their opinion-expression try to identify and then follow majority opinion or the 'consensus'. The main source of information about the consensus will be the media and, in effect, journalists, who may have considerable power to define just what is the prevailing 'climate of opinion' at a given time on a given issue, or more widely. The general term 'spiral of silence' has been given by Noelle-Neumann to this phenomenon because the underlying logic holds that the more a dominant version of the opinion consensus is disseminated by mass media in society, the more will contrary individual voices remain silent, thus accelerating the media effect — hence a 'spiralling' process. Her evidence suggests that such a process occurred in Germany in the 1960s and 1970s, to the benefit of the ruling Social Democratic Party, because of a generally left tendency among journalists of the major media. A somewhat similar view of opinion shaping by the American media in the 1970s, although with a politically different tendency, is given by Paletz and Entman (1981), who reported the propagation of a 'conservative myth' — the conventional journalistic wisdom that America had turned sharply away from the radicalisms of the 1960s. As they show, however, there was no support for this interpretation from opinion polls taken over the period in question, thus failing to uphold the 'spiral of silence' thesis.

Amongst the scarce empirical inquiries, we can mention two Swedish studies reported in Rosengren (1981) comparing trends both in newspaper editorial opinion and in public opinion. One of these, by Rikardsson, showed a very close relationship between Swedish public opinion on the Middle East issue and that of the Swedish press, both of them deviating from 'world-opinion' as measured by opinion polls in several other nations. There was no time-lag on which to base a conclusion about the direction of effect. Another study, by Carlsson, on the relationship over time between party support, economic conditions and editorial direction of the press concluded that political opinions are probably moulded first by economic conditions and second by media content. However, they found their data tending to support the standpoint of Noelle-Neumann and other proponents of 'powerful mass media'.

Structuring reality — unwitting bias
Common to much theory in this area is the view that media effects occur unwittingly, as a result of organizational tendencies, occupational practices and technical limitations. Thus Paletz and

Entman (1981) attributed the propagation of a conservative myth mainly to 'pack journalism', the tendency of journalists to work together, arrive at a consensus, cover the same stories and use the same news sources. A good deal has been said in earlier chapters about the consequences of organizational and 'media culture' factors on content, and thus, potentially, for effect. The notion that media 'structure reality' in a way directed by their own needs and interests has provided the theme for some research with strong implications for effect. An early example was the study by Lang and Lang (1953) of the television coverage of the return of McArthur from Korea after his recall, which showed how a relatively small scale and muted occasion was turned into something approaching a mass demonstration of welcome and support by the selective attention of cameras to points of most activity and interest. The reportage was seeking to reproduce from rather unsatisfactory materials what had been predicted as a major occasion. The reporting of a large demonstration in London against the Vietnam war in 1968 appeared to follow much the same pattern (Halloran et al., 1970). The coverage was planned for an event predefined (largely by the media themselves) as potentially violent and dramatic and the actual coverage strained to match this pre-definition, despite the lack of suitable reality material.

The evidence from such tendencies of an effect on how people define reality is not always easy to find. However, in their study of how children came to define the 'problem' of race and immigration Hartman and Husband (1974) do seem to show that in this respect dominant media definitions are picked up, especially where personal experience is lacking. Another, different kind of effect is documented by Gitlin (1981) in relation to media coverage of the American student radical movement in the late 1960s. Here the media played a major part in shaping the image of this movement for the American public, partly according to their own needs (e.g. for action, stars, conflict), and caused the student movement itself to respond to this image and adapt and develop accordingly. Most of the effects referred to here derive from 'unwitting bias' in the media, but the potential to define reality has been exploited quite knowingly. The term 'pseudo-events' has been used to refer to a category of event more or less manufactured to gain attention or create a particular impression (Boorstin, 1961). The staging of pseudo-events is now a familiar device in many campaigns (McGinnis, 1969), but more significant is the possibility that a high percentage of media coverage of 'actuality' really consists of planned events which are intended to shape impressions in favour of one interest or another. Those most able to manipulate actuality coverage are those with most power, so the bias, if it exists, may be unwitting on the part of the media, but is certainly not so for those trying to shape their own 'image'.

Cultivation theory

Among theories of long term media effect, some prominence should be given to the cultivation hypothesis of Gerbner (1973) which holds that television, amongst modern media, has acquired such a central place in daily life that it dominates our 'symbolic environment', substituting its message about reality for personal experience and other means of knowing about the world. The message of television is, in their view, distinctive and deviant from 'reality' on several key points, yet persistent exposure to it leads to its adoption as a consensual view of (American) society. The main evidence for the 'cultivation' theory comes from systematic content analysis of American television, carried out over several years and showing consistent distortions of reality in respect of family, work and roles, aging, death and dying, education, violence and crime. This content is said to provide lessons about what to expect from life and it is not a very encouraging message, especially for the poor, women and racial minorities.

The propagation and take-up of this 'television view' is essentially the 'cultivation' process referred to. The second main source of evidence in support of the theory comes from surveys of opinion and attitude which seem to support the view that higher exposure to television goes with the sort of world view found in the message of television. It is not easy to assess this part of the evidence and several authors have raised doubts about the interpretation of the television message (e.g. Newcomb, 1978) and about the causal relationship posited between television use data and survey data concerning values and opinions (Hughes, 1980; Hirsch, 1980 and 1981). There is also some reason to doubt whether the 'cultivation' effect would occur elsewhere than in the United States, partly because television content and use are often different and partly because the limited evidence from other countries is not yet very confirmatory. In relation to images of a violent society Wober (1978) finds no support from British data and Doob and McDonald (1979) report similarly from Canada. A longitudinal study of Swedish children (Hedinsson, 1981, p. 188) concluded, however, that evidence amounted to, 'if not a direct support, at least a non-refutation of Gerbner's theory'. However plausible the theory, it is almost impossible to deal convincingly with the complexity of posited relationships between symbolic structures, audience behaviour and audience views, given the many intervening and powerful social background factors.

A remaining point of uncertainty about the cultivation hypothesis has to do with the origin and direction of the effect. According to its authors, 'television is a cultural arm of the established industrial order and as such serves primarily to maintain, stabilize and reinforce rather than to alter, threaten or weaken conventional beliefs and behaviours' (Gross, 1977, p. 180). The statement brings the cultivation effect very close to that posited by the critical theorists of the Frankfurt School and not far from later marxist analyses. While Gerbner has paid some attention to the institutional origins of content (e.g. Gerbner, 1969) and recognized the importance of 'institutional process analysis' (Gerbner, 1977), this work has remained largely undone and the two bodies of theory remain some distance apart. One seems over-'positivistic' and the other over-theoretical and one-sided. Perhaps cultivation theory really belongs towards the end of the section that follows.

Social control and consciousness-forming

A number of media effects have already been discussed which might belong under this heading, since the idea of socialization includes an element of social control and some, at least, of the reality-defining tendencies that have been discussed seem to work in favour of an established social order. The effects still to be considered are thus not so different in kind, nor are they always easy to assess in terms of their purposefulness: to know, that is, who is doing what to whom with what objective. There are varying positions to be taken up. One is the view that the media act generally, but non-purposively, to support the values dominant in a community or nation, through a mixture of personal and institutional choice, external pressure and anticipation of what a large and heterogeneous audience expects and wants. Another view is that the media are essentially conservative because of a combination of market forces, operational requirements and established work practices. A third view holds that the media are actively engaged on behalf of a ruling (and often media-owning) class or bourgeois state in suppressing or diverting opposition and constraining political and social deviance. This is essentially the marxist view of media as an instrument for the legitimation of capitalism (Miliband, 1969; Westergaard, 1977).

These alternative theories vary in their precision, in their specification of the mechanisms by which control is exercised and in the attribution of conscious power. However, they tend to draw on much the same evidence, most of it relating to systematic tendencies in content with very little directly about effects. A good deal of the evidence concerning content has already been discussed. Most relevant here are those many assertions, based on systematic content analysis, to the effect that the content of media with the largest publics, both in news or actuality and in fiction, is supportive of social norms and conventions (an aspect of social-ization and of 'cultivation'). It has also been shown to be distinctly lacking in offering fundamental challenges to the national state or its established institutions and likely to treat such challenges offered by others in a discouraging way. The argument that mass media tend towards the confirmation of what exists is thus based on evidence both about what is present and about what is missing. The former includes the rewarding (in fiction) of 'conformist' or patriotic behaviour, the high attention and privileged (often direct) access given to established elites and points of view, the observably negative or unequal treatment of non-institutional or deviant behaviour, the devotion of media to a national or community consensus, the tendency to show problems as soluble within the established 'rules' of society and culture.

The evidence of media omission is, in the nature of things, harder to assemble but the search for it was begun by Warren Breed (1958) who, on the basis of what he called a 'reverse content analysis' (comparing press content with sociological community studies), concluded that American newspapers consistently omitted news which would offend the values of religion, family, community, business and patriotism. He concluded that ' "power" and "class" are protected by media performance'. Comparative content analyses of news in one or several countries have added evidence of systematic omission in the attention given to certain issues and parts of the world. Detailed studies of news content such as those by the Glasgow Media Group (1977; 1980) or by Golding and Elliott (1979) have documented some significant patterns of omission. More importantly, perhaps, they have shown a pattern of selection which is so consistent and predictable that a corresponding pattern of rejection can be inferred.

Golding (1980) wrote of the 'missing dimensions' of power and social process in the television news of more than one country. The absence of power is attributed to: the imbalance of media attention over the world; the concentration on individuals rather than corporate entities; the separation of policy options from the under-lying relations of political and economic power. Social process is lost by concentration on short term, fleeting events rather than deeper, long term changes. In Golding's view, the outcome is a kind of ideology showing the world as unchanging and unchangeable and one likely to preclude 'the development of views which might question the prevailing distribution of power and control' (p. 80). The explanation also lies in the complex demands of news production and its place within the media industry. Herbert Gans (1980) reached not dissimilar conclusions about the generally conservative tendencies of the main American news media and is inclined to attribute this to organizational and occupational demands rather than conspiracy. He also lays stress on the reflection in news of the characteristic outlook and social milieu of those who make the news and tend, in the absence of better information, to assume an audience much the same as themselves.

The view that media are systematically used for purposes of legitimation of the state in capitalist society has often to rely heavily on evidence of what is missing in the media. Stuart Hall (1977, p. 336), drawing on the work of both Poulantzas and Althusser, names those ideological processes in the media as: 'masking and displacing'; 'fragmentation'; 'imposition of imaginary unity or coherence'. The first is the failure to admit or report the facts of class exploitation and conflict. The second refers to the tendency to deny or ignore common working class interests and to emphasize the plurality, disconnection and individuality of social life. The third refers to the 'taking for granted' of a national consensus, common to all classes and people of goodwill and common sense. There is some evidence for the latter two of these processes and it would probably not be difficult to argue that the main mass media of western society are no more inclined to go critically into the fundamentals of capitalism than are the media of eastern Europe to question the justice underlying their forms of economy and society. Hall's own contribution to the theory has been to suggest that a view supportive of the capitalist order is 'encoded' or built into many media messages, so as to indicate a 'preferred reading' or interpretation which is not easy to resist.

An additional element in the theory of conservative ideological formation by the media lies in the observation that the media define certain kinds of behaviours and groups as both deviant from, and dangerous to, society. Apart from the obviously criminal, these include groups such as teenage gangs, drugtakers, 'football hooligans', and some sexual deviants. It has been argued that attention by the media often demonstrably exaggerates the real danger and significance of such groups and their activities (Cohen and Young, 1973) and tends to the creation of 'moral panics' (Cohen, 1972). The effect is to provide society with scapegoats and objects of indignation, to divert attention from real evils with causes lying in the institutions of society and to rally support for the agencies of law and order. It has also been suggested that the media tend to widen the scope of their disapprobation to associate together quite different kinds of behaviour threatening to society. In the pattern of coverage, the activities of some kinds of terrorism, rioting or political violence help to provide a symbolic bridge between the clearly delinquent and those engaged in non-institutionalized forms of political behaviour like demonstrations or the spreading of strikes for political reasons. In some kinds of popular press treatment, according to Hall et al. (1978), it is hard to distinguish the criminal outsider from the political 'extremist'. Within the category of anti-social elements those who rely on welfare may also come to be included under the label of 'welfare scroungers' (Golding and Middleton, 1982) and the same can happen to immigrants. The process has been called 'blaming the victim' and is a familiar feature of collective opinion forming to which the media can obviously make a contribution.

It is almost impossible to give any useful assessment of the degree to which the effects posited by this body of theory and research actually occur. Firstly, the evidence of content is incomplete, relating only to some media in some places. Secondly, it has not really been demonstrated that the media in any western country offer a very consistent ideology, even if there are significant elements of consistency both of direction and of ideology. Thirdly, we have to accept that many of the processes, especially those of selective use and perception, by which people resist or ignore propaganda apply here as well as in campaign situations, even if it is less easy to resist what is not specifically offered as propaganda and not easy to opt for what is not there. The historical evidence since the later 1960s, when theories of powerful mass media began to be revived, seems, nevertheless, to support the contention that something, if not the media, has been working to maintain the stability of capitalist societies in the face of economic crises which might have been expected to cause disaffection and delegitimation. The elements of society which seem inclined to disaffection are not the 'masses' or the 'workers' but the intellectuals and other marginal categories who do not rely on the mass media for their world view. It remains equally likely, however, that fundamental forces in society helping to maintain the existing order are reflected and expressed in the media in response to a deeply conservative public opinion.

Nevertheless, it would be difficult to argue that the media are, on balance, a major force for social change, or to deny that a large part of what is most attended to is generally conformist in tendency. It is also difficult to avoid the conclusion that, insofar as media capture attention, occupy time and disseminate images of reality and of potential alternatives, they fail to provide favourable conditions for the formation of a consciousness and identity amongst the less advantaged sectors of society and for the organization of opposition, both of which have been found necessary in the past for radical social reform. It should not be lost sight of that the media are mainly owned and controlled either by (often large) business interests or (however indirectly) the state — thus the interests which do have political and economic power. There is a good deal of prima facie evidence that such controlling power over the media is valued beyond its immediate economic yield. In any case, it is no secret that most media most of the time do not see it as their task to promote fundamental change in the social system. They work within the arrangements that exist, often sharing the consensual goal of gradual social improvement. Gans' judgement (1980, p. 68) that 'news is not so much conservative or liberal as it is reformist' probably applies very widely. The media are committed by their own ideology to serving as a carrier for messages (e.g. about scandals, crises, social ills) which could be an impulse to change, even of a quite fundamental kind. They probably do stimulate much activity, agitation and anxiety which disturb the existing order, within the limits of systems which have some capacity for generating change. Ultimately, the questions involved turn on how dynamic societies are and on the division of social power within them and these take us well beyond the scope of media-centred theory.

Effects on other social institutions

The discussion at this point has dealt with processes of effect which, although they have implications for society as a whole, are experienced primarily at the individual level. The path by which 'higher level' effects can follow is not difficult to pursue, although the extent to which effects have occurred is not easy to assess with any certainty and has not often been the object of sustained empirical investigation. As the media have developed they have, incontrovertibly, achieved two things. They have, between them, diverted time and attention from other activities and they have become a channel for reaching more people with more information than was available under 'pre-mass media' conditions. These facts have implications for any other institution which requires allocation of time, attention and the communication of information, especially to large numbers and in large quantities. The media compete with other institutions and they offer ways of reaching continuing institutional objectives. It is this which underlies the process of institutional effect. Other social institutions are under pressure to adapt or respond in some way, or to make their own use of the mass media. In doing so, they are likely to alter. Because this is a slow process, occurring along with other kinds of social change, the specific contribution of the media cannot be accounted for with any certainty.

If this argument is accepted, it seems unlikely that any institution will be unaffected, but most open to change will be those concerned with 'knowledge' in the broadest sense. These are the most universal and unselective in their reach. In most societies, this will suggest politics and education as the most likely candidates, religion in some cases and, to a lesser degree, legal institutions. In general we could expect work, social services, science, the military to be only tangentially affected by the availability and activity of mass media. Insofar as we can regard leisure and sport as an institution in modern society they should perhaps be added to politics and education as the most directly interrelated with the mass media. The case of education is an interesting one. We find a set of circumstances which at first sight seem favourable to the application of mass media, or the technologies of mass media, to existing purposes, yet in practice rather little use is being made of them. Developed educational institutions have resisted any extensive change of customary ways or adaptation of content to take advantage of new ways of communicating to large numbers (McQuail, 1970). The mass media have often been regarded as a threat to the values of the institution, but also accepted in those spheres where innovation is taking place, for instance for the extension of education to adults or for more general purposes in developing countries. This conflict and correlated resistance is partly a consequence of the early definition of mass media as belonging to the sphere of entertainment and leisure and partly due to normal institutional conservatism.

The case of politics, as conducted in those societies with a broadly liberal-democratic basis, provides more evidence of adaptation and change to the circumstances of a society where the mass media are the main source of public information. In this case, the modern mass media inherited from the press, and retained, an established political function as the voice of the public and of interest groups and as the source of information on which choices and decisions could be made by a mass electorate and by politicians. We can see an interaction between a profound change in media institutions as a result of broadcasting and a response by an established political system which was resisting profound changes. The challenge to politics from mass media institutions has taken several forms, but has been particularly strong because the press was already involved in political processes and because the introduction of broadcasting was a political act. The diversion of time from political activity was less important than the diversion of attention from partisan sources of information and ideology to sources which were more accessible and efficient, often more attractive as well as authoritative, and which embodied the rather novel political values of objectivity and independent 'expert' adjudication. As we have seen, it has increasingly seemed as if it is the mass media which set the 'agenda' and define the problems on a continuous, day-to-day basis while political parties and politicians increasingly respond to a consensus view of what should be done.

The communication network controlled by the modern mass party cannot easily compete with the mass media network and access to the national platform has to be competed for on terms which are partly determined by the media institutions themselves. Parts of the story have been well told by Blumler (1970), Seymour-Ure (1974) and Paletz and Entman (1981). Recurring ideas about the effects of media change on political institutions include the following: that personalities (leaders) have become relatively more important; that attention has been diverted from the local and regional to the national stage; that face-to-face political campaigning has declined; that partisanship and ideology are less important than finding pragmatic solutions to agreed problems; that opinion polls have gained in influence; that electorates have become more volatile (more inclined to change allegiance); that general news values have influenced the attention-gaining activities of political parties. As always, it is hard to separate out the effects of media change from broad changes in society working both on the media and on political institutions and there is much room for dispute about what is the real cause of a given effect.

8 THEMES OF MEDIA THEORY AND ISSUES OF MEDIA POLICY: SOME PATHS TO THE FRONTIER

The limits of media theory

The assembling of theories which has been attempted in the fore-going chapters may be seen as having more than one purpose. Prin-cipal amongst these has been the wish to provide a provisional record, in summary form, of the outcome of research and thought about the media. However, in a short concluding chapter, the question to be addressed concerns the lessons that might be derived from this body of work about a number of the issues of media policy and politics which currently arise within many national societies and in the international debate about mass media. While these issues can be little more than outlined in so short a space, the exercise may serve as a reminder that the study of media is not an end in itself but should produce some benefits in grappling with 'real-life' problems and choices.

Anyone who has read this far or is otherwise familiar with the field will be aware of the shortcomings and limitations of media theory. It is often imprecise in formulation; it is rarely a sound basis for specific predictions; its component propositions have rarely been systematically tested; it is subject to great variability and qualifica-tion according to the ideological views of its proponents. The same theoretical problem can often appear in variant, seemingly incon-sistent, or even contradictory, formulations. For some, the cardinal failing of media theory is that it connects so poorly with the actual practice of mass communication and a knowledge of it is not widely regarded as part of the necessary equipment of a successful communicator. For that purpose a very little knowledge of media systems and audiences goes a long way in supplementing intuition, skill, creativity and personal flair.

While it is true that the kind of theory assembled in this book was never intended as an aid to 'better communication', it is not irrelevant to note that media theory has often seemed insensitive to questions of aesthetics and intrinsic quality, to the nuances of forms and performances and has disappointed many scholars who share a view of the importance of mass media, but regret the absence, in most media research, of a cultural perspective (e.g. Carey and Kreiling, 1974; Carey, 1977).

While the 'bias' of media theory and research is no more than the bias of most social science, it does seem to represent a weakness when we are dealing with a field of human experience that is particularly resistant to generalization, systematic treatment and reduction to formulae. Media theory thus suffers the dual disadvantage of being often at odds with the creative practitioner and having made little progress towards a 'science of mass communication', in the sense of a body of dependable propositions that could be used for more effective media operation. Of course, the apparatus of audience and market research and public opinion polling does deliver much that is of practical value, but not much more than was possible twenty or thirty years ago. However, the points that follow are not meant to make good these deficiencies, but are addressed to those concerned with the performance and promise of media in society and with issues of media policy. While tentative, they are not without substance or value.

There are many possible ways of identifying policy issues, but they can all be found a place under one or other of the following four headings: questions to do with the protection of individuals and institutions of society from the media — the concern to limit potential harm; those to do with the application of media to some positive social purpose — to advance some objective of the public good; those to do with the management of media change; those to do directly with political power — of the media and over the media. This is a very general framework, but good enough for the purpose of linking the policy sphere with lessons of media theory.

Main themes of media theory

The form in which the following summary is given reflects the condition of theory as described. In place of clear statements about the degree and direction of various media tendencies or interactions between media and society we have a number of rather tentative observations often entailing alternative positions, so that media theory appears sometimes as a set of options or unresolved disagreements. There is no single reason for this, but it stems from the insufficiency of evidence, the variations of circumstances, the essential ambiguity and duality of many of the phenomena involved. While seven themes will be distinguished, it will be apparent that they often overlap and sometimes recur.

Media as either socially fragmenting
or unifying
The impact of media on the quality and 'health' of social life has

been a recurring preoccupation of media theorists and the results of their work are as mixed and divided as are conceptions of what does constitute a 'healthy' social formation. On the one hand, the media are associated historically with the break-up of communal, close-knit forms of social life and with the development of more open, calculative and less intense forms of attachment. Media culture has developed as a culture which is metropolitan and universalistic rather than local and particularistic. As such, the media have opened up wider areas of the life of society to public surveillance, if not control and, when left to themselves, have tended to contribute to increased freedom by offering cultural and informational alter-natives over and above those otherwise available, even if the alternatives tend everywhere to be much the same. The central issue has to do with whether the media act as a centralizing and unifying force or a decentralizing and fragmenting one. Beyond that, the question arises as to whether the given tendency has negative or positive aspects. Thus 'unifying' can denote nation-building, modernization, progress and political strength and a capacity for mobilization for common ends. Or it can be associated with homogenization, manipulation and suppression. Decentralization and 'fragmentation' may in their positive aspects denote diversity, choice, freedom, change, the opportunity for personal development, while their obverse signals loss of identity, social disintegration, privatization, atomization, loneliness, powerlessness. Theory thus yields neither a pessimistic nor an optimistic conclusion but sets out rather divergent possibilities.

The non-centrality and dependence of the media

The distinction implied here is between those who view media as an independent driving force or initiator in society, either through their technology or their dominant message, and those who see them as essentially dependent, reactive to other primary movements, sub-ordinate to the power exercised elsewhere in society. In the theory as summarized in the book as a whole, rather more weight is given to the latter view, for several reasons: because the subordination of media to the state is usually institutionalized and they usually draw on or defer to sources of legitimate authority; because they seem to respond and react to demands and expectations from their audiences rather than seek to shape them; because media use seems to be shaped, and messages interpreted, according to the disposition of the receiver and the collective influences of culture and social group; because, however useful and valued, the media do not seem for most people to be objects of very strong sentiments — they are extensively, but not deeply, valued.

While there are good grounds for asserting the marginality or dependence of media in relation to society and social life, there are also reasons why this may not be a permanent feature of the situation, as media continue to consume more time, become more important as industries and extend their functions. It may be eventually or already necessary to abandon notions of both media subordination and media determinism and treat media as an 'open system' not clearly demarcatable from society or other institutions.

The media as an object
of social and cultural definition

Media acquire definitions composed of a mixture of observed fact, 'image', valuation and prescription. There are thus sets of ideas about what the media actually do and what they ought to do which guide expectations and set limits. Such definitions tend to be established early in the history of a given medium and are often adaptations of ideas relating to pre-existing media and communication forms. They are not easy to manipulate and have features that are often rather arbitrarily derived from the historical circumstances of their origin. The importance of such definitions lies mainly in their influence on ideas of what is appropriate as media content and media behaviour in given circumstances. They can thus informally regulate and limit the purpose for which media can be used. They are resistant to revision and tend to discourage the 'deviations' which are sometimes envisaged in plans and policies to use entertainment media for approved social and cultural ends.

The ambiguity and multiplicity
of media purpose and message

The theoretical discussion has, at various points, highlighted the fact that media serve at more or less the same time, not only many, but also divergent purposes. These purposes are a mixture of the sacred and profane, the material and spiritual, the enduring and the ephemeral. They are also inextricably connected with questions of social control and order, and with processes of social change. Sometimes they are about nothing in particular. The media are consequently open to use for quite different ends by different interests, groups and sectors of society. While such differences may be reconciled to some extent by understandings built into the dominant social definitions, there are considerable elements of unresolved contradiction or tension.

Together with multiplicity of purpose goes ambiguity of meaning. Attempts to 'decode' the meaning of content and to use it as a criterion of evaluation or a means of prediction have found no sure scientific foundation. There is as yet no agreed way of 'reading' what is present in the media in an 'objective' way. It is not clear what media content can tell us about the society, its producers or its audiences. This is not so problematic for the normal media user, who is provided with conventions for distinguishing degrees of factualness and objectivity. However, the message of theory seems to be that we might better regard media content as a unique cultural form, a 'media culture' fashioned according to its own conventions and codes and forming a more or less independent element in the social reality rather than a message *about* that social reality. Thus even where media act as carriers for other institutions, they tend to alter the substance, to conform to the demands of 'media culture'.

Media freedom and independence

Notwithstanding what has already been written about the dependence of the media on society and public, the idea that media are independent and exercise an exclusive sphere of professional competence cannot be ignored. It lives in the public definitions of media; it is institutionalized in some normative theories of the press; it comes to light in the study of media organizations and occupations. One strand of theory has dealt with the tendency for media personnel to seek to maximize their control over the nature and circumstances of their work. In this respect they are little different from members of other service organizations or professions, but there are specific consequences for mass communication which theory has highlighted.

Firstly, media seek to protect or enlarge their sphere of autonomy in relation to sources of ultimate political and economic power by developing an objective, open, neutral, balancing stance which establishes a 'distance' from power, without conflict. Secondly, efforts to control the circumstances of work within media organizations lead to some degree of routinization, standardization, loss of creativity. Thirdly, attempts to limit or manage the demands of the audience lead to some measure of detachment from the public and are accompanied by stereotyping of audience wishes and a potentially manipulative response to audience demand. Media theory has tended to emphasize the resulting distancing and disengagement of media from their society. It is sometimes suggested, at the same time, that media find it harder to maintain a genuine detachment from the power pressures of society than from demands or needs of the audience. The nature of media systems and institutions favours the ideal of independence, but leaves media more scope for detachment from audience than from the state, clients, sources and owners. The giving of purpose to mass communication does often originate within media organizations, but is otherwise located more in the societal 'top' or other institutions than in the public or community ostensibly to be served.

Media power

The concept of media power can be formulated in a variety of ways and the lessons of media theory, here as elsewhere, are fragmentary and sometimes inconsistent. Two main questions are at issue: (1) the effectiveness of media as an instrument for achieving given power ends — persuasion, mobilization, information, etc.; (2) *whose* power do the media exercise — that of society as a whole, of a particular class or interest group, or individual communicators? An extension of this last question is whether, in general, the media act to increase, sustain or diminish existing inequalities of power in society.

Several relevant points have already been made: the media are in several senses *dependent* and thus limited in what they can achieve for anyone; they are also allowed some independence and thus freedom to pursue their own objectives. The predominant message from media theory on the latter point is that the media tend not to use their neutrality to challenge existing power relations and are somewhat vulnerable to 'assimilation' by external holders of power in society. Amongst other somewhat inconsistent messages are the following. Firstly, within limits set by circumstances of distribution, audience dispositions and other trends in society, communication effects and longer-term changes, corresponding to directions implied in media content, can and do occur. In short, theory supports the view that media can achieve reasonably delimited objectives and thus be 'effective' according to their chosen purposes. Secondly, it seems that media, for many reasons, despite, or even because of their aspirations to neutrality, more often than not do serve, by action or omission, to protect or advance the interests of those with greater economic or political power in their own societies.

This is not to say that the power of the media is only that of a dominant class, but whatever wider social power the media have comes mainly from 'outside' and to be effective, the media require authority, legitimacy and social support which cannot be sufficiently generated from within. This does not exclude the possibility that the media will be open to forces of progressive social

change, to expressing popular demands or to advancing the
interests of the public they serve. However, the normal operation of
media does not seem to favour the giving of initial support to
demands for change and the 'interests of the public' tend to be re-
interpreted according to the working needs of the media. In the
critical choice between using the media for the interests of senders
(society, advocates, communicators and the media) or those of
receivers (the public or audience, sub-groups within it), a choice
which parallels that between manipulation and communication, the
balance seems somewhat tilted towards the first of the two.

The mixing of normative and objective elements

A last strand in media theory, which can be briefly stated, relates to
the difficulty of disentangling what is objective and value-free from
what is normative and value-laden, the 'is' from the 'ought'. There is
virtually none amongst the issues just raised which can be formulated or settled without reference to one or more value positions.
Media theory is essentially normative and so also is social theory. It
is only within a narrow range, holding constant questions of value
and purpose, that one can pose and test objective propositions. In
so doing, one will almost certainly have crossed a boundary into the
fundamentals of psychology, or economics, or information theory,
or whatever.

Some lessons for policy

Protection from the media

The most recurrent public policy problems seem to have fallen under
this heading, with the media suspected of undermining the
socializing effects of other, more official, agencies of society —
family, school, church, politics, etc., by offering and even implicitly
encouraging 'deviant' or disapproved models of social and cultural
behaviour. Thus media are freely accessible to individuals, often by-
passing controls and able to offer, especially under the protection of
entertainment and fictional forms, content which might, variously:
stimulate individual or collective aggression; demotivate people or
divert them from serious tasks; spread debased or debilitating
forms of culture; undermine attempts to develop or maintain a
national, indigenous or minority culture. At the same time such
problem definitions may often connect with widespread perceptions
of what is morally or socially desirable.

Although mass media theory does tend to confirm the above

assumption about the way media work, it also offers some cautionary lessons. Firstly, we are reminded of the resilience and self-protective capacity of individuals, groups and even cultures in the face of seeming harm. The media may even have an 'inoculative' effect in respect of more 'real' experiences. Secondly, theory draws attention to the strength of existing controls by society over media and over audience behaviour. Thirdly, caution is called for in the assessment of what is 'negative', given the uncertainty about the meaning of content, and especially about its relation to 'reality'. In general, developments of media theory have encouraged a widening of the scope of what might be thought harmful, to take account of such supra-individual matters as: the protection of cultural forms; threats to diversity and the representation of minority or oppositional viewpoints; the consequences of 'disinformation'; the consequences of national media tendencies for international relations. Media theory gives less support to solutions based on piecemeal censorship and more to institutional solutions of various kinds, including: developments in media self-responsibility; better ways of relating media to audiences and to those they depict or give access to; revisions of normative theory which will be responsive to some of the wider issues mentioned and to variations in societal conditions. Finally, developments in media theory have tended to raise the status of normative and qualitative criteria in the whole set of media definitions and arrangements and divert attention away from a preoccupation with quantitative, behavioural evidence as a source of diagnosis and as a prerequisite for action.

The harnessing of media
to positive social purpose
The diversity of possible objectives is great, but the general line of thought from theory reverses that outlined above. The media need not subvert other agencies of society, but can supplement or increase their power. They can: extend educational and cultural opportunity; raise 'levels' of culture and diffuse information more widely in society; help in giving identity and consciousness to local, ethnic, political or cultural groups; encourage good relations between societies; foster social and economic change. In sum, the media may be perceived as a 'pro-social' force, according to different versions of the good. Such a perception is especially likely to be found in developing societies, although not universally so, and it is not absent in the developed world, especially in societies with advanced ideas about communication welfare.

Whether or not media will follow such a path, if left to themselves, depends very much on the institution and forms of organization. Where media respond solely or mainly to market forces, the kinds of objective mentioned are not likely to predominate, simply because the consumer market does not usually give rise to such demands, nor do public definitions of media, as outlined, lend themselves very well to such motivated applications. Whether attempts to apply the media to 'positive social purpose' originate within the media or outside, they are subject to severe limitations which are mainly outside their own control. Direct effects on attitudes and behaviour are possible, but not very predictably and with even less certainty about lasting consequences. On the positive side, developments of media theory seem to have opened up more prospects for achieving results in the sphere of information. These were neglected or under-valued in earlier theory of media effects. In addition, the limitation seemingly uncovered by theories of social influence and of mediation according to functionality can be used as a guide to 'better' com-munication practice, in which media activities are planned much more closely in relation to the needs, capacities and interests of those who are expected to benefit. Further, while the assimilation of media to the power of class and sectional economic interests has often been postulated, occasionally demonstrated and often deplored, a corollary proposition is that the media, appropriately backed by sources of legitimate authority and popular support, can achieve positive social objectives. The apparent success of media in supporting socially agreed objectives has often been neglected, undervalued, or subject to query from the media themselves. Finally, it should be emphasized that the outcome of positive intervention, by whatever means, is bound to be unpredictable in its outcome, as to degree and direction, even under seemingly favourable conditions of social support. The media remain limited by their social definition as to what they can achieve, media processes are too complex and too little self-contained for rational manipulative plan-ning from 'above' and the audience is often 'obstinate'.

The management of media change

The most immediate pressures on policy are experienced at points of major technical innovation, having mainly to do with the need to meet, or control, demand and the consequences of innovation for established media. Currently, a series of major technological changes is threatening the established 'media order', especially in the form of: video cassettes and discs; cable distribution of signals; broadcasting satellites; interactive computer-based communication systems; the 'electronic newspaper'. These fast-arriving developments challenge many of the ground rules governing existing television and radio arrangements, take away or redistribute audiences, have potentially far-reaching economic consequences for press media and undermine some of the established purposes assigned to media in society. Insofar as the media do have social purposes, however acquired, these have either to be protected by new rules or new media have to be guided actively to meeting old or new social purposes.

Media theory, as interpreted above, suggests, firstly, that the stage of introduction of media is critical for establishing subsequent possibilities. If there is to be 'social purpose', beyond what may attend market expansion, it is essential to recognize and 'legitimate' this from the beginning. The possibilities for doing so are likely to depend very much on the condition of 'normative theory' in a given society. It is unlikely that new rules can sharply deviate from what is already regarded as, on balance, just and proper. A reading of media history, rather than theory, might suggest, however, that early, perhaps arbitrary, kinds of regulation, can have long-term unintended consequences. The body of normative theory is not very helpful on the specifics of regulative policy for managing media change, but it indicates a general tripartite choice between: market freedom and de-regulation; arrangements which favour, or give competence to, the media themselves (not the same as the market); and those which give more direct say to 'society' and its constituent groups by various forms of intervention. One lesson of media theory, in any case, is that the 'media' and 'society' are likely to have somewhat divergent conceptions of how best to meet the needs of the public. Even if the public is often omitted from crucial decision-making except by proxy, it does tend to have some eventual say in developments, setting limits both to what is done for its own alleged 'good' or done to it for its own 'harm'. This echoes a lesson already mentioned, that one should not be too confident about the effectiveness of planned intervention in such an open and adaptive system of work and culture.

Media and politics

All the questions that have been posed resolve themselves ultimately into issues of political principle and choice, but there are a number of basic and directly political issues which have arisen in the history of mass media and to which all societies have found solutions, however arbitrary, provisional or even fictive. Most central is the question of media autonomy: how much freedom should media have in political matters — as reporter, advocate, channel?

Secondly, how should access to, and control over, the media as a political power resource be allocated? Several possible answers are contained in the normative theories described in Chapter 3, but quite a few of the realities are either not stated or not recognized in these rules and conventions. Perhaps most underestimated is the overriding competence which is almost universally claimed by, or ascribed to, the nation state. The media are still from, of and for their own nation and culture and are subordinate to the policy of their own society or that which effectively governs international relations. One further point from a reading of media theory is that most of the actuality of political control and of the myth, insofar as it is one, of media potency has more to do with what those with power fear for, or dream of, than with what the media can or do actually achieve. At this point, media theory begins to shade into, and is subordinate to, political theory. We can describe some of the manner and results of the exercise of political power over and by the media but to go further takes us into other territory. It is to be hoped that this discussion has indicated some paths leading to the frontier.

REFERENCES

Adorno, T. and M. Horkheimer (1972), 'The Culture Industry: Enlightenment as Mass Deception', in *The Dialectics of Enlightenment*, New York, Herder and Herder.

Altheide, D. L. (1974), *Creating Reality*, Beverly Hills and London, Sage Publications.

Altheide, D. L. and R. P. Snow (1979), *Media Logic*, Beverly Hills and London, Sage Publications.

Althusser, L. (1971), 'Ideology and Ideological State Apparatuses', in *Lenin and Philosophy and Other Essays*, London, New Left Books.

Baker, R. K. and S. Ball (eds.) (1969), *Violence and the Media*, Washington, DC, GPO.

Ball-Rokeach, S. and M. L. DeFleur (1976), 'A Dependency Model of Mass Media Effects', *Communication Research*, 3: 3-21.

Barthes, R. (1967), *Elements of Semiology*, London, Jonathan Cape.

Barthes, R. (1972), *Mythologies*, London, Jonathan Cape.

Barthes, R. (1977), *Image, Music, Text: Essays*, London, Fontana.

Bass, A. Z. (1969), 'Refining the Gatekeeper Concept', *Journalism Quarterly*, 46: 69-72.

Bauer, R. A. (1958), 'The Communicator and the Audience', *Journal of Conflict Resolution*, 2(1): 67-77. Also in Dexter and White, 1964: 125-139.

Bauer, R. A. (1964), 'The Obstinate Audience', *American Psychologist*, 19: 319-328.

Bauer, R. A. and A. Bauer (1960), 'America, Mass Society and Mass Media', *Journal of Social Issues*, 10(3): 3-66.

Bauman, Z. (1972), 'A Note on Mass Culture: On Infrastructure', in McQuail, 1972: 61-74.

Becker, L. (1982), 'The Mass Media and Citizen Assessment of Issue Importance: A Reflection on Agenda-Setting Research', in Whitney et al., 1982: 521-536.

Beharrell, B. and G. Philo (eds.) (1977), *Trade Unions and the Media*, London, Macmillan.

Bell, D. (1961), *The End of Ideology*, New York, Collier Books.

Bell, D. V. J. (1975), *Power, Influence and Authority*, London and Toronto, Oxford University Press.

Belson, W. A. (1967), *The Impact of Television*, London, Crosby Lockwood.

Benet, J. (1970), 'Interpretation and Objectivity in Journalism', in A. K. Daniels and C. Kahn-Hut (eds.), *Academics on the Line*, San Francisco, Jossey Bass.

227

Benjamin, W. (1977), 'The Work of Art in an Age of Mechanical Reproduction', in Curran et al., 1977: 384-408.

Berelson, B. (1949), 'What Missing the Newspaper Means', in Lazarsfeld and Stanton, 1949: 111-129.

Berelson, B. (1952), *Content Analysis in Communication Research*, Glenoe, Ill., Free Press.

Berelson, B. (1959), 'The State of Communication Research', *Public Opinion Quarterly*, 23(1): 1-6.

Berelson, B. and P. J. Salter (1976), 'Majority and Minority Americans: An Analysis of Magazine Fiction', *Public Opinion Quarterly*, 10: 168-190.

Blau, P. and W. Scott (1963), *Formal Organisations*, London, RKP.

Blumer, H. (1933), *Movies and Conduct*, New York, Macmillan.

Blumer, H. (1939), 'The Mass, the Public and Public Opinion', in A. M. Lee (ed.), *New Outlines of the Principles of Sociology*, New York, Barnes and Noble.

Blumer, H. (1969), *Symbolic Interactionism*, Englewood Cliffs, NJ, Prentice Hall.

Blumer, H. and P. M. Hauser (1933), *Movies, Delinquency and Crime*, New York, Macmillan.

Blumler, J. G. (1964), 'British Television: The Outline of a Research Strategy', *British Journal of Sociology*, 15(3): 223-233.

Blumler, J. G. (1969), 'Producers' Attitudes towards the Television Coverage of an Election', in Halmos, 1969: 85-115.

Blumler, J. G. (1970), 'The Political Effects of Television', in Halloran, 1970: 69-104.

Blumler, J. G. (1979), 'Looking at Media Abundance', *Communications*, 5: 125-158.

Blumler, J. G. and D. McQuail (1968), *Television in Politics: Its Uses and Influence*, London, Faber.

Blumler, J. G. and E. Katz (eds.) (1974), *The Uses of Mass Communications*, Beverly Hills and London, Sage Publications.

Boorstin, D. (1961), *The Image: A Guide to Pseudo Events in America*, New York, Athenaeum.

Boyd-Barret, O. (1977), 'Media Imperialism', in Curran et al., 1977: 116-135.

Boyd-Barret, O. (1982), 'Cultural Dependency and the Mass Media', in Gurevitch et al., 1982: 174-195.

Bramson, L. (1961), *The Political Context of Sociology*, Princeton, Princeton University Press.

Breed, W. (1955), 'Social Control in the Newsroom: A Functional Analysis', *Social Forces*, 33: 326-355.

Breed, W. (1956), 'Analysing News: Some Questions for Research', *Journalism Quarterly*, 33: 467-477.

Breed, W. (1958), 'Mass Communication and Socio-Cultural Integration', *Social Forces*, 37: 109-116.

Brown, J. R. (ed.) (1976), *Children and Television*, London, Collier-Macmillan.

Brown, J. R. (1978), *Characteristics of Local Media Audiences*, Farnborough, Hants., Saxon House.

Brown, J. R. and O. Linné (1976), 'The Family as a Mediator of Television's Effects', in Brown, 1976: 184-198.

Burgelin, O. (1972), 'Structural Analysis and Mass Communication', in McQuail, 1972: 313-328.

Burns, T. (1969), 'Public Service and Private World', in Halmos, 1969: 53-73.

Burns, T. (1977), *The BBC: Public Institution and Private World*, London, Macmillan.

Cantor, M. (1971), *The Hollywood Television Producers*, New York, Basic Books.

Cantril, H., H. Gaudet and H. Hertzog (1940), *The Invasion from Mars*, Princeton, Princeton University Press.

Carey, J. (1969), 'The Communication Revolution and the Professional Communicator', in Halmos, 1969: 23-38.

Carey, J. (1977), 'Mass Communication Research and Cultural Studies: An American View', in Curran et al., 1977: 409-425.

Carey, J. (1978), 'The Ambiguity of Policy Research', *Journal of Communication*, 28(2): 114-119.

Carey, J. and A. L. Kreiling (1974), 'Popular Culture and Uses and Gratifications', in Blumler and Katz, 1974: 225-248.

Chaney, D. (1972), *Processes of Mass Communication*, London, Macmillan.

Chibnall, S. (1977), *Law and Order News*, London, Tavistock.

Clark, T. N. (ed.) (1969), *On Communication and Social Influence* (Collected Essays of Gabriel Tarde), Chicago, Chicago University Press.

Clausse, R. (1968), 'The Mass Public at Grips with Mass Communication', *International Social Science Journal*, 20(4): 625-643.

Cohen, B. (1963), *The Press and Foreign Policy*, Princeton, Princeton University Press.

Cohen, S. (1972), *Folk Devils and Moral Panics*, London, McGibbon and Kee.

Cohen, S. and J. Young (eds.) (1973), *The Manufacture of News*, London, Constable.

Comstock, G., S. Chaffee, N. Katzman, M. McCombs and D. Roberts (1978), *Television and Human Behavior*, New York, Columbia University Press.

Cooper, E. and M. Jahoda (1947), 'The Evasion of Propaganda', *Journal of Psychology*, 23: 15-25.

Cox, H. and D. Morgan (1973), *City Politics and the Press*, Cambridge, Cambridge University Press.

Curran, J., M. Gurevitch and J. Woollacott (eds.) (1977), *Mass Communication and Society*, London, Arnold.

Curran, J. and J. Seaton (1981), *Power without Responsibility*, London, Fontana.

Curran, J., A. Douglas and G. Whannel (1981), 'The Political Economy of the Human Interest Story', in A. Smith (ed.), *Newspapers and Democracy*, Cambridge, Mass., MIT Press: 288-316.

Darnton, R. (1975), 'Writing News and Telling Stories', *Daedalus*, Spring: 175-194.

Davis, D. K. and S. J. Baran (1981), *Mass Communication and Everyday Life*, Belmont, Cal., Wadsworth.

Dawson, R. E. and K. Prewitt (1969), *Political Socialization*, Boston, Little Brown.

DeFleur, M. L. (1964), 'Occupational Roles as Portrayed on Television', *Public Opinion Quarterly*, 28: 57-74.

DeFleur, M. L. (1970), *Theories of Mass Communication* (2nd ed.), New York, David McKay.

Dennis, J. (ed.) (1973), *Socialization to Politics*, New York, Wiley.

Dewey, J. (1927), *The Public and its Problems*, New York, Holt Rinehart.

Dexter, L. A. and D. M. White (eds.) (1964), *People, Society and Mass Communication*, New York, Free Press.

Donohue, G. A., P. J. Tichenor and C. N. Olien (1975), 'Mass Media and the Knowledge Gap', *Communication Research*, 2: 3-23.

Doob, A. and G. E. McDonald (1979), 'Television Viewing and the Fear of Victimization: Is the Relationship Causal?', *Journal of Social Psychology and Personality*, 37: 170-179. Reprinted in Wilhoit and de Bock, 1980: 479-488.

Eco, E. (1977), *A Theory of Semiotics*, London, Macmillan.

Edelman, M. J. (1967), *The Symbolic Uses of Politics*, Urbana, Ill., University of Illinois Press.

Edelstein, A. (1966), *Perspectives in Mass Communication*, Copenhagen, Harcks Forlag.

Eisenstein, E. (1978), *The Printing Press as an Agent of Change*, 2 vols. New York, Cambridge University Press.

Elliott, P. (1972), *The Making of a Television Series — A Case Study in the Production of Culture*, London, Constable.

Elliott, P. (1974), 'Uses and Gratifications Research: A Critique and a Sociological Alternative', in Blumler and Katz, 1974: 249-268.

Elliott, P. (1977), 'Media Organisations and Occupations — An Overview', in Curran et al., 1977: 142-173.

Ellis, T. and J. Child (1973), 'Placing Stereotypes of the Manager into Perspective', *Journal of Management Studies*, 10: 233-255.

Engwall, L. (1978), *Newspapers as Organisations*, Farnborough, Hants., Saxon House.

Ennis, P. (1961), 'The Social Structure of Communication Systems: A Theoretical Proposal', *Studies in Public Communication*, (University of Chicago), 3: 120-144.

Enzensberger, H. M. (1970), 'Constituents of a Theory of the Media', *New Left Review*, 64: 13-36.

Enzensberger, H. M. (1972), 'Constituents of a Theory of the Media', in McQuail, 1972: 99-116.

Etzioni, A. (1961), *Complex Organisations*, Glencoe, Ill., Free Press.

Festinger, L. A. (1957), *A Theory of Cognitive Dissonance*, New York, Row Peterson.

Findahl, O. and B. Höijer (1981), 'Studies of News from the Perspective of Human Comprehension', in Wilhoit and de Bock, 1981: 393-403.

Fiske, J. (1982), *Introduction to Communication Studies*, London, Methuen.

Fiske, J. and J. Hartley (1978), *Reading Television*, London, Methuen.

Fjaestad, B. and P. G. Holmlov (1976), 'The Journalist's View', *Journal of Communication*, 2: 108-114.

Frank, A. G. (1971), *Capitalism and Underdevelopment*, Harmondsworth, Mddx., Penguin.

Frank, R. S. (1973), *Message Dimensions of Television News*, Lexington, Mass., Lexington Books.

French, J. R. P. and B. H. Raven (1953), 'The Bases of Social Power', in D. Cartwright and A. Zander (eds.), *Group Dynamics*, London, Tavistock.

Friedson, E. (1953), 'Communications Research and the Concept of the Mass', *American Sociological Review*, 18(3): 313-317.

Furu, T. (1971), *The Functions of Television for Children and Adolescents*, Tokyo, Sophia University Press.

Galtung, J. and M. Ruge (1965), 'The Structure of Foreign News', *Journal of Peace Research*, 1: 64-90. Also in J. Tunstall (ed.), *Media Sociology*, London, Constable, 1970.

Gans, H. J. (1957), 'The Creator-Audience Relationship in the Mass Media', in B. Rosenberg and D. M. White (eds.), *Mass Culture*, New York, Free Press.

Gans, H. J. (1980), *Deciding What's News*, New York, Vintage Books.

Garnham, N. (1979), 'Contribution to a Political Economy of Mass Communication', *Media Culture and Society*, 1(2): 123-146.

Geiger, K. and R. Sokol (1959), 'Social Norms in Watching Television', *American Journal of Sociology*, 65 (3): 178-181.

Gerbner, G. (1964), 'On Content Analysis and Critical Research in Mass Communication', in Dexter and White, 1964: 476-499.

Gerbner, G. (1964), 'Ideological Perspectives and Political Tendencies in News Reporting', *Journalism Quarterly*, 41: 495-506.

Gerbner, G. (1967), 'Mass Media and Human Communication Theory', in F. E. X. Dance (ed.), *Human Communication Theory*, New York, Holt, Rinehart. Reprinted in McQuail, 1972: 35-58.

Gerbner, G. (1969), 'Institutional Pressures on Mass Communicators', in Halmos, 1969: 205-248.

Gerbner, G. (1973), 'Cultural Indicators — The Third Voice', in G. Gerbner, L. Gross and W. Melody (eds.), *Communications Technology and Social Policy*, New York, Wiley: 553-573.

Gerbner, G. (1977), 'Comparative Cultural Indicators', in G. Gerbner (ed.), *Mass Media Policies in Changing Cultures*, New York, Wiley.

Gerbner, G. and L. P. Gross (1976), 'Living with Television: The Violence Profile', *Journal of Communication*, 26 (2): 173-199.

Gerbner, G. and G. Marvanyi (1977), 'The Many Worlds of the World's Press', *Journal of Communication*, 27 (1): 52-66.

Gieber, W. and W. Johnson (1961), 'The City Hall Beat: A Study of Reporter and Source Roles', *Journalism Quarterly*, 38: 289-297.

Giner, S. (1976), *Mass Society*, London, Martin Robertson.

Gitlin, T. (1978), 'Media Sociology: The Dominant Paradigm', *Theory and Society*, 6: 205-253. Reprinted in Wilhoit and de Bock, 1981: 73-122.

Gitlin, T. (1981), *The Whole World is Watching — Mass Media in the Making and Unmaking of the New Left*, Berkeley, University of California Press.

Glasgow Media Group (1977), *Bad News*, London, Routledge and Kegan Paul.

Glasgow Media Group (1980), *More Bad News*, London, Routledge and Kegan Paul.

Golding, P. (1977), 'Media Professionalism in the Third World: The Transfer of an Ideology', in Curran et al., 1977: 291-308.

Golding, P. (1980), 'The Missing Dimensions — News Media and the Management of Social Change', in Katz and Szecskö, 1980: 63-81.

Golding, P. and P. Elliott (1979), *Making the News*, London, Longman.

Golding, P. and S. Middleton (1982), *Images of Welfare — Press and Public Attitudes to Poverty*, Oxford, Basil Blackwell and Martin Robertson.

Goodhart, G. J., A. S. C. Ehrenberg and M. A. Collins (1975), *The Television Audience: Patterns of Viewing*, Farnborough, Hants., Saxon House.

Gouldner, A. (1976), *The Dialectic of Ideology and Technology*, London, Macmillan.

Graber, D. (1976), *Verbal Behavior and Politics*, Urbana, Ill., University of Illinois Press.

Graber, D. (1980), *Crime News and the Public*, New York, Praeger.

Gramsci, A. (1971), *Selections from the Prison Notebooks*, London, Lawrence and Wishart.

Greenberg, B. S. (1964), 'Person-to-Person Communication in the Diffusion of a News Event', *Journalism Quarterly*, 41: 489-494.

Greenberg, B. S. (1974), 'Gratifications of Television Viewing and their Correlates for British Children', in Blumler and Katz, 1974: 71-92.

Gross, L. P. (1977), 'Television as a Trojan Horse', *School Media Quarterly*, Spring: 175-180.

Gurevitch, M., T. Bennet, J. Curran and J. Woollacott (1982), *Culture, Society and the Media*, London, Methuen.

van der Haak, K. (1977), *Broadcasting in the Netherlands*, London, IIC/RKP.

Hagen, E. (1962), *On the Theory of Social Change*, Homewood, Ill., Dorsey Press.

Hall, S. (1973), 'The Determination of News Photographs', in Cohen and Young, 1973: 176-190.

Hall, S. (1977), 'Culture, the Media and the Ideological Effect', in Curran et al., 1977: 315-348.

232

REFERENCES

Hall, S. (1982), 'The Rediscovery of Ideology: Return of the Repressed in Media Studies', in Gurevitch et al., 1982: 56-90.

Hall, S., J. Clarke, C. Critcher, T. Jefferson and B. Roberts (1978), *Policing the Crisis*, London, Macmillan.

Halloran, J. D. (1965), *The Effects of Mass Communication*, Leicester, Leicester University Press.

Halloran, J. D. (ed.) (1970), *The Effects of Television*, London, Granada.

Halloran, J. D., R. L. Brown and D. Chaney (1970), *Television and Delinquency*, Leicester, Leicester University Press.

Halloran, J. D., P. Elliott and G. Murdoch (1970), *Communications and Demonstrations*, Harmondsworth, Mddx., Penguin.

Halmos, P. (ed.) (1969), *The Sociology of Mass Media Communicators, Sociological Review Monographs*, 13.

Hardt, H. (1979), *Social Theories of the Press: Early German and American Perspectives*, Beverly Hills and London, Sage Publications.

Harrison, S. (1974), *Poor Men's Guardians*, London, Lawrence and Wishart.

Hartman, P. and C. Husband (1974), *Racism and the Mass Media*, London, Davis Poynter.

Hawkes, T. (1977), *Structuralism and Semiology*, London, Methuen.

Hedinsson, E. (1981), *Television, Family and Society — The Social Origins and Effects of Adolescent TV Use*, Stockholm, Almquist and Wiksel.

Himmelweit, H. T., P. Vince and A. N. Oppenheim (1958), *Television and the Child*, London, Oxford University Press.

Himmelweit, H. T. and J. Swift (1976), 'Continuities and Discontinuities in Media Taste', *Journal of Social Issues*, 32(6): 133-156.

Hirsch, F. and D. Gordon (1975), *Newspaper Money*, London, Hutchinson.

Hirsch, P. M. (1977), 'Occupational, Organisational and Institutional Models in Mass Communication', in Hirsch et al., 1977: 13-42.

Hirsch, P. M. (1980), 'The "Scary World" of the Non-viewer and Other Anomalies — A Reanalysis of Gerbner et al.'s Findings in Cultivation Analysis', Part I, *Communication Research*, 7(4): 403-456.

Hirsch, P. M. (1981), 'On Not Learning from One's Mistakes', Part II, *Communication Research*, 8(1): 3-38.

Hirsch, P. M., P. V. Miller and F. G. Kline (eds.) (1977), *Strategies for Communication Research*, Beverly Hills and London, Sage Publications.

Hopkins, M. (1970), *Mass Media in the Soviet Union*, New York, Pegasus.

Horton, D. and R. R. Wohl (1956), 'Mass Communication and Para-social Interaction', *Psychiatry*, 19: 215-229.

Hovland, C. I., A. A. Lumsdaine and F. D. Sheffield (1949), *Experiments in Mass Communication*, Princeton, Princeton University Press.

Howitt, D. and G. Cumberbatch (1975), *Mass Media, Violence and Society*, New York, John Wiley.

Huaco, G. A. (1963), *The Sociology of Film Art*, New York, Basic Books.

Hughes, H. M. (1940), *News and the Human Interest Story*, Chicago, University of Chicago Press.

Hughes, M. (1980), 'The Fruits of Cultivation Analysis: A Re-examination of Some Effects of TV Viewing', *Public Opinion Quarterly*, 44(3): 287-302.

Hutchins, R. (1947), Commission on Freedom of the Press, *A Free and Responsible Press*, Chicago, University of Chicago Press.

Hyman, H. and P. Sheatsley (1947), 'Some Reasons Why Information Campaigns Fail', *Public Opinion Quarterly*, 11: 412-423.

Innis, H. (1950), *Empire and Communication*, Oxford, Clarendon Press.

Innis, H. (1951), *The Bias of Communication*, Toronto, University of Toronto Press.

Jackson, I. (1971), *The Provincial Press and the Community*, Manchester, Manchester University Press.

Janowitz, M. (1952), *The Community Press in an Urban Setting*, Glencoe, Ill., Free Press.

Janowitz, M. (1975), 'Professional Models in Journalism: The Gatekeeper and Advocate', *Journalism Quarterly*, 52(4): 618-626.

Jay, M. (1973), *The Dialectical Imagination*, London, Heinemann.

Johns-Heine, P. and H. Gerth (1949), 'Values in Mass Periodical Fiction 1921-1940', *Public Opinion Quarterly*, 13: 105-113.

Johnstone, J. W. L., E. J. Slawski and W. W. Bowman (1976), *The News People*, Urbana, Ill., University of Illinois Press.

Jowett, G. and J. M. Linton (1980), *Movies as Mass Communication*, Beverly Hills and London, Sage Publications.

Katz, D. (1960), 'The Functional Approach to the Study of Attitudes', *Public Opinion Quarterly*, 24: 163-204.

Katz, D. (1971), 'Platforms and Windows: Broadcasting's Role in Election Campaigns', *Journalism Quarterly*, 48: 304-314. Reprinted in McQuail, 1972: 353-371.

Katz, E. (1977), *Social Research and Broadcasting: Proposals for Further Development*, London, BBC.

Katz, E. and P. F. Lazarsfeld (1955), *Personal Influence*, Glencoe, Ill., Free Press.

Katz, E., M. L. Lewin and H. Hamilton (1963), 'Traditions of Research on the Diffusion of Innovations', *American Sociological Review*, 28: 237-252.

Katz, E., M. Gurevitch and H. Hass (1973), 'On the Use of Mass for Important Things', *American Sociological Review*, 38: 164-181.

Katz, E., J. G. Blumler and M. Gurevitch (1974), 'Utilization of Mass Communication by the Individual', in Blumler and Katz, 1974: 19-32.

Katz, E. and T. Szecskö (eds.) (1980), *Mass Media and Social Change*, Beverly Hills and London, Sage Publications.

Kelman, H. (1961), 'Processes of Opinion Change', *Public Opinion Quarterly*, 25: 57-78.

Kerner, O. et al. (1968), *Report on the National Advisory Committee on Civil Disorders*, Washington, DC, GPO.

Key, V. O. (1961), *Public Opinion and American Democracy*, New York, Alfred Knopf.

Kingsbury, S. M. and M. Hart (1937), *Newspapers and the News*, New York, Putnams.

Klapper, J. (1960), *The Effects of Mass Communication*, New York, Free Press.

Kornhauser, W. (1959), *The Politics of Mass Society*, New York, Free Press.

Kornhauser, W. (1968), 'The Theory of Mass Society', in *International Encyclopedia of the Social Sciences*, New York, Macmillan and Free Press, Vol. 10: 58-64.

Kracauer, S. (1949), 'National Types as Hollywood Presents Them', *Public Opinion Quarterly*, 13: 53-72.

Kraus, S. and D. K. Davis (1976), *The Effects of Mass Communication on Political Behavior*, University Park, Pennsylvania State University Press.

Krugman, H. E. (1965), 'The Impact of Television Advertising: Learning without Involvement', *Public Opinion Quarterly*, 29: 349-356.

Kumar, C. (1975), 'Holding the Middle Ground', *Sociology*, 9(3): 67-88. Reprinted in Curran et al., 1977: 231-248.

Lang, K. and G. E. Lang (1953), 'The Unique Perspective of Television and its Effect', *American Sociological Review*, 18(1): 103-112.

Lang, K. and G. E. Lang (1959), 'The Mass Media and Voting', in E. J. Burdick and A. J. Brodbeck (eds.), *American Voting Behavior*, New York, Free Press.

Lasswell, H. (1948), 'The Structure and Function of Communication in Society', in L. Bryson (ed.), *The Communication of Ideas*, New York, Harper.

Lasswell, H., D. Lerner and I. de Sola Pool (1952), *The Comparative Study of Symbols*, Stanford, Stanford University Press.

Lazarsfeld, P. F., B. Berelson and H. Gaudet (1944), *The People's Choice*, New York, Duell, Sloan and Pearce.

Lazarsfeld, P. F. and F. M. Stanton (1949), *Communications Research 1948-9*, New York, Harper and Bros.

Lerner, D. (1958), *The Passing of Traditional Society*, New York, Free Press.

Lewis, G. H. (1980), 'Taste Cultures and their Composition: Towards a New Theoretical Perspective', in Katz and Szecskö, 1980: 201-217.

Lippman, W. (1922), *Public Opinion*, New York, Harcourt Brace.

Lowenthal, L. (1961), *Literature, Popular Culture and Society*, Englewood Cliffs, NJ, Prentice Hall.

Lull, J. (1982), 'The Social Uses of Television', in Whitney, Wartella and Windahl, 1982: 397-409.

Maccoby, E. (1954), 'Why Do Children Watch TV?', *Public Opinion Quarterly*, 18: 239-244.

Marcuse, H. (1964), *One Dimensional Man*, London, Routledge and Kegan Paul.

Mattelart, A. (1979), *Multinational Corporations and the Control of Culture*, Brighton, Harvester Press.

McBride, S. et al. (1980), *Many Voices, One World*. Report by the International Commission for the Study of Communication Problems. Paris, Unesco and London, Kogan Page.

McCombs, M. E. and D. L. Shaw (1972), 'The Agenda-setting Function of the Press', *Public Opinion Quarterly*, 36: 176-187.

McCormack, T. (1961), 'Social Theory and the Mass Media', *Canc   Journal of Economics and Political Science*, 4: 479-489.

McCormack, T. (1980), 'Revolution, Communication and the Sense of History', in Katz and Szecskö, 1980: 167-185.

McCron, R. (1976), 'Changing Perspectives in the Study of Mass Media and Socialization', in J. Halloran (ed.), *Mass Media and Socialization*, Leicester, IAMCR: 13-44.

McGinnis, J. (1969), *The Selling of the President*, New York, Trident Press.

McGranahan, D. V. and L. Wayne (1948), 'German and American Traits Reflected in Popular Drama', *Human Relations*, 1(4): 429-455.

McGuire, W. J. (1973), 'Persuasion, Resistance and Attitude Change', in I. de Sola Pool et al. (eds.), *Handbook of Communication*, Chicago, Rand McNally: 216-252.

McLelland, D. W. (1961), *The Achieving Society*, Princeton, NJ, van Nostrand.

McLeod, J. M., L. S. Ward and K. Tancill (1965), 'Alienation and Uses of the Mass Media', *Public Opinion Quarterly*, 29: 583-594.

McLeod, J. M. and L. B. Becker (1974), 'Testing the Validity of Gratification Measures through Political Effects Analysis', in Blumler and Katz, 1974: 137-164.

McLuhan, M. (1962), *The Gutenberg Galaxy*, Toronto, Toronto University Press.

McLuhan, M. (1964), *Understanding Media*, London, Routledge and Kegan Paul.

McQuail, D. (1969), *Towards a Sociology of Mass Communication*, London, Collier-Macmillan.

McQuail, D. (1970), 'Television and Education', in Halloran, 1970: 181-218.

McQuail, D. (ed.) (1972), *Sociology of Mass Communications*, Harmondsworth, Mddx., Penguin.
McQuail, D. (1975), *Communication*, London, Longman.
McQuail, D. (1977), *Analysis of Newspaper Content*. Royal Commission on the Press 1974-77, Research series No. 4. London, HMSO.
McQuail, D., J. G. Blumler and J. Brown (1972), 'The Television Audience: A Revised Perspective', in McQuail, 1972: 135-165.
McQuail, D. and M. Gurevitch (1974), 'Explaining Audience Behaviour', in Blumler and Katz, 1974: 287-306.
McQuail, D. and S. Windahl (1982), *Communication Models*, London, Longman.
Mead, G. H. (1934), *Mind, Self and Society*, Chicago, University of Chicago Press.
Mendelsohn, H. (1964), 'Listening to Radio', in Dexter and White, 1964: 239-248.
Mendelsohn, H. (1966), *Mass Entertainment*, New Haven, Conn., College and University Press.
Mendelsohn, H. (1973), 'Some Reasons why Information Campaigns can Succeed', *Public Opinion Quarterly*, 37: 50-61.
Merton, R. K. (1949), 'Patterns of Influence', in Merton, 1957: 387-470.
Merton, R. K. (1957), *Social Theory and Social Structure*, Glencoe, Ill., Free Press.
Meyersohn, R. (1968), 'Television and the Rest of Leisure', *Public Opinion Quarterly*, 32(1): 102-112.
Mickiewicz, E. P. (1981), *Media and the Russian Public*, New York, Praeger.
Miliband, R. (1969), *The State in Capitalist Society*, London, Weidenfeld and Nicolson.
Mills, C. W. (1951), *White Collar*, New York, Oxford University Press.
Mills, C. W. (1956), *The Power Elite*, New York, Oxford University Press.
Moles, A. (1973), 'Television Organizations and Audience Influence — the Typology of "Feedback"', in *Broadcasters and their Audiences*, Roma, Edizioni RAI.
Molotch, H. L. and M. J. Lester (1974), 'News as Purposive Behavior', *American Sociological Review*, 39: 101-112.
Morin, E. (1962), *L'Esprit du temps: essai sur la culture de masse*, Paris, Grasset.
Morin, V. (1976), 'Televised Current Events Sequences or a Rhetoric of Ambiguity', in *News and Current Events on TV*, Roma, Edizioni RAI.
Murdock, G. and P. Golding (1977), 'Capitalism, Communication and Class Relations', in Curran et al., 1977: 12-43.
Murdock, G. and P. Golding (1978), 'Theories of Communication and Theories of Society', in *Communication Research*, 5(3): 339-356.
Murphy, D. (1976), *The Silent Watchdog*, London, Constable.

Newcomb, H. (1978), 'Assessing the Violence Profile of Gerbner and Gross: A Humanistic Critique and Suggestion', *Communication Research*, 5(3): 264-282.
Noble, G. (1975), *Children in Front of the Small Screen*, London, Constable.
Noelle-Neumann, E. (1973), 'Return to the Concept of Powerful Mass Media', *Studies of Broadcasting*, 9: 66-112.
Noelle-Neumann, E. (1974), 'The Spiral of Silence: A Theory of Public Opinion', *Journal of Communication*, 24: 43-51.
Nordenstreng, K. (1974), *Informational Mass Communication*, Helsinki, Tammi.
Novak, K. (1977), 'From Information Gaps to Communication Potential', in M. Berg et al., *Current Theories in Scandinavian Mass Communication*, Grenaa, Denmark, GMT.

Paletz, D. L. and R. Dunn (1969), 'Press Coverage of Civil Disorders: A Case-study of Winston-Salem', *Public Opinion Quarterly*, 33: 328-345.
Paletz, D. L. and R. Entman (1981), *Media, Power, Politics*, New York, Free Press.

Park, R. (1940), 'News as a Form of Knowledge', in R. H. Turner (ed.), *On Social Control and Collective Behavior,* Chicago, University of Chicago Press, 1967: 32-52.

Pearlin, L. (1959), 'Social and Personal Stress and Escape Television Viewing', *Public Opinion Quarterly,* 23: 255-259.

Peirce, C. S. (1931-35), *Collected Papers,* eds. C. Harteshorne and P. Weiss. Cambridge, Mass., Harvard University Press, Vols II and V.

Peterson, R. C. and L. L. Thurstone (1933), *Motion Pictures and Social Attitudes,* New York, Macmillan.

Peterson, T., J. W. Jensen and W. L. Rivers (1965), *The Mass Media and Modern Society,* New York, Holt, Rinehart & Winston.

Philips, D. P. (1980), 'Airplane Accidents, Murder and the Mass Media', *Social Forces,* 58(4): 1001-1024.

Phillips, E. B. (1977), 'Approaches to Objectivity', in Hirsch et al., 1977: 63-77.

Poulantzas, N. (1975), *Classes in Contemporary Society,* London, New Left Books.

Ray, M. L. (1973), 'Marketing Communication and the Hierarchy-of-Effects', in P. Clarke (ed.), *New Models for Communication Research,* Beverly Hills and London, Sage Publications: 147-176.

Rice, R. E. and W. J. Paisley (eds.) (1981), *Public Communication Campaigns,* Beverly Hills and London, Sage Publications.

Riley, M. W. and J. W. Riley (1951), 'A Sociological Approach to Communications Research', *Public Opinion Quarterly,* 15(3): 445-460.

Rivers, W. L., W. Schramm and C. G. Christians (1980), *Responsibility in Mass Communications,* New York, Harper and Row.

Robinson, J. P. (1972), 'Mass Communication and Information Diffusion', in F. G. Kline and P. J. Tichenor (eds.), *Current Perspectives in Mass Communication Research,* Beverly Hills and London, Sage Publications.

Robinson J. P. (1976), 'Interpersonal Influence in Election Campaigns: 2 Step Flow Hypotheses', *Public Opinion Quarterly,* 40: 304-319.

Rogers, E. (1962), *The Diffusion of Innovations,* Glencoe, Ill., Free Press.

Rogers, E. (1976), 'Communication and Development: The Passing of a Dominant Paradigm', *Communication Research,* 3: 213-240.

Rogers, E. and F. Shoemaker (1973), *Communication of Innovations,* New York, Free Press.

Rosengren, K.-E. (1973), 'News Diffusion: An Overview', *Journalism Quarterly,* 50: 83-91.

Rosengren, K.-E. (1974), 'International News: Methods, Data, Theory', *Journal of Peace Research,* 11: 45-56.

Rosengren, K.-E. (1976), 'The Barsebäck "Panic"'. Lund University (mimeo).

Rosengren, K.-E. (ed.) (1980), 'Mass Media and Social Change: Some Current Approaches', in Katz and Szecskö, 1980: 247-263.

Rosengren, K.-E. (1981), *Advances in Content Analysis,* Beverly Hills and London, Sage Publications.

Rosengren, K.-E. and S. Windahl (1972), 'Mass Media Consumption as a Functional Alternative', in McQuail, 1972: 166-194.

Roshco, B. (1975), *Newsmaking,* Chicago, University of Chicago Press.

Roshier, R. J. (1973), 'The Selection of Crime News by the Press', in Cohen and Young, 1973: 28-39.

Rositi, F. (1976), 'The Television News Programme: Fragmentation and Recomposition of our Image of Society', in *News and Current Events on TV,* Roma, Edizioni RAI.

Rosten, L. C. (1937), *The Washington Correspondents,* New York, Harcourt Brace.

Rosten, L. C. (1941), *Hollywood: the Movie Colony, the Moviemakers*, New York, Harcourt Brace.
de Saussure, F. (1915), *Course in General Linguistics*, English trans. London, Peter Owen, 1960.
Schiller, H. (1969), *Mass Communication and American Empire*, New York, Augustus M. Kelly.
Schlesinger, P. (1978), *Putting 'Reality' Together: BBC News*, London, Constable.
Schmid, A. P. and J. De Graaf (1982), *Violence as Communication*, Beverly Hills and London, Sage Publications.
Schramm, W. (1964), *Mass Media and National Development*, Stanford, Stanford University Press.
Schramm, W., J. Lyle and E. Parker (1961), *Television in the Lives of Our Children*, Stanford, Stanford University Press.
Schudson, M. (1978), *Discovering the News*, New York, Basic Books.
Seymour-Ure, C. (1974), *The Political Impact of the Mass Media*, London, Constable.
Shaw, D. L. (1967), 'News Bias and the Telegraph: A Study of Historical Change', *Journalism Quarterly*, 44: 3-12.
Shibutani, T. (1966), *Improvised News*, New York, Bobbs-Merrill.
Siebert, F., T. Peterson and W. Schramm (1956), *Four Theories of the Press*, Urbana, Ill., University of Illinois Press.
Sigal, L. V. (1973), *Reporters and Officials*, Lexington, Mass., D. C. Heath.
Sigelman, L. (1973), 'Reporting the News: An Organisational Analysis', *American Journal of Sociology*, 79: 132-151.
Singer, B. D. (1970), 'Mass Media and Communication Processes in the Detroit Riots of 1967', *Public Opinion Quarterly*, 34: 236-245.
Singer, B. D. (1973), *Feedback and Society*, Lexington, Mass., Lexington Books.
Smith, A. (1973), *The Shadow in the Cave*, London, Allen and Unwin.
Smythe, D. W. (1977), 'Communications: Blindspot of Western Marxism', *Canadian Journal of Political and Social Theory*, 1: 120-127.
de Sola Pool, I. (1973), 'Newsmen and Statesmen — Adversaries or Cronies?', in W. L. Rivers and N. J. Nyham (eds.), *Aspen Papers on Government and Media*, London and New York, Praeger.
Spilerman, S. (1976), 'Structural Characteristics and Severity of Racial Disorders', *American Sociological Review*, 41: 771-792.
Star, S. A. and H. M. Hughes (1950), 'Report on an Education Campaign: The Cincinatti Plan for the UN', *American Journal of Sociology*, 55: 389-400.
Steiner, G. (1963), *The People Look at Television*, New York, Alfred Knopf.
Surgeon General's Scientific Advisory Committee (1972), *Television and Growing Up: The Impact of Televised Violence*, Washington, DC, GPO.

Teheranian, M. (1979), 'Iran: Communication, Alienation, Revolution', *Intermedia*, 7(2): 6-12 (London, IIC).
Thompson, E. P. (1963), *The Making of the English Working Class*, London, Gollancz.
Tichenor, P. J., G. A. Donohue and C. N. Olien (1970), 'Mass Media and the Differential Growth in Knowledge', *Public Opinion Quarterly*, 34: 158-170.
Tracey, M. (1977), *The Production of Political Television*, London, Routledge and Kegan Paul.
Trenaman, J. S. M. and D. McQuail (1961), *Television and the Political Image*, London, Methuen.
Tuchman, G. (1973-74), 'Making News by Doing Work: Routinizing the Unexpected', *American Journal of Sociology*, 79: 110-131.

238   REFERENCES

Tuchman, G. (1978), *Making News: A Study in the Construction of Reality*, New York, Free Press.
Tuchman, G., A. K. Daniels and J. Benet (eds.) (1978), *Hearth and Home: Images of Women in Mass Media*, New York, Oxford University Press.
Tunstall, J. (1970), *The Westminster Lobby Correspondents*, London, Routledge and Kegan Paul.
Tunstall, J. (1971), *Journalists at Work*, London, Constable.
Tunstall, J. (1977), *The Media are American*, London, Constable.
Tunstall, J. (1982), 'The British Press in the Age of Television', in Whitney et al., 1982: 463-479.

Vidmar, N. and M. Rokeach (1974), 'Archie Bunker's Bigotry: A Study of Selective Perception and Exposure', *Journal of Communication*, 24: 36-47.

Weaver, D. H. (1981), 'Media Agenda-setting and Media Manipulation', *Massacommunicatie*, 9(5): 213-229. Reprinted in Whitney et al., 1982: 537-554.
Weber, M. (1948), 'Politics as a Vocation', in H. Gerth and C. W. Mills (eds.), *Max Weber Essays*, London, Routledge and Kegan Paul.
Wells, A. (1972), *Picture-Tube Imperialism? The Impact of US TV in Latin America*, New York, Orbis.
Westergaard, J. (1977), 'Power, Class and the Media', in Curran et al., 1977: 95-115.
Westley, B. and D. MacLean (1957), 'A Conceptual Model for Mass Communication Research', *Journalism Quarterly*, 34: 31-38.
Whale, J. (1969), *The Half-Shut Eye*, London, Macmillan.
White, D. M. (1950), 'The Gate-Keeper: A Case Study in the Selection of News', *Journalism Quarterly*, 27: 383-390.
Whitney, D. C., E. Wartella and S. Windahl (eds.) (1982), *Mass Communication Review Yearbook*, Vol. 3. Beverly Hills and London, Sage Publications.
Wilensky, H. (1964), 'Mass Society and Mass Culture: Interdependence or Independence', *American Sociological Review*, 29(2): 173-197.
Wilhoit, G. C. and H. de Bock (eds.) (1980) and (1981), *Mass Communication Review Yearbook*, Vol. 1 and Vol. 2. Beverly Hills and London, Sage Publications.
Williams, R. (1961), *Culture and Society*, Harmondsworth, Mddx., Penguin.
Williams, R. (1973), 'Base and Superstructure', *New Left Review*, 82.
Williams, R. (1975), *Television: Technology and Cultural Form*, London, Fontana.
Williams, R. (1976), *Keywords*, London, Fontana/Croom Helm.
Wober, J. M. (1978), 'Televised Violence and Paranoid Perception: The View from Gt. Britain', *Public Opinion Quarterly*, 42: 315-321.
Wolfe, K. M. and M. Fiske (1949), 'Why they Read Comics', in Lazarsfeld and Stanton, 1949: 3-50.
Wolfenstein, M. and N. Leites (1947), 'An Analysis of Themes and Plots in Motion Pictures', *Annals of the American Academy of Political and Social Sciences*, 254: 41-48.
Wright, C. R. (1960), 'Functional Analysis and Mass Communication', *Public Opinion Quarterly*, 24: 605-620.
Wright, C. R. (1974), 'Functional Analysis and Mass Communication Revisited', in Blumler and Katz, 1974: 197-212.

Zassoursky, Y. (1974), 'The Role of the Soviet Means of Mass Information in the Growth of Scientific and Communist Class Consciousness', Proceedings of IAMCR Congress, Leipzig.

NAME INDEX

Goodhart, G.J., 162
Gordon, D., 166
Gouldner, A., 42
Graber, D., 134, 136
Gramsci, A., 61
Greenberg, B., 164, 196
Gross, L., 136, 205
Gurevitch, M., 63, 67, 163

Haak, van der, K., 153
Hagen, E., 41
Hall, S., 61, 63, 64, 109, 140, 207, 208
Halloran, J.D., 118, 159, 177, 203
Hardt, H., 77
Harrison, 21, 22
Hart, M., 128
Hartley, J., 66, 141
Hartman, P., 136, 203
Hauser, P.M., 176
Hawkes, J., 130
Hedinsson, E., 159, 161, 200, 204
Himmelweit, H.T.H., 162, 163, 201
Hirsch, F., 166
Hirsch, P.M., 113, 204
Hoijer, B., 195
Holmlov, P.G., 108
Hopkins, M., 92
Horkheimer, M., 62
Horton, D., 159
Hovland, C.I., 176, 184
Howitt, D., 187
Huaco, G., 23
Hughes, H.M., 141, 177
Hughes, M., 204
Husband, C., 135, 203
Hutchins, H., 90
Hyman, H., 192

Innis, H., 42, 43

Jackson, I., 78
Jahoda, M., 191
Janowitz, M., 77, 108, 152
Jay, M., 62
Johns-Heine, P., 125
Johnson, W., 114
Johnstone, J.W.L., 106, 108
Jowett, G., 24, 158

Katz, D., 186
Katz, E., 18, 157, 163, 164, 171, 191, 193, 194
Kelman, H., 185
Kerner, O., 189

Key, V.O., 193
Kingsbury, S.M., 128
Klapper, J., 177, 179, 184
Kornhauser, W., 58
Kracauer, S., 133
Kraus, S., 192, 197
Kreiling, A.L., 215
Krugman, H.E., 184
Kumar, C., 109

Lang, G., 177, 203
Lang, K., 177, 203
Lasswell, H., 78, 133
Lazarsfeld, P.F., 157, 176, 191, 193
Leites, N., 133
Lerner, D., 41, 44, 194
Lester, M.J., 117
Lewin, K., 167
Lewis, G.H., 155
Linne, O., 161
Linton, R., 24, 158
Lippman, W., 108, 114, 139
Lowenthal, L., 125
Lull, J., 158

McBride, S., 94
Maccoby, E., 159
McCombs, M., 196
McCormack, T., 47, 78, 79
McCron, R., 201
McDonald, G.E., 158
McGinnis, J., 203
McGranahan, D.V., 133
McGuire, W.J., 182, 183
MacLean, M., 75
McLelland, D.W., 41
McLeod, J., 159, 164
McLuhan, M., 27, 42
McQuail, D., 67, 136, 145, 163, 164, 187, 196, 197, 210
Marcuse, H., 62, 156
Marvanyi, G., 135
Marx, K., 59, 62, 92
Mattelart, A., 44
Mead, G.H., 67
Mendelsohn, H., 78, 158
Merton, R.K., 64, 74, 156, 157
Meyersohn, R., 175
Mickiewicz, E.P., 92
Middleton, S., 136, 208
Miliband, R., 205
Mill, J.S., 87
Mills, C.W., 58, 59, 152
Milton, J., 87, 88

SUBJECT INDEX

Denis McQuail

is currently Professor of Mass Communication, University of Amsterdam, the Netherlands. After graduating from Corpus Christi College, Oxford, with a BA in Modern History and a Diploma in Public and Social Administration, he received a PhD in Social Studies from the University of Leeds. He has since been affiliated to the Television Research Unit, University of Leeds; the University of Southampton; and the Annenberg School of Communication, University of Pennsylvania. His major publications include: *Television and the Political Image* (with J. Trenaman) 1961; *Television in Politics: Its Use and Influence* (with J. G. Blumler), 1968; *Towards a Sociology of Mass Communications,* 1968; *Sociology of Mass Communication* (editor), 1972; *Communication,* 1975; *Review of Sociological Writing on the Press,* 1976; *Analysis of Newspaper Content,* 1977; *Communication Models for the Study of Mass Communication* (with Sven Windahl), 1982.